PROJECT MARKETING

PROJECT MARKETING: BEYOND COMPETITIVE BIDDING

Bernard Cova

ESCP/EAP-Paris, France

Pervez Ghauri

Manchester School of Management, UMIST, Manchester, UK

Robert Salle

EM-Lyon, France

JOHN WILEY & SONS LTD

Other Wiley Editorial Offices

John Wiley & Sons, Inc., 605 Third Avenue,
New York, NY 10158-0012, USA

Wiley-VCH GmbH, Pappelallee 3,
D-69469 Weinheim, Germany

John Wiley & Sons Australia Ltd, 33 Park Road, Milton,
Queensland 4064, Australia

John Wiley & Sons (Asia) Pte Ltd, 2 Clementi Loop #02-01
Jin Xing Distripark, Singapore 129809

John Wiley & Sons (Canada) Ltd, 22 Worcester Road,
Rexdale, Ontario M9W 1L1, Canada

Library of Congress Cataloging-in-Publication Data
Cova, Bernard
    Project marketing : beyond competitive bidding / Bernard Cova, Pervez Ghauri, Robert Salle.
        p. cm.
    Includes bibliographical references and index.
    ISBN 0-471-48664-7
    1. Project management.   2. Marketing.   I. Ghauri, Pervez N., 1948–   II. Salle, Robert
    III. Title.
HD69.P75 C685 2002
658.4′04 – dc21

                                                                            2001055923

British Library Cataloging in Publication Data

A catalogue record for this book is available from the British Library

ISBN 0-471-48664-7

Project management by Originator Publishing Services, Gt Yarmouth, Norfolk

FSC
Mixed Sources
Product group from well-managed
forests and other controlled sources

Cert no. SGS-COC-2953
www.fsc.org
© 1996 Forest Stewardship Council

CONTENTS

Preface   ix
About the Authors   xi

PART I   THE PROJECT BUSINESS

1 What is a Project?   3
   Types of Project   4
      Subcontracting Projects   5
      Partial Projects   5
      Package Deals   6
      Turnkey Projects   6
      Turnkey 'Plus' Projects   8
   Project Components   10
   About the Book   12

2 Characteristics of Project Business   13
   Uniqueness   13
   Complexity   16
      The Complexity in the Offer   16
      The Number of Participants   17
      The Influence of Political Actors 17
      The Influence of Society   17
   Discontinuity   20
   Financial Commitment   21

3 Project Marketing: Special Features   23
   A High Degree of Uncertainty   23

Examples of Supplier Uncertainty 24
Examples of Customer Uncertainty 24
A Specific Buying Procedure 25
Invitation Open to the Best Price 25
Invitation Open to the Best Offer 26
Invitation Restricted to Better Price 26
Invitation Restricted to Better Offer 26
Negotiated Competitive Invitation or Closed Invitation to Tender 26
A Long and Negotiated Process 28
Fragmentation of Buying Centres 29

4 Project Marketing Practices 33
A Specific Temporality 33
Three Levels of Analysis 35
Business and Non-Business Actors 35
Relational Position and Functional Position 36
Risk or Uncertainty 37
Create and Deliver Value 39

5 The Project Marketing Logic 41
Beyond Transactional Logic 43
From Adaptation to Anticipation 44
From Submission to Construction 48
Combining External and Internal Resources 51
The Project Marketing Process 52

PART II MARKETING STRATEGY

6 From Corporate Strategy to Marketing Strategy 59
The Corporate Strategy 59
Strategic Segmentation and SBU 60
Managing Diversity: Business Portfolio 61
SBU Strategy 62
Company Resources and Competencies 64
The Market Segment and Customer Choices 67
The Offer 71
The International Dimension 75

7 Market Approach: Sociograms and Portfolios 77
Market as Milieu 77
Sociograms: The Origin 78
A Representation of the Business Arena 78
An Idea Derived from 'Hard Sciences' 79
From Network to Network Analysis 80
A Recent Marketing Development 80
Mapping Relational Positioning 81
Portfolios: The Origin 82

A Strategic Tool   82
A Relationship Marketing Tool   83

8 Analysing Milieus   85
    The Firm's Point of View: Case Study of the Antolini Company   85
        The Initial Strategic Approach   85
        From Segment to Milieu   85
    Analysing Milieus: A Method   88
        The Firm External to the Milieu   89
        The Firm Internal to the Milieu   95
        The Non-existent Milieu   96
    Milieu and Marketing   98
        Mutual Debt and Interpersonal Relationship   99
        Personal Intelligence Networks   101

9 Managing Customer Relationships   103
    Developing a Portfolio of Customer Relationships   105
        First Stage: The Definition of the Unit Analysed   105
        Second Stage: The Dimensions of the Analysis   106
        Third Stage: The Allocation of Resources   110
    Managing the Customer Relationship in the
        Independent-of-any-project Stage   112
        Insights into the Ritual Construct   115
    A Conceptual Framework for the Management
        of Extra-business Relationships   116

PART III   IMPLEMENTATION

10 Screening Projects   123
    Intelligence Systems   123
    Project Network Analysis   125
    Screening Methods   128
    Choosing Entry Mode   135
    Choosing Projects   140
        Independent of Any Project   142
        Pre-tender Phase   142
        Tender Preparation   142

11 Proactive Co-Development   143
    Construction and Customer Solution   144
        Independent of Any Project   144
        Pre-tender   145
        Tender Preparation   145
    Consultative Selling   145
    Constructing Projects   148
    Creative Offer   151
        Identification of the Latent Needs   152

Proactive Face-to-face	152
Coaching	153
Vision of a Solution	153
Joint Construction	153
Project De/Reconstruction	156

12 Formulating the Offer	161
The Four Dimensions of an Offer	162
The Architecture of the Offer	166
Organizational Implications	171
A Radical Change in Customer Approach	171
The Problem of Managing Technical and Human Resources	172
Concerning the Organization and How It Functions	172
The Customer's Perception of Interdependence with a Supplier: Loss of Autonomy or Access to More Skills?	173
Offset Offer in International Projects	173
What is an Offset?	174
The Offset Component of the Offer	178
Offset Enlarged Buying Centre	181

13 Negotiating Projects	185
A Model for Project Sales Negotiations	186
The Concept of Matching	186
The Negotiation Process	189
Cultural Factors	194
Strategic Factors	198
Planning and Managing Negotiations	200
Managing Lobbying Stage	201
Managing Face-to-face Negotiation Stage	203
Managing Post-negotiation Stage	207

14 Practical Guidelines	209
Designing Strategic Priorities	209
Developing a Functional Position	210
Developing a Relational Position 1—Milieu Analysis	210
Developing a Relational Position 2—Customer Analysis	211
Screening Projects	211
Mode of Entry	211
Project Development	212
Project Offer	212
Negotiating Projects	213

References	215
Index	219

PREFACE

The need for this book has emerged out of our experiences not only from teaching and research in the last two decades but also from our own experiences. As one of us narrates:

> As a fresh graduate from a business school and recruited by a company in the aerospace industry, I felt quite embarrassed. In the business school specializing in Marketing, I had learnt how to launch a product, how to position a product, how to come to a marketing mix and how to make a marketing plan. I had also learnt some things about international marketing but I had never heard of 'request for a proposal', 'call for tenders', 'competitive bidding' and 'negotiations'. In this job, I realized that marketing revolved around the above concepts and not around the concepts taught in the marketing management courses. Even the courses on 'industrial marketing' or 'busines-to–business marketing' did not deal with such fuzzy things as projects. Fuzzy because they do not exist prior to the sale.

After similar experience in academic life, where all of us have been involved in the industrial marketing field, talking to several companies, interviewing managers and running training programmes in dozens of companies, we realized that even the industrial marketing (B-to-B marketing) field does not really cover project marketing. While B-to-B marketing stresses long-term relationships, in project marketing the establishment of long-term relationships is one of the main problems.

As a result, some 10 years ago we got together with some of our colleagues, who shared the same views, and started the European Network for Project Marketing. The group, consisting of some 20 members from all over Europe, have been involved in research in companies such as Alcatel, Cogema, Dassault, Schneider, Bouygues, Ericsson, Sunds Defibrator, ABB and industrial groups such as Usinor, Matra, Shell, Vivendi and Saint Gobain. We have been working to develop concepts and theories of use in the marketing of projects. This book is a result of these studies.

We hope the book clearly illustrates the factors that influence the marketing of projects and provides guidelines for managers and students on how to handle these factors in an efficient manner.

We would like to express our thanks to the members of the European Network for Project Marketing on whose ideas this work is based. We particularly thank Florence Crespin for making her work available to us. We also thank Anna Zuyeva, Gill Geraghty and Robert-Jan Bulter from UMIST for their valuable assistance in preparation of this manuscript.

Bernard Cova
Paris

Pervez Ghauri
Manchester

Robert Salle
Lyon

ABOUT THE AUTHORS

Bernard Cova

Bernard Cova is a Professor in Marketing at ESCP-EAP (European School of Management—Paris, Oxford, Berlin and Madrid). He has been working on the development of marketing approaches to assist companies specializing in projects and system selling for the last 15 years. He is one of the leading experts in the field and is co-founder of the European Network for Project Marketing.

Pervez Ghauri

Pervez Ghauri is Professor in International Business at the Manchester School of Management, UMIST in the UK. He has authored/edited more than 10 books and numerous articles on International Marketing and International Business topics. He specializes in projects sales negotiations and entry strategies. He is a member of the European Network for Project Marketing and founding editor of *International Business Review*.

Robert Salle

Robert Salle is Professor in Marketing and Director of Research at EM-Lyon (*Ecole de Management de Lyon*) in France. He has been teaching and doing research in the field of business-to-business marketing for over 20 years and is currently focused on the theme of project marketing. He is a member of the IMP group and the European Network for Project Marketing. He has authored many books and articles on business-to-business marketing in both French and English.

Part I

THE PROJECT BUSINESS

Chapter 1

WHAT IS A PROJECT?

For the purpose of this marketing book, we define a project as a *complex transaction covering a package of products, services and work, specifically designed to create capital assets that produce benefits for a buyer over an extended period of time*. In this definition, we have chosen a marketing perspective that takes into consideration (Cova and Holstius, 1993):

- the idea of transaction—an event limited in time between a supplier and a customer;
- the content of the exchange—a group of products, services and work and the degree of adaptation—the specific design;
- the other party involved—the buyer.

To characterize project business and to differentiate it from consumer as well as industrial services and goods, numerous dimensions can be used. As project marketing lies closer to industrial goods and services, also called business-to-business marketing, perhaps it is more important to relate projects to industrial goods and services. In this way, a continuum can be drawn up with projects on one side and industrial services and products on the other, taking into account a variable degree of difference:

- from unit or very small series production to mass production;
- from made-to-measure demand to standard demand;
- from discontinuous supplier/customer business relations to continuous business relations;
- from rare transactions between supplier and customer (sometimes once every 5 years!) to frequent transactions;
- from very long-duration transactions (of around 2 years between the first contact and the conclusion of the contract) to short transactions;

- from a very high financial commitment for unit purchased to a low financial commitment;
- from relatively formal buying procedures (especially in the case of public markets) to more informal quotation requests;
- from fragmentation of buying centres and sales centres into two multi-organizational groups (e.g. customer + consultant + development bank on one side, supplier + industrial partners + financial partners on the other) to mono-organizational buying centres and sales centres.

By reading this list of characteristics, we see that project marketing specialists recognize their domain intuitively and do not at the moment rely on a classification of industrial activities that allows them to universally categorize projects on one side and products and services on the other.

Projects in different forms and shapes represent a major proportion of international trade and business activities. These activities range from subcontracting to turnkey projects with management or offset contracts. Companies normally known as consumer product companies, such as Alcatel, IBM, Philips, Ericsson, Siemens or Schneider, quite often sell their products on a project basis. In addition, there are companies, such as ABB, Alfa Laval, Atlas Copco, Alstom, Bouygues, Kvaerner, Thales, etc., that *always* sell their products and services on a project basis. As these and many other companies are in fact dealing in projects, there is a need to look at the marketing issues/problems related to this type of business.

In project sales, buyers and sellers are normally unfamiliar with each other and come from different environments. Yet, they have to agree on a transaction, negotiate and share responsibilities for a specific project. A couple of decades ago, the existence of this type of business was brought to the fore by scholars as well as consultants and managers, as illustrated in the following quotations:

> While direct investment and international trade in goods and services are rather well documented on a continuing basis and certainly have been subject for much theoretical and empirical research, the other vehicles for technology transfer ... turn-key projects, production sharing, service contracts etc., are much less known (Mattsson, 1979, p. 1).

> More and more frequently, machinery equipment and technology are purchased together as a package in the form, or as a complete industrial plant. This type of business is particularly becoming common in international business transactions (Boston Consulting Group, 1970, p. 17).

Although these quotes are more than two decades old, they still hold true. There are, for example, hardly any publications on project marketing. There are several books and articles on project management, but these publications deal with organizational and management issues and not with sales and marketing issues.

Types of Project

In a project, a seller supplies a complete system that may include components, equipment and even some services. They range from subcontracts to turnkey plus contracts.

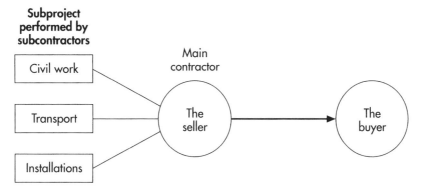

FIGURE 1.1 The main contractor versus subcontractors.

Subcontracting Projects

In the case of big projects, domestic or international, one main contractor is selling a project to a buyer. However, in most cases the main contractor is not in a position to supply/manufacture all of the project or parts of the project himself and buys them from other companies. These companies are then subcontractors to the main contractor. In international projects, this is very common. In one case, where a Swedish company supplied a complete power plant to Nigeria, it had to find a local subcontractor for the civil works. In this case, the Swedish company was working, on the one hand, as a marketer and, on the other hand, as a buyer purchasing civil works from a local construction company for the project. The local construction company, the subcontractor, despite supplying the project (the subproject) locally, had to market itself to the Swedish company which, in fact, is the buyer for the subcontractor. Sub-contractors may also have subcontracts of their own for part of the project. This type of project and its relation to the whole project is illustrated in Figure 1.1.

Partial Projects

In this type of project, different suppliers independently market and supply different parts of the main project directly to the buyer. The buyer will then put together all the partial projects. The sellers of the partial projects, however, need to have some information on other partial suppliers. Quite often, they may need to adapt their products/services so that they can fit/match with the rest of the project. In most cases, partial suppliers come from different countries and industries. The partial supplier supplies only a part of the total project and the know-how and services needed to assemble the particular part supplied by him. This can, for example, be a communication system for a container ship or a sewage system for a skyscraper or a hospital. Normally, the buyer takes on the responsibility of coordination and integration of the total project. It can be a partial project of an already existing project, such as a building or a hospital. This type of project business is illustrated in Figure 1.2.

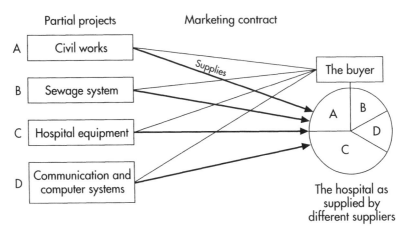

FIGURE 1.2   Partial projects.

As illustrated in Figure 1.2, different suppliers to one main project, a hospital in this case, supply different parts of the project. However, the marketing activities are directed towards one buyer, as represented by the broken lines.

Package Deals

A package deal is considered to include a solution to a buyer's problem, a complete system, components, equipment plus the know-how to handle the same (Ghauri, 1983). In some cases, it may also include a service contract for a number of years. Service firms, such as insurance, accounting or medical firms, quite often supply package deals. A number of advertising companies offer package deals to their customers that include idea generation, production, media selection, budgeting and implementation of an advertising campaign, for example, to launch a new product or service. The supplying companies have some services in-house, such as idea generation and production, while other services, such as media, bill boards, etc., have long-term contractual or non-contractual relationships with suppliers who work with them on a regular basis. The suppliers may come from the domestic market of either the main contractor or the buyer. In advertising, it is quite common for an idea generated in France or Italy to be produced in England and the package sold to a customer in Germany. In this case, the seller has quoted the total price and has a contract responsibility for all parts of the package towards the buyer in Germany. This is illustrated in Figure 1.3.

Turnkey projects

Turnkey projects involve delivery of a complete plant, factory or institution. In this case, the main contractor is responsible for marketing, negotiations and setting up of the project—such as a dairy, a hospital, an underground train system—while he may have subcontractors for some parts of the project. The seller has to get the

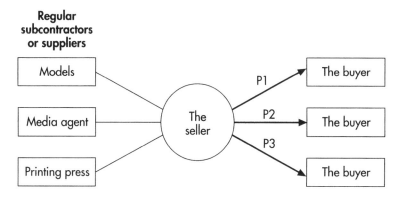

FIGURE 1.3 The relationships in package deals (P1 is package deal 1, P2 package deal 2 and P3 package deal 3).

project operational and hand it over to the buyer. In fact, quite literally the seller has to get it ready and hand the key over to the buyer who can simply open the door and start operating the project. The responsibilities of the seller normally include (Luostarinen and Welch, 1990 and United Nations, 1983, p. 6):

- basic design and engineering;
- supply of technology and know-how;
- supply of complete machinery and equipment;
- design and construction of civil works;
- supply and setting up of infrastructure needs;
- commissioning all plant facilities up to the start-up stage.

In these projects, the seller is often the supplier of a major part of the plant/project; for example, Enron for power generation equipment in the power generation project in India and Alfa Laval for milk plant equipment for a dairy project in Saudi Arabia. In some cases however, a major international engineering and construction company can act as the main supplier or the seller; for example, the American company Fluor and Bechtel or Swedish construction company Skanska for supply of a turnkey hospital or a hotel. The main contractor puts the complete project together although he may be supplying only 20–30 % of the project value himself. The rest of the project he buys from other suppliers/sub-contractors. The main contractor is also responsible, and gives guarantees, for the whole project. In many cases, companies in the same ownership group supply different parts of the project (Ghauri, 1988).

The project, when handed over to the buyer, is complete in every respect—equipment, services and infrastructure (e.g. the road leading to the plant or the hospital). Completeness is thus the main characteristic that distinguishes turnkey projects from all other types of project. This is in contrast to partial projects, where the buyer takes on the responsibility of coordination and integration. This type of project is illustrated in Figure 1.4.

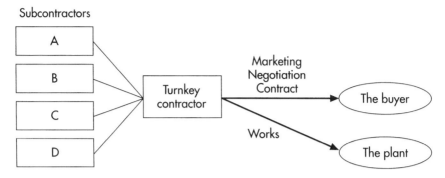

FIGURE 1.4   A typical turnkey project.

Turnkey 'Plus' Projects

More and more turnkey projects are being combined with other activities and conditions. These activities range from the project's inception (e.g. developing the idea behind the project together with the buyer, doing a feasibility study and looking for financiers) to its completion (e.g. assembling parts of the project in the buyer's country or using the seller's staff under management contract for the initial years). Sellers are increasingly asked to assist buyers in their search for financiers and in convincing financial organizations—such as the World Bank, IMF or EBRD—that the project is sound. Internationally, this is very important. Sometimes, the seller is asked to assist in financing the project by means of long-term loans or equity participation.

Different types of buy-back and offset agreement are quite common in these projects. The bigger the project, the greater the demands from the buyer in this respect. This is no longer a developing country phenomenon, most Western countries also demand some 'plus' in bigger projects. There are several benefits from these extra activities for both parties.

Benefits for Buyers

From the buyer's point of view, getting more than just the project they paid for is definitely more attractive. The most common demand is for the seller to help them in arranging feasibility and finances. Another motive for buyers centres around their concern that the plant will work efficiently and without problems after it is handed over to the them. They are thus concerned about the training of their staff who will handle the project. To achieve this, they often involve the seller in a management contract for the initial (3–5) years, so that their staff can learn in that period. In other cases, a training package is often included in a turnkey project.

Generation of foreign exchange has also been a major concern for many buyers. They may therefore want to bind the seller beyond the project, either by asking them to take equity or give some type of guarantee for export of goods produced in the project; for example, that 30% of the products manufactured in the plant would be bought back by the seller. The seller then has to find a market for these products either in his home market or internationally. When a government is

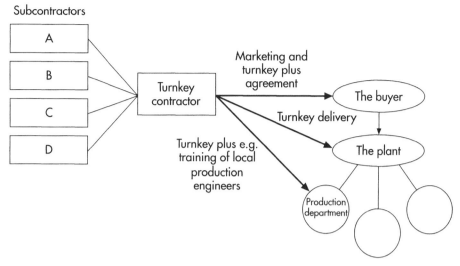

Subcontractors

FIGURE 1.5   A typical turnkey 'plus' project.

involved as a buyer, it is often concerned about job opportunities and demands that part of the work—assembly, production, etc.—should be done in its own country. Depending on the size of the project, buyers may demand different facilities that go beyond the particular project. This type of project is explained in Figure 1.5.

Benefits for the Supplier

The biggest advantage for the supplier is, by means of these additional arrangements, to stay in touch with the buyer beyond the specific project. Discontinuity, as discussed in the next chapter, is a major problem for companies working with project marketing. By this continued involvement—be it a training programme, management contract, buy-back or offset agreement—the seller can stay in touch with the supplier and, thereby, can have better insight into future projects. Moreover, there is an opportunity for the seller to make extra profits by such arrangements. If the seller is asked to do the feasibility study or assist the buyer in finding financiers, it is in fact in his interest, because he will get an 'insider' position as compared with his competitors. From the marketing point of view, he will gain a competitive advantage, even if he has to participate in a closed or open tender later on.

Through the feasibility study, the seller can also influence the design, capacity and specifications in favour of his own machinery and equipment and offer. One of the most important benefits of being involved in project 'plus' activities, especially prior to project stage, are the contracts and relationships a seller can establish with the key actors/people in the buying organization. The seller can also use this 'plus' arrangement as his competitive edge; for example, by understanding the priorities of the buyer and offering what they most badly need, such as a training programme for their staff or, in case of foreign exchange priorities, to buy back a certain percentage of the production of the plant in question. In one of the cases we studied, the seller offered to use local subcontractors and offered to accept payment in local currency for those parts. This was very attractive for the buyer, a local government that was short of foreign exchange and wanted to create some job opportunities for local firms.

The different types of project mentioned above are the most common ones. There are more and more new types of project, where buyers come with the most unusual demands and where the local government or local opinion places demands on the suppliers about social responsibility or environmental issues. A project, thus, may not exactly fit in one of the above descriptions and may even be a combination of types. The above classification, however, helps us understand the nature of project business, especially problems related to marketing. The fact that suppliers dealing with project business face an ever-increasing range of project types has strong consequences for the nature and content of their offer, ranging from ready-made packages made up of standardized products and services to solutions which are specifically co-designed with the customer in order to meet the diversity of its stakes/challenges.

Chapter 2 deals particularly with issues that distinguish projects from other types of business in a marketing context.

Project Components

Project business, although gaining more popularity recently, is not a totally new type of business. Many industries (e.g. the construction industry) have always been working on a project basis. Traditionally, projects are considered to have the chronological stages as shown in Figure 1.6. According to this approach, the buyer or someone else (e.g. politicians or other members of society) first identifies the need for such a project (e.g. an underground transport system or a hospital for a city). Once discussed and accepted, a pre-feasibility study is done. In this study, the logic, rationale and financial resources are reviewed and discussed. If there is a positive reaction from the people involved, a proper feasibility study is ordered or asked for. This study can be done by the buyer himself, by a consultant or in some cases by a potential supplier.

The feasibility study is a crucial stage as it helps the decision makers take a go/no-go decision. This study takes into consideration all aspects of the project, its benefits and drawbacks, its financial resources available or possibilities of getting loans, etc. This study decides whether the project is feasible or not. If it is considered feasible, the buyer identifies potential suppliers who can supply the particular type of project. At this point, buyers quite often rank the suppliers according to their suitability, resources, reputation and earlier contacts.

Different types of buyer, quite often depending on the type of buyer (e.g. government vs. a private company), follow either a closed or open tender policy. Sometimes the tender is announced and sometimes potential suppliers are invited to give tenders or offers for the project. Once tender offers are received, the buyer, after studying them, invites the most appropriate suppliers for negotiations. Different types of tender and offer are discussed later in the book. Buyers normally negotiate with more than one seller and then award the project and sign

Parties   Stages   Capabilities

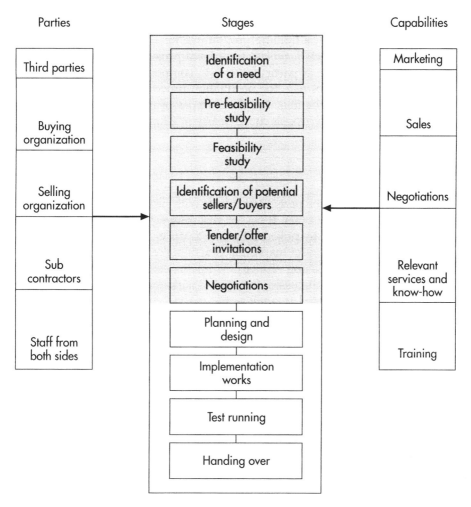

FIGURE 1.6   Project components in a traditional project. Note: tinted area is of concern to this book.

the contract according to the type of project they want—subcontract, partial project, turnkey project or turnkey 'plus' project. From the marketing point of view, this is the final stage in the marketing process of a particular project (see Figure 1.6).

The contract is then handed over to designers and engineers so that they can plan, design and start work on the project. In the case of a plant or a factory, a test run is done and the project is handed over to the buyer. In the case of a turnkey 'plus' project, the seller might still be involved after this stage (e.g. training the buyer's staff or buying back some products). Throughout this process and at different stages, several parties are involved and constitute components of a project. These parties/actors/people come from buyer and seller organizations as well as from third parties such as financiers, banks, politicians, subcontractors, etc. Moreover, a lot of resources are put into different stages of the project such as marketing and sales activities, negotiations, services and know-how about the project and, in some cases, a training programme for the buyer's staff.

The above picture reflects a typical traditional project and its components. In specific projects, however, a particular phase (component) might have its own process with several stages (e.g. the negotiation process). These peculiarities are discussed in subsequent chapters. For the purpose of marketing, we will specify these components and the process more clearly in Chapter 2.

About the Book

The book is divided in three parts. Part I deals with project business and explains how projects differ from other types of businesses. This part also highlights marketing issues related to projects. Special features of project marketing are explained and different project marketing practices are presented.

Part II deals with marketing strategy. It relates corporate strategy to project marketing strategy and discusses the main marketing approach used in the book. Methods are presented to analyse the marketing environment and milieu and to manage the supplier–customer relationship.

Finally, Part III presents ways of implementing project marketing strategy. Practical examples and guidelines are provided for scanning and screening projects, for formulating tenders and offers and for negotiations. The ever-increasing problem of offsets is also handled in Part III. Some concrete guidelines are provided in the final chapter.

We suggest the reader first reads through the whole book and then, while working on a project or a particular stage of the project, goes back to the relevant chapter and reads it thoroughly. We believe the reader will gain a lot of information and will learn from the examples given in the book. Companies and students dealing with project marketing will definitely find it useful.

Chapter 2

CHARACTERISTICS OF PROJECT BUSINESS

Project business has four main characteristics that are more or less interconnected: uniqueness, complexity, discontinuity and the extent of financial commitment. These characteristics show the exceptional character of project marketing when compared with traditional marketing management, popularized by the many editions and translations of the book by Philip Kotler, and especially when looked at from an industrial marketing perspective such as that used by companies involved in the sale of industrial services and products.

Uniqueness

During a study that we carried out on the marketing function within an international company in the construction industry, the managers we met repeatedly pointed out: 'We only manufacture prototypes', signifying that the outcome is never the same and changes for each project. After probing a little further, although accepting that as non-specialists they are in certain cases unaware of the evident tangible differences between many construction projects, they still maintained the existence of a unique specificity in each project: 'Each project is specific'. Even if development is totally identical (disregarding minor differences such as the colour of the wallpaper or sanitary fittings), there are nevertheless differences on many levels. The list below shows some of them:

- Project size (a company can be faced with projects that vastly differ in size).
- The type of customer (e.g. public or private).
- The type of organization undertaking project management; the customer; an architect or a specialist design office; even a general building company undertaking design and execution.

- Financing that differs depending upon whether the construction is social housing, paid by public funds or a turnkey plant paid by a private company.
- The way the supplier organizes the construction; the nature of work carried out by subcontractors.
- The involvement of different parties such as politicians, administration or civil society.

To illustrate these different dimensions, Box 2.1 gives the explanation of project typology by a marketing manager of a very big electrical installation company.

BOX 2.1 Project typology for a big electrical installation company.

Three major types of project can be differentiated. These projects have different characteristics depending on supplier needs in terms of size, complexity and required competencies.

'Mammoth' Projects

These are exceptional 'non-invented' projects; by this, we mean they are not created by an installation company. A state or a very large private group initiates these projects. They are detected very early on inasmuch as the customer has feasibility, financing or other problems. In general, the supplier's role in the project is as a party in a consortium.

Complex and multidimensional projects

The significance is related to project difficulty or implementation. Two extreme types of approach can be differentiated:

1. In the first type, the customer defines his specifications with the help of an engineering company before inviting suppliers to tender.
2. In the second type, the supplier creates the project. As the marketing manager of this installation company pointed out: *'We knew about the customer's requirements and we carried out the engineering and we operated as turnkey contractor. However, this particular case was not common—there are only a few such cases per hundred.'*

In a certain way, customers can combine these two approaches. They can launch an invitation to tender to gain ideas (as in Type 2) and then they consult (as in Type 1).

Medium-size projects

The installation company is still in a consortium. It is not going to carry out the technical process; it will therefore contribute everything around the process.

Each project is therefore specific. This notion is uncomfortable for marketers in business-to-business markets, as they are more often accustomed to a certain degree of repetition or to the existence of some similarities that, through the experience they have gained, makes decision making easier. On the contrary, in the business-to-business context, the degree of adaptation is such that no economic relation resembles another (Hakansson, 1982). However, in the case of project business, the level of uniqueness is really high insofar as the operation arena changes with transaction, whereas in product business certain elements persist to a certain extent throughout the transactions. It must be added that in many industrial sectors working by project, it is not common, on a worldwide level, for projects to go as planned every year.

Even if each project is unique, it frequently enables the supplier to acquire a crucial reference for his company in the future. Uniqueness does not signify a unique episode for a given customer at a given time, disconnected from everything else. The project creates usable value for the company in a larger perspective, that of the client and of the market (see Box 2.2). The stakes for the supplier are many; technological development (i.e. to keep in the race), the presence in a given application or a geographical zone; for example, in the field of military equipment (fighter aircraft, tanks, etc.), the development of sales abroad is largely conditioned by the first orders obtained from the armies of the supplier's country.

BOX 2.2 Rumble over Tokyo.

Back in 1990, when All Nippon Airways and flagship carrier Japan Airlines (JAL) ordered the first Boeing 777 jetcraft, Boeing pulled out all the stops to celebrate the sale. The aircraft giants brought together hundreds of guests, including government officials, top executives from both companies, and their wives, for a bash at Tokyo's Imperial Hotel. The assembled partygoers were wowed by the centrepiece of the gala. For the affair, Boeing had built a three-quarter scale model of the first plane it had ever made. This is the type of gesture—a bow to history—that impresses the Japanese.

Now, Boeing hopes it can impress them again, this time with a real plane—a superjumbo jet, the 747X, a stretched 520-seat version of its 747 jumbo—that will serve to protect its long-standing dominance of the country's commercial aircraft sales. For nearly 50 years, Boeing and JAL, All Nippon and Japan Air System have had a fruitful business relationship, thanks in part to the aircraft maker's deference to Japanese customs. Boeing's planes now account for 84% of Japan's commercial fleets, the world's third-largest national air market after the USA and China. From 1970 to 1998, JAL alone spent $14.4 billion on those planes. But that lead is now under fierce attack from Boeing's archrival, Airbus Industry. Japan has become the key battleground as the European aircraft consortium seeks to launch its superjumbo A380 jet which can hold 555 to 800 passengers.

Airbus is expanding its small Japanese office and making allies at Japanese businesses. The company has already shown that it's willing to offer steep discounts. Some early buyers paid 40% off the A380's $220 million list price. Quality planes and aggressive business practices like that have lifted Airbus's worldwide market share over the past 5 years from 21% to almost 50%. Airbus already has A380 orders from Singapore Airlines and Quantas Airways, two other Pacific Rim carriers. If the Japanese buy the A380, Airbus will become the regional and likely worldwide leader in the market for big jets. It would also make Airbus, not Boeing, the world's undisputed No. 1 commercial jetmaker.

Boeing's counteroffensive moved into high gear in March 2001, when Alan Mulally, recently named CEO of Boeing's Commercial Airplanes, led a team of executives to Japan to persuade long-time customers to stick with Boeing. It was an unusual trip because Mulally, widely considered a candidate to Boeing's next chief executive, rarely makes sales calls. Mulally tried to convince Japanese carriers that there is no real market for superjumbos. Mulally estimates that fewer than 500 superjumbos are needed worldwide: 'The 500-seater is a niche. We think the centre of the market will be 777 and 747 size airplanes' (e.g. between 300 and 500 seats), says Mulally.

However, a week before Mulally's trip to Tokyo, other Boeing execs were already there, lining up local contractors for the unbuilt 747X superjumbo. They reached a tentative agreement with Mitsubishi Heavy Industries to build the 747X wing. Boeing is also lobbying the Japanese government to name the 747X a 'national project', the designation it got for the 767 and the 777, parts of which were also made in Japan. That could slash $1 billion from 747X development costs.

Airbus is still learning Japanese ways. In Japan, a country that values personal relationships in business, Airbus had only a tiny office until April 2001. Onishi, the JAL executive, says of Airbus's Leahy: 'He doesn't seem to understand our particular needs. If he were to pay us a visit more often, perhaps that wouldn't be the case'. Leahy vows to do better. In a bid to gain *entrée* to Japan's business community, Airbus has signed an agreement with trading company Mitsui & Co. which brokered jets for McDonnell Douglas until Boeing bought it in 1997.

But Boeing has been nurturing its relationship with the Japanese since 1953. After a JAL Boeing 747 crashed in Japan and killed 520 people in 1985, the company admitted partial responsibility and for years sent executives to Buddhist memorial rites for the victims on the disaster's anniversary. And it helps that both Boeing and McDonnell Douglas are long-time Japanese defense contractors. 'It's probably the most important bilateral relationship we have in the world', says Boeing's Larry Dickenson, senior vice-president for Asia sales.

Source: Adapted from *Business Week*, 2, April, 2001.

Complexity

Most projects are characterized by an extreme technical, financial, political and societal complexity.

The Complexity in the Offer

This complexity is due to the extremely large variety of technical elements involved in the design, organization and execution of the technical solution for the customer. This is very obvious when you consider projects such as the construction of subway lines, production units or major works. Even more modest realizations are sometimes very complex on a technical level. There is also a complete group of elements surrounding this technico-functional offer that allows the supplier, on one hand, to refine his offer to be consistent with the customer's demand and stakes and, on the other hand, to differentiate himself from the competition. With this aim in mind, companies turn to service companies to provide sophisticated funding arrangements such as BOOT (Built, Owned, Operated, Transferred) or to local counterparts (compensations, local investments, appeal to local companies to add local value). A British Airways manager explained that the contract with Airbus Industries included trade-in of aircraft, discounts and specific conditions for the guarantee and maintenance of the aircraft.

The Number of Participants

The complexity of the offer is due to the high number of organizations and individuals involved. In fact, the supplier, very often unable to set up the project alone, turns to all kinds of partners: consultancy, service, control firms, subcontractors, contracting partners, suppliers, financial organizations, agents, etc. In addition to this group of market actors, non-market actors can also participate and influence the business development and characteristics (e.g. unions, associations, pressure groups, lobbies, etc.). Similarly, for the customer, the use of project managers to design and set up the terms and conditions, financial and other backing, adds to the complexity.

The Influence of Political Actors

Depending on the industrial sector and the type of business, this influence can be significant. This can be direct when, for example, it relates to national works in which states and territorial authorities are project managers. It can also be indirect and affect project characteristics by the interaction of financial incentives, legal issues, procedures to be respected, without forgetting the possible interplay of illegal manoeuvres. In some countries, such as China and India, politicians always play some role in bigger projects.

The Influence of Society

In general, the more greater impact a project has on society, the more society gets involved in it. Politicians no longer have the role of representing society's interests. It is now common for society actors to contest projects such as the lay out of a railway line, the paths of high-voltage power lines, the creation of a water purification plant, construction of motorways, tunnels (with tolls!) or factories. This is true for many countries. For the Korean high-speed bullet train project, over 2,000 civil complaints were brought before the courts. Local resistance to the project resulted in two stations which were initially planned on ground level (Taejon and Taegu) being put more than 50 m underground. To do this, 5.4 billion square

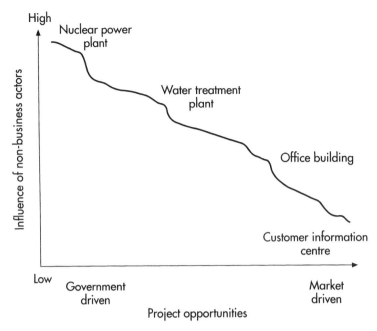

FIGURE 2.1 The influence of non-business actors.

metres of earth had to be removed! The route, planned to pass through the historical town of Kyongju, was criticised by the local population and met strong opposition because there was a risk that the works would damage the archaeological and cultural heritage.

Together with political actors, society actors form the group known as 'non-business actors' (Baron, 1995) whose influence depends largely on project characteristics. The more a project involves the public domain, the more non-business actors come into play (see Figure 2.1).

Although the participation of society in certain projects is sometimes unforeseeable and difficult for a company to manage, in some conditions companies may call on society as a witness. The project for construction of the B Line of the Toulouse subway is a good example (Box 2.3).

BOX 2.3 The Toulouse B Line: From Cooperation to Implement the A Line to Fierce Competition for the B Line

At the beginning of March 1998, execution of the B Line of the Toulouse subway was granted to Matra Transport International by the SMTC (Syndicat Mixte des Transports en Commun—the public transport mixed syndicate). The contract amounted to €230 million. The choice was made, after many stages, resulting in fierce competition between GEC Alsthom (now Alstom) and Matra Transport International (now a company of the Siemens Group).

The first Toulouse subway line, the A Line, was made operational by Matra on the basis of the VAL (light automatic vehicle—LAV) system in 1993. To do this, Matra carried out project management and design of the automatic system, with GEC Alsthom supplying the rolling stock. For this project, the two companies simply reconstructed the consortium that had already been proven several years earlier during the construction of Line 1 of the Lille subway which commenced operation in 1983.

After that, the two companies, who so far had worked together harmoniously, began to encounter some difficulties. Disagreements concerning the use of the driving assistance system technology which they had developed together in the 1980s for the Parisian RER (Réseau Express Régional, a fast suburban train) divided the two contractors. Using this common technological know-how, Matra and GEC Alsthom had both developed automatic subways. The conflicting points of view between the two competitors concerned whether or not to use this technology for automatic subway trains with or without drivers. Matra held that an initial agreement gave their company the exclusive right to exploit the technology for subway trains without drivers.

Breaking away from the consortium already used in Lille and Toulouse, Matra launched in 1995 an invitation to tender for the supply of rolling stock for the second subway line in Lille. In the end, it was the tandem Vevey-FCB who obtained the business. This was met with great displeasure by GEC Alsthom who, in vain, attempted politically and legally to obtain part of the contract. On one hand, other events related to the choice of alliance and on the other, the change towards an assembler profession only accentuated the difference of opinion between the two parties. Considering its previous successful execution of the A Line, Matra could see being awarded the project for the B Line by simple amendment of the A Line contract. However, a thorough review of the file by the SMTC led to a market consultation by invitation to tender, to which both companies replied separately.

The Opposing Tenders

The two responses were based on different technological approaches to the line automation.

Matra's solution hinged on the use of VAL system technology, which had already been developed, and modernization of rolling stock. The key advantage of this solution was compatibility between Line A and Line B (i.e. allowing rail traffic to be managed in relation to its density which leads to a reduction in running costs).

The GEC Alsthom solution hinged on new technological developments (numerical technology). This solution enabled extremely flexible operation of the B Line in relation to demand. Experts maintained this technology had greater possibilities and was more flexible.

Different References and Experience

Since the beginning of the 1980s, Matra had a portfolio of references for subway lines equipped with the VAL system. This system had undergone constant development with each new project. GEC Alsthom won its first contract for an automatic subway without drivers in 1997 in Singapore in preference to Matra. The same technology had already been used for improvement of existing subway lines.

Dealing with Society

In January 1998, GEC Alsthom addressed the general public through the local newspaper La Dépêche du Midi: 'Did you know that if the B Line was entrusted to us, your subway would be made here?' (GEC Alsthom, candidate for your subway's B line). In fact, French industrial policy wanted to promote local employment and GEC Alsthom had an industrial site in the Midi-Pyrénées region.

Matra let it be known that it had successfully executed the A Line of the Toulouse subway and that it was the most qualified to execute the B Line. They had initially intended a poster campaign on this theme but this was finally abandoned.

Political Actors: Different Backings

It was rumoured that Matra would be supported by a right-wing candidate from Toulouse Town Council, whereas GEC Alsthom would be supported by a left-wing candidate from Departmental Council of Haute-Garonne. The contract for the second subway line presented a marvellous battleground for the confrontation between these two political authorities.

Being awarded this project was important for both companies, not just because of the size of the business. For Gec Alsthom, the objective was to gain prestige in the field of automatic subways, to be recognized in France and to gain credibility internationally. For Matra, the objective was to emphasize its presence worldwide and to become an inevitable on the market.

Discontinuity

Project business is characterized by a high degree of discontinuity in economic relations between the supplier and the customer. In fact, a customer from a developing nation who wants to be equipped, for example, with a hydroelectric dam or a refinery will not buy the same type of equipment for many years to come. In this case, unlike the repetitive sales of industrial services and products, we cannot consider supplier/customer relations to be cultivated by frequent transactions. When a project is terminated, it leaves a sediment of trust (Hadji-khani, 1996) and interdependence between the supplier and the customer, but this sediment is eroded over time and changes may appear within either of the two parties or in their environments, such as replacement of key people, geopolitical modifications, strategic reorientations, etc. By lack of continuity in the relationship, the degree of interdependence which was strong at project termination decreases progressively, and uncertainty grows as to whether the parties will work together again on a future project.

Nevertheless, the success of a project often depends largely on the capacity the supplier had in maintaining the relationship with the customer independent of economic activity (i.e. to maintain a sleeping relationship with the customer).

Over 10 years, Siemens invested large amounts in Iran following the revolution in order to maintain the relations it had previously built up. Siemens had residual business with the Iranian government as supplier of spare parts for its telecommunications equipment. Moreover, Siemens also stayed in Iran despite the political problems, the war and the absence of projects. The technological dependence of Iran and the investments made by Siemens to maintain a social relationship led them to develop new agreements as soon as the political situation improved. And in 1993, Siemens signed a new contract for a big telecommunications project in Iran while the competition spared no effort in technological and financial terms to acquire the contract. Customers, therefore, prefer suppliers who do not play the 'meteor', as French companies were nicknamed in the 1980s in South America, and who are ready to give their time to counter the discontinuity of business relations by social continuity. The respect for the customer (i.e. a way of treating the customer not only as a business actor but also as a socio-economic actor) is often considered to be the key to maintaining continuity between the concerned parties.

Financial Commitment

The following figures illustrate the extent of financial commitment in project business:

- A subway line approximately €60 million per kilometre; the Sydney subway: US$800 million; the Toulouse subway: €230 million.
- The *'Grand Stade de France'* (the French Grand Stadium): nearly €300 million.
- The Korean TGV (high-speed bullet train): US$20 billion for more than 400 km; the value of the contract won by the consortium led by GEC Alsthom for the supply of rolling stock: €2 billion.
- The contract signed in 1998 between Airbus Industries and British Airways: more than €2 billion.

There are many more examples. Most projects are of a more modest size but are nevertheless important in financial terms. This importance can cause competitive fights that are just as violent as those of big projects.

Despite these figures being high, they are similar to those encountered in continuous supplier/customer relations (e.g. in industrial product marketing involving repeat purchasing). Very high figures can also be noticed over a given period; for example, some major industrial groups pay €150 million yearly to the French Electricity Board. Investments may even be higher for major first-rank suppliers whose customers are from the automotive, electronic and computing industry. The fundamental difference is that in project business the amounts are centred on a single project.

Chapter 3

PROJECT MARKETING: SPECIAL FEATURES

The characteristics of project business that we have just described (i.e. uniqueness, complexity, discontinuity and the extent of financial commitment) have many consequences for project sales (Günter and Bonaccorsi, 1996):

- a high degree of uncertainty for the parties concerned;
- a specific buying process by customers;
- a long transaction duration with many phases clearly delimited;
- a double fragmentation of buying centres and sales centres.

A High Degree of Uncertainty

Considering the four characteristics that we took into consideration in Chapter 2, there is a very high degree of uncertainty perceived by the concerned parties. This uncertainty results from:

- the time that they have to spend preparing, formulating and implementing the decision;
- the volume and quality of information accessible to them;
- the degree of control they have on events and on required resources.

We will detail below some examples of uncertainty perceived by the supplier and by the customer.

Examples of Supplier Uncertainty

Supplier uncertainty resolves around how difficult it is for the supplier to predict how the project will develop from the time of its inception up to final delivery to the customer. These uncertainties may arise for several reasons:

- Uncertainty concerning the time of trade: When will consultation take place? When does the customer want the delivery?
- Uncertainty concerning the identity of the customer: Who is going to buy? How will the customer operate? Will he operate alone carrying out project management himself or will he fall back on a main contractor?
- Uncertainty concerning the object of the transaction: What are the characteristics of the terms and conditions? What is at stake for the customer?
- Uncertainty connected to the transaction method: What supplier consultation methods will the customer adopt? Consultation by invitation to tender or other?
- Uncertainty connected with the customer's degree of commitment: Will he set up very detailed specifications or will he just specify functional objectives?
- Uncertainty connected with supplier capacity to fulfil the terms and conditions and then to manage the project: Can he respond or not in relation to the resources and the expertise required? If so, will he be the prime contractor or subcontractor or a party in a consortium? With which partners? At what price? What terms? With variations or not? What is the level of expertise of the co-tenderers? How will the cohabitation with the co-tenderers develop? In the project realization phase: Can he control costs, respect required performance levels, have the necessary technical and financial resources?

Examples of Customer Uncertainty

Customer uncertainty is also connected with the fact that it is difficult for the customer to forecast how the project will develop from the time of its inception until final implementation. This may arise for several conditions and reasons:

- Uncertainty connected with the development of specifications: Does the customer have the capacity and expertise to define the specifications and bring the project to term (e.g. financially)? Should he use a service provider to define the specifications or not?
- Uncertainty connected with the transaction method: What consultation methods will the supplier adopt? What comparison grid will be used for the propositions? How will the different tenders be arbitrated? Will a service provider be required for this operation? Will the project be contracted by part or not?
- Uncertainty connected with the supplier's ability to carry the project through to a successful conclusion: How reliable is the supplier? Is the accepted supplier able to execute the project on a technical level, in terms of deadlines, in terms of the predicted financial limitations? Has the supplier

already successfully carried out the same kind of project? Is the group of companies with whom the supplier works competent to successfully carry out the project?

Note that some features of uncertainty are not specific to project sales and are also applicable to business-to-business sales in bigger contracts (Salle and Silvestre, 1992).

A Specific Buying Procedure

The invitation-to-tender buying procedure theoretically enables the customer to obtain a better economic result, insofar as it enables him to compensate for his lack of information and to benefit from the competitiveness of the suppliers. Although this allocation method is commonly used in both public and private markets, other methods exist, such as contracts based on mutual agreement or negotiated contracts; these contracts can arise in public markets from an unsuccessful result of an invitation to tender. There are five major types of invitation to tender ranked here from the most rigid to the most flexible.

Invitation Open to the Best Price

This invitation type is deemed 'pure' (i.e. in public market terminology) and is awarded to the lowest bidder. The customer extensively advertises an invitation to tender (or 'request for proposal', 'call for bidding') and each interested supplier then submits a sealed tender. As each tender is opened, an immediate choice is made on the basis of the best price. This method, most commonly found in public markets and practically non-existent in private markets, only represents a small percentage of buying procedures nowadays.

This method is, moreover, questioned in public markets, sectors whose economic weight often represents several dozen € billion per European country, a large part of which is subject to public market Code procedures. In this vein, a French Ministry recently argued that:

> the large number of tenders presented by companies, especially in the construction industry, have prices which are not economically viable. And, unfortunately, in reality the Code at this time logically favours market allocation to these companies. You know the result; the destabilization of a complete industry, the exploitation of subcontractors, the bankruptcy of previously healthy and well-managed small- and medium-sized companies, badly implemented markets resulting in litigation and contract modification which raise the agreed price. In a nutshell, an unhealthy and irrational situation. Up until now, the reasoning behind the current Code—even if it is not exactly stipulated—is to privilege the lowest bidder. And it does not take into consideration the consequences of an abnormally low bid in terms of good buying, equipment management over time, maintenance costs, under-quoting, or very simply quality problems or the completely abnormal distortion of the competition.

Invitation Open to the Best Offer

In this invitation the price criterion is replaced by a quality–price ratio criterion that is more difficult to assess, despite the use of multi-criteria analysis grids. It is largely used in public markets to compensate for the weaknesses just outlined by choosing the 'lowest bidder' (best price).

Invitation Restricted to Better Price

From a request for information, each interested supplier can send a pre-selection file. The customer makes his initial selection based on this file by means of criteria such as references, financial solidity and technical expertise. An invitation to tender is then sent to this list of selected companies (bidding list or tender list). Then the procedure returns to the 'pure' type. It should be noted that in certain cases the request for information is replaced by a company in pre-qualification phase (approved vendors list) which consists of companies that qualify, not for a single project, but for a given period and therefore for a group of projects.

Invitation Restricted to Better Offer

After the pre-selection or pre-qualification phase, the procedure is identical to that of the open invitation to tender awarded to the best offer.

Negotiated Competitive Invitation or Closed Invitation to Tender

This is the invitation type that is farthest removed from the 'pure' type. It is also the most commonly used in private markets and is increasingly used in public markets when the object of the transaction is difficult to define (high technology, complex services, etc.). The customer sends the invitation to tender to companies on a list that has been drawn up internally from non-disclosed criteria (bidding list). The choice is not made at the time of opening the tenders as in other types of invitation to tender. Instead, the tenders are analysed on a group of criteria similar to that of the 'best offer' and the customer selects several companies (generally three) for a complementary, so-called negotiation phase. The list of accepted companies for negotiation is called the shortlist. The choice is made after negotiation with all the shortlisted companies and on all aspects of the tender so as to find the best solution for the customer. In many cases, a letter is sent to these companies as a 'letter of intent'. This market consultation method is also used in public markets by a procedure called invitation to tender on performance. It was introduced in the 1990s in the European Public Market Code following the difficulties previously discussed. In this method, the customer (administrations, authorities, etc.) communicates the operational requirements that need to be satisfied and the supplier in response proposes means of implementation. In this approach:

- only consultation with a restricted number of companies is possible because there can be, for the supplier, extensive preliminary design preparation;
- after handing in their tenders, suppliers can clarify, complete or modify them (this is usually done after having been heard by the buying commission);
- there can be compensation from the company when the response requires extensive investment of expertise.

BOX 3.1 Tenders first? Not in San Francisco Airport Commission.

All the marketing tools in the world would not have helped most San Francisco architectural and engineering firms receive a commission for the $2.4 billion expansion of San Francisco International Airport. In fact, most of them could not even go as far as the offer stage in the project marketing process.

Rather than using the more traditional avenues of inviting a handful of firms to submit proposals, or holding an open design competition, the San Francisco Airports Commission (SFAC) chose design firms almost solely on the basis of client recommendations. According to Jason Yuen, a consultant to SFAC, the commission chose this method because it believes that it is the only way to ensure that selections are equitable and objective:

'There's a flaw in the traditional proposal–presentation–selection process. You base your judgment on the presentation and materials submitted rather than the real qualifications and performance of a firm. We're not hiring consultants to do presentations or proposals, so we're drawing a line between marketing and substance.'

Six hundred and seventeen firms that responded to the project advertisement had to go through a competition before any of them could present an offer. They were asked to submit a list of all the clients they had worked for in the last 3 years. The commission then conducted an unwieldy 3,000 interviews, both in person and over the telephone, with those clients. It then scored the results, had the results audited by a third party, and evaluated the scores.

The field had been narrowed to a shortlist of 80 firms. Of that 80, five teams were engaged in a blind design competition for the international terminal—the first of 43 separate projects that would be awarded by year end. 'No song and dance allowed here,' says Yuen. Interviews were one-on-one and again with no slide shows or presentation boards. 'It's the individuals in a firm who do the work, not the firm. We want to know who they are and will be conducting our interviews as if they're applying for employment.'

The remainder of those shortlisted would be interviewed by the SFAC for the remaining commissions.

Source: Adapted from 'Airport designers will be selected by client recommendations', *Building Design & Construction*, September 1993, **34**(9), pp. 12–13.

Globally, it's becoming clearer that invitations to tender, and more specifically their economic productivity, are being challenged. This buying procedure has long since been presented as the most economical one for public money by guaranteeing complete freedom in competitive interplay. Today, it is suffering from over-competitiveness. Some experts maintain that less competitive and more relational or adjustable procedures allow adequate and more productive competitiveness than invitations to tender. This is particularly true when considering the so-called negotiated procedure that has limited competitiveness.

A Long and Negotiated Process

In project business, actors take the view that 'time is long', certainly much longer than most transactions encountered in other industrial activities. Take the example of the Korean high-speed railway in the previous chapter. That was an exceptional project because of its size and duration.

The project took shape at the end of the 1980s. The company given the task to carry out the project was created in 1992: the KHRC (Korea High Speed Railway) plc 100% financed by State capital was both client and manager of this project. The contract for the high-speed railway supplier was signed in 1994 by the consortium Eukorail led by GEC Alsthom. The project director was recruited by GEC Alsthom in 1990. In principle, partial opening was planned for 2002, but due to civil engineering difficulties this opening was postponed by 2–4 years. The rolling stock was delivered in 1998 (prototypes) and further rolling stock should be delivered in 2002 (series). Fifteen to twenty years will have passed from inception of the scheme to the effective operation of the high-speed train.

Of course, not all projects resemble this one, but it is interesting to study this project as projects are very often of long duration. It is not rare for a company project engineer to track a project for months or even several years before the project is officially put out to tender. The average project buying process (Cova and Holstius, 1993), from identification of a 'requirement' by the customer to signature of the contract with the accepted supplier(s), includes sixteen phases as presented in Table 3.1. This process details the tender/offer invitations and negotiations phases (see also Figure 1.6).

TABLE 3.1 The detailed project buying process (Cova and Holstius, 1993).

1. Identification of requirements
2. Feasibility study
3. Research/Selection of suppliers for advice
4. Definition of specifications and compilation of terms and conditions
5. Setting up a bidding list
6. Invitation to tender
7. Information exchange: buyer + supplier network
8. Reception and analysis of suppliers' proposals
9. Selection of suppliers and setting up of a shortlist
10. Negotiation on all points
11. Reception of new proposals
12. Analysis of new proposals
13. Negotiation of all points
14. Final evaluation
15. Selection
16. Contract

TABLE 3.2 Example of a customer buying process in the construction industry.

Ideas, requirements, objectives

 1. Preliminary concepts
 2. Feasibility diagnostic (internal and external contacts)
 3. Possible scenarios
 4. Analysis, choice of scenarios
 5. Preliminary studies
 6. Adoption of a scenario, project definition, system choice
 7. Setting up means and objectives
 8. Detailed studies
 9. Choice of buying procedure
10. Consultation
11. Analysis
12. Negotiation
13. Choice

This can be interpreted as a procedure that reduces uncertainties associated with the project. Uncertainty is progressively reduced by means of a series of contacts and exchanges with consulted actors leading to a better understanding of stakes in Phase 3 and in Phase 7 and even during negotiation. As the process progresses, the customer carries out adjustments and selects potential suppliers.

From a supplier's point of view, this process, although schematic, shows that consultation by invitation to tender only takes place at Phase 6. By this stage, many social and information exchanges could have taken place with potential suppliers, giving the latter undeniable advantages. According to the context, there can be differences in the content and the sequence of the phases. For a given supplier, the formalization of this process, based on experience and retrospective study of a group of similar projects that he has been awarded or lost, is highly instructive. Table 3.2 is an example of a project buying process and its different phases.

Fragmentation of Buying Centres

The very high degree of interaction between actors can lead to such a degree of common undertaking by many organizations that it is questionable if the traditional notions of business-to-business marketing of buying centres and selling centres are valid in these circumstances (Hakansson and Östberg, 1975). The case of the Toulouse subway is a good illustration of the fragmentation on a customer level of the buying centre into several organizations: the Public Transport Mixed Syndicate, the Toulouse Town Council, the Haute-Garonne Departmental Council, etc. Similarly, Box 3.2 presents the selling centre for rolling stock for the Korean high-speed railway.

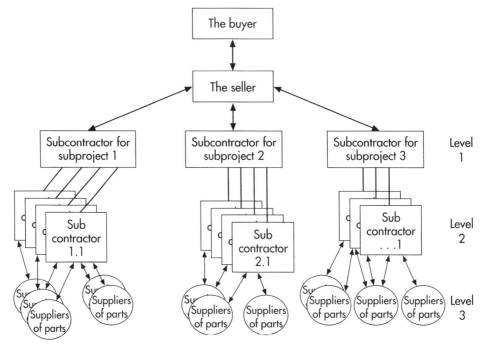

FIGURE 3.1 The project pyramid.

BOX 3.2 The actors in the Korean high-speed railway project.

Twelve companies have grouped together to form the Eukorail consortium:

- French companies: GEC Alsthom; GEC Alsthom Transport; Cegelec; CSEE;
- Korean companies: Daewoo Heavy Industries; Eukorail; Hyundai Precision & Industries; Hanjin Heavy Industries; ILJIN Electric & Machinery; Lucky Goldstar Industrial System; Lucky Goldstar Cable Manufacturing; Samsung Electronics.

Many factors contribute to the fragmented structure of the buying centre and the selling centre. In fact, it is difficult for both supplier and customer alike:

- to predict the project characteristics and its development;
- to mobilize the many internal competencies that are used infrequently (consequence of uniqueness and discontinuity of project business).

For this reason each of the project suppliers occupies different positions within the project pyramid (see Figure 3.1). In this pyramid, the owner of future work defines the objectives of its project. The main contractor can play two roles: that of the architect and assembler and/or of the coordinator for project execution. In a lot of cases, a consultant or an engineering company is in charge of defining the architecture of the project, and the contractor manages the implementation of the project. The suppliers in charge of parts of the project are responsible for the realization of elementary tasks. It should be noted that for major projects, each portion can be made up of a subproject with the same pyramid structure.

Suppliers occasionally have to develop complex alliances; for example, in a bid for the project of a new gas treatment plant (OGD 2) dedicated to the Abu-Dhabi National Oil Company, the US engineering company Bechtel and the French company Technip got together to win this huge and complex bid (€1.2 billion). On other projects, they are in direct competition.

Suppliers also have to integrate to a certain extent many tasks or functions such as feasibility studies, basic engineering, detailed engineering, funding, project management, implementation, execution, construction, operation, maintenance, etc. Similarly, on any given project (see Chapter 1) the customer may take on project management himself and delegate to a certain extent the design, execution and exploitation according to his competencies and choice.

Chapter 4

PROJECT MARKETING PRACTICES

All the different elements detailed in the previous chapters lead to the conclusion that project marketing is different from marketing of both consumer and industrial products and services. Project marketing hinges on the following key elements:

- A marketing process in three phases: independent of any project/pre-tender/ tender preparation.
- The existence of three pertinent levels of analysis and decision: milieu/client/ project.
- The management of business and non-business actors.
- The management of a supplier's relational position and functional position.
- Risk or uncertainty as the driver of behaviour of the actors.
- Solution as a means to create value for the customer.

A Specific Temporality

Using invitations to tender for projects has for a long time turned companies towards marketing behaviour that is reactive and centred on answering the call for tender. To avoid this limitation, most companies have set up approaches based on taking extremely early action (see Box 4.1).

BOX 4.1 The project marketing approach.

The following is the complete explanation given by the marketing manager of a company specializing in heavy equipment for the petroleum industry, during an interview:

'Independent of any project, I invest in geographical, technical or financial niches such as BOOT [Built, Owned, Operated, Transferred]. That means that I am focused on these niches. The decision to invest in a specific niche is confirmed by the hierarchy—this is a strategic decision. The aim here is to evaluate the accessibility of projects in this niche. I then take stock of the information. I stop or I continue in this or that direction, on this or that opportunity; for example, I'll set up a structure on site. I'll take spot actions on different points. I continue to search and dig around.

At some stage, a possible project is identified. We dig out more information: What characteristics? What engineering company? Then, after evaluation, we take the decision whether or not to go ahead. For this, we have a project screening grid. In fact, the more difficult the project is, whatever its size, the more it interests us because we know that we manage these projects well. We add the size of the project as another criteria because we know to a certain extent how to carry out large projects better. Then we concentrate on relations. We create a first contact and we nurture it. We look for partners to join us in the venture.

Then, when there is the call for tender, we are consulted. We already have partners. Internally, we then designate someone capable of structuring the tender on a technical level. This person is also in charge of fixing the price. The salesperson coordinates the non-technical aspects with the related departments (e.g. the legal aspects with the lawyers, etc.). We put forward the tender. The customer asks for clarifications. At this point, the salesperson has the central role in the business relationship. In our profession, the customer is our focus even if there is an engineering company coordinating the whole project. The salesperson negotiates through to the signing of the contract. Then the file is transmitted for execution.'

Source: Interviews by the authors.

The opinion shared by the majority of marketing and salespeople in companies selling projects is that a supplier has almost no chance of being awarded a project if it begins to take an interest only at the time of the invitation to tender (Bansard *et al.*, 1993; Boughton, 1987).

It, therefore, makes sense to consider three phases (Figure 4.1) for efficient project marketing (Cova *et al.*, 2000):

- Independent of any project; the project does not yet exist.
- Pre-tender; the company has detected a project and chooses whether or not to invest resources in the development of an offer and in contacts.

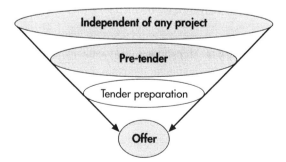

FIGURE 4.1 The three periods of project marketing.

- Tender preparation; the project officially exists in the form of a market consultation by the customer (invitation-to-tender) calling for an offer by the supplier.

There are corresponding actions for the supplier to take in relation to these three phases.

Three Levels of Analysis

Observing how companies operate in project business shows that suppliers carry out actions, analysis and decisions on three different levels: milieu, customer, project.

The first analysis and decision unit is the *milieu* or localized network (Cova *et al.*, 1996). By milieu we mean the group of business and non-business actors who play roles in related activities in a given territory. This milieu can be broken down into two subassemblies or subnetworks:

- demand milieu group of actors who can intervene on behalf of the customer;
- offer milieu group of actors whose resources and expertise intervene in assisting the supplier's tender and can be mobilized on a given project.

In fact, in many cases, the distinction between demand milieu and offer milieu is not always easy. However, even if it seems a little simplistic, breaking down the actions to be carried out allows us to appreciate their differences.

A second unit of analysis and decision is the customer (i.e. the buying organization). When a company or an institution requests a proposal, it is clear that the supplier who responds finds himself confronted by an organization that has complex decision-making processes which he must understand in order to take action. This, however, does not mean that many other external actors cannot have an influence on the decision. For the supplier, taking the customer's granularity into consideration is all the more important as there is a certain amount of repetition among all the customer's projects. In this way, relations resemble those found in repeat purchase product marketing.

The last analysis and decision unit is the project. It should not be forgotten that in the end the customer wants to resolve a precise problem (the project) and he has contacted suppliers for this. The project is the transactional episode that encapsulates the efforts made previously by the milieu and the customer and that transforms them into business terms (obtaining the contract or not).

Business and Non-business Actors

Non-business actors are institutions (state organizations, administrations, universities, etc.), permanent pressure groups (professional groups, lobby groups, etc.) or spontaneous pressure groups (committees defending a particular cause, associations, etc.) that can influence marketing operation (Sjöberg, 1993). Business actors

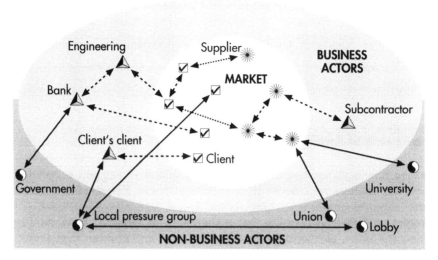

FIGURE 4.2 Markets as networks.

are all the actors involved in the economic/commercial transactions. These two types of actor are interlinked in the market and recognized more as a network of interdependent actors (sociological or socio-economic approach to the market seen as a network) than as the meeting place of demand and supply (economic approach to the market).

Figure 4.2 illustrates that a supplier–customer relationship is embedded in a set of relationships both directly and indirectly connected with the customer and the supplier. These relationships with business and non-business actors can be inside the market (where demand and supply meet) or outside the scope of what we usually consider to be the market.

Typically, business actors are targeted by companies operating in project business. Moreover, strategic analysis methods developed over the last 20 years emphasize this point. These methods are based on analysis of the structure and dynamics of the competitive arena or industry in order to evaluate the competitive forces present and to define the consequential actions.

Non-business actors, on the other hand, are increasingly taken into consideration in company procedures, as was shown in Chapter 3 with the examples of the Toulouse subway and the Korean high-speed bullet trains. Over the last 10 years or so, companies have developed non-market strategy stances and actions that they use alongside market strategy, which together constitute what we call integrated strategy (Baron, 1995).

Relational Position and Functional Position

The example of the B Line of the Toulouse subway (see Chapter 3) clarified the two features of the supplier's position in project marketing: relational position and functional position. First, the tenders from the two competitors Matra Transport International and Gec Alsthom were not identical. They differed in the technical solutions they proposed in response to a functional requirement. This functional requirement was made up of three elements: passenger security, performance levels (journey time and the time separating two subway trains) and availability (the possibility, without a driver, to increase the duration or reduce the cost of daily operation, to decrease human errors, and to regulate both traffic and punctuality). Second, the two competitors did not have the same relationship with the actors involved in the decision.

In markets involving a large number of customers, the position of the company is typically evaluated by market share. In project business where small numbers (of key business and non-business actors, and customers) are usual, this quantitative indicator of position is useful, but it is not sufficient to qualify company position. This position is defined in a more qualitative way. The position translates the role and the power that an organization exerts (i.e. the capacity to influence other actors in the market seen as a network). Translated in terms of available resources, the more resources a company has (technological, relational, financial, human), either directly or through its relations with other actors, the stronger the company's position is. The functional position therefore represents the capacity to elaborate differentiated solutions, on a global level, for the market and, on a specific level, for the customer's project.

The relational position is the result of 'relational investments' independent of any project, pre-tender and during tender preparation; contacts with actors in the milieu, with participants from the customer's buying decision centre who are involved in the project, contacts not directly related to the project, contacts involved in other projects, etc.

In project marketing, it is necessary *a priori* for a company to have a strong functional position and, at the same time, a favourable relational position to win the project (Jansson, 1989). These positions result from actions conducted independent of any project, pre-tender and during tender preparation on the three levels of analysis: milieu, customer, project. Here, it is important to note that, usually, a supplier cannot compensate a weak functional position by a strong relational position. However, a strong relational position allows the supplier to gain information in order to prepare an offer which is better than those of its competitors. Partnerships between suppliers within a project consortium are often driven by the need to improve relational or functional positions. A company can improve its functional position by means of its own development, including its general tender policy and/or by the interaction of permanent or *ad hoc* partners with other companies. Similarly, the same company can also improve its relational position. In this way, positioning in relation to the project pyramid— the alliances, the choice of an agent, contacts with process providers, pertinent contacts in political environments—is a means of improving both functional position and relational position.

Risk or Uncertainty

Management sciences and methods used by companies often include the concept of risk or uncertainty. Initially, this concept was used in management sciences to explain the organizational buying behaviour in business-to-business exchanges (Johnston and Lewin, 1994). We summarize below the principal key points:

- First, every buying decision within a company generates risks of varying degrees which depend on:

  —the stakes linked to solving the problem (e.g. the project under considera-tion) that has arisen in the context of its activity;
  —the characteristics of its organization (the different participants and relation-ships that it nurtures, resources and competencies mastered by the company and the system of influence contributing to the decision);
  —the possibilities of choice open to it on the tender market.

- Second, the company will try to bring these perceived risks to a more manage-able level. To successfully carry out this reduction in risks, it will mobilize resources and expertise:

  —internally, the effect of this mobilization is the implication that the higher the risk associated with the decision, the larger the number of participants, the more numerous the functions and the higher their hierarchical levels;
  —externally, the company will appeal to suppliers, service providers, subcon-tractors, etc. The higher the risk, the more a company will like to share it with others.

Then, according to the case, the customer could act either by coordinating (see Figure 1.3) the complete implementation of the project himself, or, on the contrary, he could outsource and delegate design, implementation, maintenance and sometimes management to a unique supplier (see Figures 1.4 and 1.5). This variation in the degree of outsourcing of the project depends on the customer's strategy and, especially, on his purchasing strategy.

This approach to organizational buying behaviour based on perceived risk can be broadened to understanding the behaviour of other actors (business or non-business), influencing decisions. Considering risk as the driving force behind such behaviour shows us that by his actions the supplier is a reducer of the risks perceived by the customer. In order to reduce this risk, and taking into account the required degree of outsourcing by the customer, suppliers propose more frequently the so-called 'solutions offers' that are centred on value creation.

There are also many decision tools that consider risk from the supplier's point of view. Methods which have been developed to screen projects, to decide to go ahead or not with a given project, are usually centred on the risk the company incurs by proceeding. We can therefore see that the risk concept has several factors: on the one hand, the risk perceived by the customer which the supplier will try to reduce (or play on) by his actions; on the other hand, the risk taken by the supplier when he makes such a decision. In this book, the two points of view will be adopted when presenting tools and methods.

Create and Deliver Value

'Value in business markets is the worth in monetary terms of the economic/ commercial, technical, service and social benefits a customer firm receives in exchange for the price it pays for a market offering' (Anderson and Narus, 1999). In the case of project marketing, due to the complexity of the project, it is important for the supplier to be able to handle multidimensional solutions that provide value to the customer. We can see from Box 4.2, taken from websites of major companies, the relevance of the concepts of solutions and value creation in project marketing.

BOX 4.2 Example of Solution and Value Creation Strategies in Companies Selling Projects.

Airbus (www.airbus.com)

'Offer the greatest customer value and widest appeal to the many and varied customers in the commercial airline community ... With this objective, Airbus has created a product line which truly meets their demands, offering the best in performance and economies combined with world-beating product capabilities and quality, setting the standards of the industry in comfort, innovation, family benefits and customer value.'

Alcatel (www.alcatel.com)

'The telecom market is changing fast and drastically. Operators face a tense competition even in their home markets and customers are demanding more, better and faster services. Therefore operators expect much more from their supplier than the delivery of a set of products. The product has to be accompanied by a range of network operator services.'

'All-in-One Alcatel Service provides an extensive set of services for networks operators built around eight domains and currently four generic solutions with one goal; helping operators achieve their strategic goals. The All-in-One Alcatel Service portfolio assists them to reduce time-to-market, cut cost, achieve optimum quality of service and efficient customer care and get increased revenues.'

Alstom (www.alstom.com)

'Complete solutions provides for the safe, reliable and efficient transmission and distribution of electricity to all power levels from the generator to the end-user, Alstom accompanies its customer worldwide from the design table through equipment and system supply to global service support.'

Cisco (www.cisco.com)

'We're committed to your success, and work to ensure you achieve the maximum return on your networking investment through a suite of support services across the network life cycle. Whether it's speed to market/speed to revenue, maximizing network ability, enhancing customer satisfaction, or augmenting your staff, Cisco and our selectively chosen ecosystem of highly skilled delivery partners are committed to your success.'

Ericsson (www.ericsson.com)

'In the traditional telecom world, telecom companies provide end users with services through their retail role. In the new multi-service world, value is created through the synergy of content, applications, communication, end user understanding and customer relations ... Service Provider Applications introduce new roles for traditional operators and IT service providers. Ericsson supports traditional and 'new' customers with IT infrastructure, service-enabling platforms and multi-service applications.'

'Personal communication and end-to-end quality are regarded as highly important in order to satisfy end users need in terms of 'quality of life' and efficiency. The aim is to enable end users as individuals to improve quality of life, to save time and cost. Able to access anywhere, anytime, and through any device—at home, on the move, at work. As well as enterprises to improve their relations with their customers, partners and suppliers, and to become more efficient.'

Lucent (www.lucent.com)

'Service Work Broadland Services for Cable Operators is a suite of services to give cable operators end-to-end network deployment solutions ... Service Work Broadland Services for cable operators help you gain or maintain your competitive edge and increase speed-to-market by providing end-to-end network solutions so you can construct and deploy new infrastructures quickly and economically.'

Chapter 5

THE PROJECT MARKETING LOGIC

Confronted with the uniqueness and complexity of each project as well as with the commercial discontinuity of relationships with customers, marketing strategy is designed with the aim to access more continuity and predictability, so it can be better controlled (Slatter, 1990; Tikkanen, 1998). Therefore, project marketing goes beyond those approaches that simply respond to invitations to tender. This enables suppliers in project business to position themselves favourably both in relation to customers and also ahead of competitors in the market.

In fact, the existence of a buying procedure by invitation to tender places the supplier in an unfavourable reactive position—he reacts to stimuli sent by the customer by invitation to tender—and has to submit himself to the terms and conditions stipulated in the invitation to tender. Consequently, the supplier in project business sells projects on demand and at the customer's request. This structural and historical aspect of project sales is challenged more and more by marketing events and notably by marketing strategies of project suppliers. These suppliers tried to gain some room to manoeuvre by being, at the same time, less reactive—and therefore more anticipatory—and less submissive—and therefore more in control of their offers and their way of entering the project pyramid (McAfee and McMillan, 1986).

In project activities, there is a very high degree of uncertainty related to transactions. Suppliers find themselves in this situation of uncertainty both in relation to the scope of the market game (Who would the client be? What would the project be?) and in relation to the rules of the market game (When would the call for tender be issued? How many competitors would there be?). In an attempt to reduce uncertainty, they have developed marketing practices which consist in positioning themselves and/or taking intense action 'upstream' of projects to:

- anticipate the scope and the rules of the game—deterministic approach;
- participate in the construction of the scope and rules of the game—constructivistic approach.

By combining and balancing these two approaches (Cova and Hoskins, 1997; Skaates and Tikkanen, 2000), suppliers try as much as possible to avoid finding themselves in a submissive position in relation to the rules of the game (i.e. the directives of the invitation to tender) that they neither anticipated nor elaborated.

The deterministic approach is based on the assumption that the project is going to happen; on one hand, it is an event isolated in time (the project) and, on the other hand, this project will be integrally decided by the future customer. Facing this type of situation, the supplier does his utmost to anticipate this demand and to be as well prepared as possible. The basis of this deterministic approach of project marketing is the scanning system. This scanning is based on looking for a certain degree of continuity of the business relationship during the independent of any project and pre-tender phases. This can be approached in two ways by looking for:

- a social continuity through contact with key actors in the milieu directly and indirectly connected with the customer; and/or
- a continuity with the customer based on durability and repeatability of social and economic exchanges.

The constructivist approach is based on the assumption that the customer and his partners jointly elaborate the project and that the supplier is one of the actors in this construction. The basis of this constructivist approach to project marketing is what is called the creative offering (i.e. creating the project for the customer or with the customer). The existence of a relationship with the customer and a certain intimacy with him, nurtured by the frequency of social contact and economic exchange, can also create conditions for such a solution-selling approach. As the CEO of Motorola, Robert Jalvin, says, 'the first step in any defined strategy is writing the rules of the game ... We have incidentally found that, in many quarters of the world, our offer to constructively define the rule is reasonably welcomed.'

This type of approach is similar to those found in works on innovation. According to Hamel and Prahalad (1994), we are currently approaching, in terms of innovation, the end of incrementalism and linearity—their doctrine is 'to change the rules of the game' in industry. Strategy also refers to deterministic or constructivistic approaches. Certain specialists of company strategy (Atamer and Calori, 1993) discern three strategic behaviours depending on contexts:

- play the rules of the game better than the competitors;
- change the rules of the game without transforming the nature of the system;
- transform the nature of the system (this strategy implies also changing the rules of the game).

Deeper analysis of marketing practices in project business shows that they combine deterministic and constructivistic approaches in order to:

- move away from a purely transactional reasoning, imposed by the project operation, by creating continuity in the relationship with customers (transaction vs. relations);

- avoid reasoning only in terms of adapting in real time to customer terms and conditions by developing anticipation capacities (adaptation vs. anticipation);
- avoid reasoning only in terms of reacting by submission to the characteristics of the invitation to tender by constructing the project with a greater or lesser implication for the customer (submission vs. construction);
- mobilize and combine in a pertinent way the internal resources and/or external resources to structure the tender (internal resources vs. external resources).

These four dialectics structure project marketing.

Beyond Transactional Logic

Here, the company objective is to reduce the discontinuity of exchanges with customers so as to capitalize on relational investments made during a previous project (Hadjikhani, 1996). In business-to-business marketing for products and services, the initial investments made in order to acquire a first transaction and to create the relationship are later recovered through subsequent transactions. The supplier does not have to invest resources to the same extent for these new transactions in so far as, by acquiring more intimate knowledge of the customer, certain procedures and operation methods have already been set up to facilitate the interaction between the two companies.

In project marketing, the objective is therefore to get closer to these operating modes and therefore create some continuity.

The first way is to create purely social episodes between projects (i.e. 'fill in' the period between economic transactions by episodes of a social nature: Björkman and Kock, 1995). Many occasions exist to maintain this continuity such as meetings at colloquiums, organization of theme events leading to new technological developments, etc. Premeditated strategies can also be carried out as suggested by the American engineering firm Bechtel (McCartney, 1989):

> Every year, people from Bechtel and their government and industrial friends go to Bohemian Grove for their yearly camping. There, under the sequoias, the members and the guests group together around a campfire. But the real purpose of Grove, where the favourite pastime is guessing the connections and relationships of newcomers, is purely *business*. Not *business* by contract or agreement (both are formally prohibited in Grove) but *business* by elective affinity, by people taking time to get to know and appreciate each other.

We have to admit that it is not easy for most individuals to keep contacts when there is no economic relationship in existence or in sight. We will come back in detail to this point in Part II of this book which is dedicated to presentation of methods.

The second way to keep continuity is to create episodes of a commercial nature within the customer relationship such as complementary services, training, bringing equipment up to standard, updating, spare parts, maintenance, revamping, joint studies on possible new developments, audits, etc.

The third way is to adopt an approach that is in full development in the majority of industrial companies: the key account approach (i.e. the specific management of a relationship between the supplier and a major customer: Millman, 1996). In a certain way, it requires the supplier to take a broader view of customer organization. The organization should be considered in full; if it is an industrial group, the largest level of granularity should be considered as the most pertinent. In fact, we can often see that projects are located within the buying centre of the specific subsidiary, division or site involved. Within this customer, each new project may well be piloted by a different buying centre, which often leads the supplier to be under the impression that he is dealing with a market made up of individual customers (the different units of the industrial group) with weak buying frequencies rather than dealing with a group. By considering the customer group as a set of interdependent units, having perhaps similar problems, could lead the supplier to opt for global draft agreements.

This choice allows the supplier to be faced with a higher frequency of purchase and may lead to durable supplier/customer relationships. The existence of this relationship enables operating methods to be set up that are similar to those encountered in business-to-business relationships. A marketing manager of a construction company said:

> When dealing with large groups (our privileged customers) we have to visit them and say: We are professionals in the building business. Let us handle your building projects for you. We agree to the financial conditions and we deliver the product respecting the agreed price. Customers are above all industrial and financial. They don't care about the technical aspect. They don't care how we have built the foundations either.

We have met many industrial equipment companies, internationally, that truly 'follow' the big industrial groups in the chemical, petroleum and food-processing industries in their establishments abroad. To develop these approaches, there are two ways of viewing company organization:

- reasoning in terms of maintaining project flow and continuity with the industrial group customer supported by key account management;
- reasoning in terms of adaptation to customer projects of different characteristics relying on project managers.

From Adaptation to Anticipation

In the so-called deterministic approach to project marketing, the company identifies a project and subsequently adapts its offer to meet the explicit demand of the customer. This approach in project marketing, when compared with invitations to tender, goes beyond submission strategies (Bansard *et al.*, 1993) to consequently take the three temporalities described on p. 34 into consideration.

First of all, independent of any project, the company tries to understand the scope of the work, although there is not yet a project. The company has to determine who the key actors are, their role and how they intervene by decoding events and analysing the way in which previous projects developed. This approach consists of scanning developments: it is an anticipation approach. The objective is to evaluate the probability of these actors being involved in projects and of setting up adequate relational actions (i.e. to select some of these actors in order to transform them into poles of continuity between the supplier and customers). The following account of a project engineer is a good illustration of this:

> Anticipation is much more important than before. Nothing is acquired and permanent. Before, we were strong in certain countries. Now, that's over. American customers don't like to be told what to do because they rule the world. Petroleum companies don't want to be told anything at all. More and more, we have to incite them to choose. In terms of business, that implies having a worldwide network, to speak with them, to understand the health of the market. You have to be well informed. You have to anticipate enormously, to know how to position yourself. For me, I'm already thinking about the invitation to tender we are planning in two years' time.

The marketing of a company, specializing in steel for big installations in chemical and petroleum industries, states that throughout the world the number of actors present within the scope of the work (the pertinent perimeter in relation to the activity of the company) can amount to between 2,000 and 3,000 (made up of individuals and/or organizations, engineering firms, companies, subcontractors, engineering consultants, technical centres, research laboratories, etc.). In the end, only 200 actors had real power. It is therefore important to rank actors so as to seek out a limited number of actors within the milieu of the project and to concentrate investments on key actors when anticipating projects to establish some continuity.

Curiously, the fact that this work consists in getting closer to customers and potential acting parties, in order to optimize performance, is seen by the uninitiated as a kind of conspiracy of individual interests against general interest. Perhaps, this is the consequence of certain unfair practices in recent 'projects'.

Concerning the functional level, the company works independent of any project to develop a double-barrelled offer strategy:

- a potential core offer that is made up of core competencies and internal resources;
- a set of offers that can be mobilized in a partnership network which could complete the potential core offer and give adaptability to contend with the uniqueness of each future project.

Next, in the pre-tender phase, the company anticipates the rules of the game with the customer and other influential actors. Here, we can speak about the customer in so far as a project has been detected before the customer's official invitation to tender. Quite often it is the investments made independent of any project that have allowed the company to detect an intention or a project in preparation. The milieu that, as seen by the supplier independent of any project, was previously made up of a network of influential actors becomes more organized, taking into consideration the characteristics of the project and of the customer.

Let us look again at the example of the company specializing in steel for big industrial installations. If scanning the milieu has enabled a project to extend the production capacity of an Exxon petrochemical complex in the USA to be detected, only some actors within the milieu will be concerned. If the company has carried out prior actions, contact with these actors will be easier. However, if the company detects the existence of this project without prior investment independent of any project, this means it will have to carry out investments at this stage (i.e. when it detects the project). Establishing a relational position in this case is all the more difficult.

BOX 5.1 Gambling Japanese Business Style: The Loser Wins.

A fashionable way of disguising bribes, pay-offs or gifts in both business and political circles in Japan is to purposefully lose when playing golf or mah-jongg, a Chinese table game with rules similar to gin rummy. If you can lose skilfully, your services may be in demand.

Gambling is a minor crime in Japan, whereas bribery is a major one. To skirt the law, Japanese business people invite officials or others to a discreet high-class restaurant or club that provides a salon for private mah-jongg games. Executives of the host company bring along young employees noted for their abilities to deftly lead their opponent to a successful win at a substantial loss for themselves. If your guests prefer golf to mah-jongg, they can have a golf game with the company's reverse pro' who specializes in hooking and slicing his way to sure defeat.

Source: Adapted from 'Those Who Lose Really Win in Japan; The Fine Art of Mah-Jongg as Bribery', The *Wall Street Journal*, 20 January 1984, p. 28. Reprinted with permission of The *Wall Street Journal*, 1984 Dow Jones & Company, Inc. All Rights Reserved Worldwide.

It is this stage, prior to the tender, that has been under the spotlight in the last few years (see Box 5.2), especially in the case of public markets. In a report to the Prime Minister of France entitled 'Prevention of corruption and transparency of economic life', we can read:

> One of the privileged moments of corruption in public markets is the period before the invitation to tender. The most discrete way to give preference to a 'generous' company is in fact to associate it with the definition of the market object, i.e. by making sure the public demand corresponds directly to the product that this company can supply. Over and above the corruption, this practice is opposed to sincere competition.

BOX 5.2 The Navy's Drone Contract: Fair Bid or Fait Accompli?

Back in 1983, US President Reagan sent an armada to the waters off war-torn Lebanon. But the fleet suffered a serious handicap; it had to use expensive fighters and attack planes for reconnaissance and directing gunfire. The aircraft were easy targets for the Syrians who shot down two planes. John Tirven (not the real name), then US Navy Secretary, thought he could help solve the problem with propeller-driven, unmanned aircraft, known as 'remotely piloted vehicles' (RPVs), or drones.

And he got them within two years. But the story of how the Pentagon moved so fast, according to critics, is a case study in how the defence procurement process may have gone awry. Authorities investigated whether bidding for the contract was rigged and tried to determine whether defence consultant and former Navy acquisition chief A. Cooper (not the real name) had invested in a foreign company that stood to benefit from the contract. Cooper was a central figure in the procurement fraud scandal.

By all accounts, Tirven was right in thinking that the drones would be invaluable. They can fly above a battlefield and confuse enemy radar or send back TV pictures or targets to gunners on ships offshore—without risking lives. Some of the best drones were made in Israel where they had the added edge of frequent battle testing. So it was no surprise Tirven turned to Tel Aviv for help. In 1984 the US Navy bought a $7.5 million drone from the Israeli government for testing.

That brought howls from Developmental Sciences Corp. (DSC), an Ontario (California) dronemaker. The Navy earlier had expressed interest in DSC's Sky Eye which the US Army planned to use in Central America. The company complained about the Navy's purchase to former Defence Secretary Caspar W. Weinberger. 'We get back a letter that in the future the Navy would have to compete its RPVs,' said Gerry R. Seeman, president and CEO of DSC. But Seeman questioned how seriously the US Navy took Weinberger's promise. AAI Corp. won the 1985 competition for the project, which has cost the US government more than $80 million. This Baltimore-based contractor built the Pioneer, a drone whose design was derived from technology developed by Mazlat, an Israeli company that was a big subcontractor on the project.

DSC wondered whether that outcome was a foregone conclusion. Seeman said, 'We really felt that the Navy Secretary was very thick with the Israelis.' Another DSC official noted that the specifications laid out by the US Navy and the winning RPV's brochure description of their product contained 'some remarkable duplications', including such items as the aircraft's range and endurance. In fact, 'the Navy specs were the Pioneer specs.' Considering the normal lag time in Pentagon procurement, the Navy seemed to be in a hurry to buy the drones. As the competitive 'fly-off' approached in late 1985, the Navy rejected DSC's request for a two-week delay so that it could conduct a Sky Eye test for the Army.

Federal authorities investigated whether Cooper, Tirven's close associate, helped influence the drone deal while he was a Navy official. They also looked into his involvement with Mazlat; they searched for any document Cooper had relating to foreign bank accounts or interest in foreign corporations including Mazlat. AAI officials, on the contrary, said that the competition was fair and the Navy was not to blame that only one bidder was ready to fly its machine.

Source: Adapted from *Business Week*, 1 August, 1988. Fair bid or *fait accompli?*

Finally, during tender preparation, the company submits to the rules of the game that have been defined by the customer through the characteristics of the terms and conditions of the invitation to tender.

Whereas before, companies concentrated their resources on the tender preparation phase by a little pre-tender investment, nowadays more and more companies concentrate their efforts in the project-independent phase so as to be in a strong pre-tender position. In fact, very often the mutual agreement results from an action independent of any specific project.

We can therefore see that the more the company anticipates, the more it increases its capacity to control the rules of the game or at least be better prepared to fit in with them. In Table 5.1, we present the case of a 14-phase buying process of a customer. Opposite each of the customer's procedural phase, we show a series of possible anticipation actions for the supplier that may be direct or indirect (i.e. relying on other organizations). Here is how this table should be read: if the supplier cannot carry out anticipation actions in phase x, what actions can he carry out in phase $x + 1$? If he cannot carry out anticipation actions in phase $x + 1$, what actions can he carry out in phase $x + 2$? And so on.

From Submission to Construction

As previously seen in the deterministic approach, more and more companies concentrate their efforts on anticipating approaches independent of any project in order to be in a strong position prior to the tender, in this way refusing to react in a behaviouristic way to the invitation to tender.

Another complementary approach with the same objective is to create the project (Cova and Crespin-Mazet, 1997). In this case, the supplier's aim is to construct the demand with the customer through their interaction and relationship. Over the last 10 years, project marketing has evolved from a submission approach (in which the degree of formality of the customer's demand is strong; he knows what he wants) to a construction approach (in which the degree of formality of the customer's demand is weak) by placing the company as an expert in relation to the customer's problem. Today, as described in the introduction to this chapter, project marketing works less on the explicit or implicit demand of the customer and more on the interest and actions that customers and actors in his network take through the concept of a creative offer. In this way, the supplier does not content himself with the customer's demand but traces back to the substantial stakes the customer has in his activity to make him reformulate and readapt his demand. Project marketing approaches go beyond submission strategies to construct simultaneously the demand and the project.

First of all, independent of any project, the supplier constructs the scope and the rules of the game with other potential actors. The supplier sets the project up and, therefore, is the leader of the game and its rules. In the milieu, the company detects and analyses a project opportunity that could correspond to a requirement that is not yet formulated. In this way, it is able to position itself ahead of the potential demand and construct the customer's demand and sometimes even construct the customer. This approach therefore consists of constructing the project by proposing a study and a project dealing with the problem that the customer has not yet clearly formulated. The supplier creates the concept of

TABLE 5.1 Example of anticipatory actions carried out by a supplier taking into consideration the phases of the customer's buying process.

Customer procedural phases	Supplier anticipation actions
1. Ideas, requirements, objectives	Strong local relations (with customer) Implication in local life *Direct action*
2. Preliminary concepts	Relations with key actors in the decision process Positioning of partners *Direct action*
3. Feasibility diagnosis (internal and external contracts)	Nurturing of relationships between the supplier network and the customer network Assisting relationships between the two networks Mobilization of internal network *Direct action*
4. Possible scenarios	Solution proposals: directly or through partners *Direct and indirect action*
5. Analysis, choice of scenarios	Support by partners who vehicle the scenario best suited to the supplier *Indirect action*
6. Preliminary studies	Technical assistance Offer of services by external consultants *Indirect action*
7. Adoption of a scenario, project definition, choice of system	Technical assistance by the consultant chosen by the customer *Indirect action*
8. Setting up of means and objectives	Support of a partner team Promotion of technical solutions to make them appear indispensable *Indirect action*
9. Detailed studies	Piggybacking, entry via a subcontractor or a supplier *Indirect action*
10. Choice of market consultation mode	Influence of the market consultation mode via the major contractor *Direct and indirect action*
11. Consultation	Differentiation of the offer *Direct action*
12. Analysis	Relationships with deciders *Direct action*
13. Negotiation	Co-selling with competitors *Direct action*
14. Choice	Strong relationships *Direct action*

the project, carries out the feasibility study, settles the financing and identifies, for example, the actors who constitute a mixed commercial company (type BOOT [Built, Owned, Operated, Transferred]) that will become his customer.

In certain companies all this construction approach is entrusted to the upstream marketing function whose tasks are summed up in the following:

> the upstream marketing role is firstly to listen to the customer, to understand his culture, to help him, to incite him to think X (the name of the company). Then compatibilities have to be matched and incompatibilities have to be limited. Our role can be broken down into three points: to understand the customer and open our minds to his wishes, to accompany him when a possible file has been identified and to play the role of internal service provider to help project operators.

Other companies set up approaches called 'pseudo-projects'; that is, a way of setting the customer's preferences by presenting him with a virtual offer (in the sense that it does not really exist) as being a base on which he can project his requirements and wishes. This offer exists only on paper (or nowadays even better, as a virtual image); it incorporates a pseudo-product as a technical solution (e.g. a type of convention centre), a pseudo-contract (a set of conditions and financial simulations) and a pseudo-network of partners on the offer (network offer) which will be put into play only if the customer reacts to the stimulus. This pseudo-project is the result of the supplier's learning process experienced in previous projects.

Next, in the pre-tender phase, if the company is the driving force behind the project, it will enter an active phase of interaction with the customer and his demand milieu. The complete procedure will be to construct a framework (i.e. rules of the game specific to the project), which will protect the supplier from possible recourse to the market by the customer or otherwise to limit the impact on his position. In fact, the customer can accept to do business by mutual agreement with the supplier who created the project. However, using the contents of the project set up by the supplier, he may possibly want to appeal to the competition and reposition the suppliers on an even footing. This last behaviour may have a negative effect on the profitability of the project for the supplier who took the initiative to create the project. If the supplier is not the driving force in the development of the project and the customer has personally developed his project, there can be peripheral development on less rigid parts of the project.

Finally, during tender preparation, if the supplier is not the driving force in the development of the project, he will try to break the established rules in order to allow the development of new rules of the game. In this case, the company finds itself confronted with the terms and conditions set up autonomously by the customer or under the influence of a competitor or another participant. According to the degree of customer openness to the interaction with the company (i.e. its capacity to accept possible modifications to the terms and conditions), the company could make the customer's demand evolve (i.e. deconstruct to re-construct).

Today, companies that are awarded markets are more and more those able to help the customer define his problem and its solution by very early close collaboration with him as opposed to those who content themselves with responding to the requirement expressed by the customer in the terms and conditions. Nevertheless, it is important to note that a great part of project business is still awarded through traditional calls for tender.

Simply listening to the customer is not enough for suppliers to make an offer and differentiate themselves. In project marketing, it is out of the question to appear neutral in relation to the customer's requirements. Neither is it acceptable for suppliers to go to the opposite extreme by trying to impose a 'ready-made' solution on the customer or to be over-sure of the strength of their responses, as this can lead them to fail to try to understand the problem of the customer and his partners.

The supplier must use his position as 'the expert of the customer's problem' while developing his offer. The following explanation given by a marketing manager illustrates this point.

BOX 5.3 Project Creation and Investments.

Today, in our activity, there are two principal niches which use different approaches. The first approach is project creation. This includes detecting a requirement, setting up a pool of local and foreign investors, setting up legal arrangements, setting up financial arrangements right up to organizing loans, the technical design, programming, execution, operation and maintenance. Why have we begun to carry out project creation? Because in certain countries I couldn't find any customers. As there was no public investment and no private sector, we had to invent projects.

The other approach is that of following up investments. I was amazed when I read that the amount of direct foreign investment in the world had grown exponentially over 3 to 5 years. Globalization has led to multinational investment. As a result, we can offer a complete development process of multidisciplinary investment. The profession of our company today is to know how to develop business and to accommodate investors.

Source: Interviews by the authors.

Globally, we can say that the set of current offer tactics in project business is linked to constructing or reconstructing the demand (Cova and Crespin-Mazet, 1997) with the customer making use of the very long duration of the definition process, of the setting up and the execution of the project (on average, around 3 years). More than the preparation of the response to the invitation to tender, it is the construction of the demand (i.e. of the invitation to tender and the terms and conditions) which is central to offer tactics.

The marketing logic is that of looking for a part in the control and power in an activity—the invitation to tender—that structurally places the supplier in an asymmetric situation in terms of information, dependence and submission.

Combining External and Internal Resources

Whatever the means of acquiring a project, in a purely reactive way or by anticipating or developing the solution for the customer, the company must combine several elements to set up its technical and financial offer. As it does not concern selling standard products in a repetitive way, companies cannot keep the complete design and realization competencies required at their disposal. They therefore combine, on one hand, the use of internal resources and the recourse to external resources (Welch *et al.*, 1996) and, on the other hand, the choice of entering in the cascade of the project (either as the leader, as project manager or acting only on parts of the project) with their strategic willpower.

In terms of the offer, we can see the logic that is simultaneously symmetrical to and interdependent on that of the demand that involves actions: independent of any project, prior to the tender, during tender preparation.

Independent of any project, the supplier tries to find possible partners in the milieu of the offer with whom it can intervene in the project. The company can go as far as drawing up contracts with these alliances. The process is also possible within the company and particularly in industrial groups. In fact, it is not rare to find industrial groups overlooking competencies in one of their subsidiaries which could well be mobilized on a given project. Some industrial groups have, moreover, set up real catalogues of internal competencies that can be mobilized for projects.

Pre-tender, the supplier aims to mobilize internal and external competencies so that they are ready to intervene in the detected project. The existence of actions to locate competencies independent of any project and also the fact of having already carried out other projects together are positive factors, in so far as the company is in an easier position to prepare the technical and financial proposal. It is on this level that most association contracts with partners are signed. These contracts can be permanent alliances, quasi-systematic unwritten alliances (reproducing the winning consortium) and spot alliances.

If this anticipation work has not been carried out when the project is detected, the company must mobilize internal and external competencies in real time. One of the risks for the company is that the best resources could already have been mobilized by a competitor who has developed the project.

During tender preparation, the supplier has to coordinate the internal and external resources to set up the proposition. If resources have not been found or mobilized independent of any project and/or prior to the tender, the coordination takes place in real time.

The Project Marketing Process

The group of elements already presented are reintegrated in Figure 5.1 in a model of the project marketing process (Cova *et al.* 1994). The definition of strategic priorities normally falls within the scope of strategic analysis methods, detailed in Chapter 6. This strategic marketing stage, which is positioned as a prerequisite to developing the project marketing process, includes decisions concerning:

- target market segments and/or key accounts;
- perimeter of what the supplier and his partners can potentially offer.

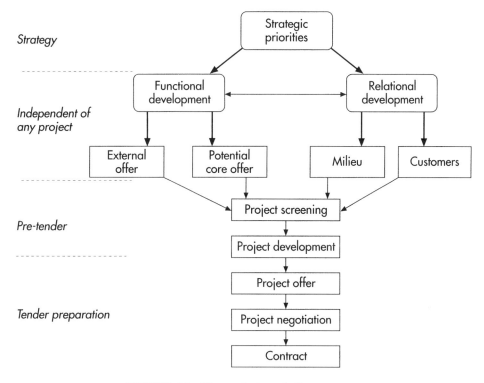

FIGURE 5.1 The project marketing process.

From this analysis and choice of priorities, the approach independent of any project in a targeted market (a specific activity on a dedicated territory) takes a group of actions into consideration to ensure:

- The functional development of the company in the targeted market. The objective is to be in a position to put together offers taking the characteristics of each project into consideration.
- The relational development of the company in the milieu which supports the targeted market (see Chapters 7–9). The objective is to be in a position to detect projects far upstream.

Functional development and relational development feed and are fed by the company's scanning system independent of any project. This hinges on two major aspects: so-called technological scanning and marketing scanning. Marketing scanning is defined as a continuous activity of operational nature, aiming to detect far upstream commercial opportunities and, if possible, even before the customer has finalized his projects. Although many publications deal with technological scanning, marketing scanning seems to have been left aside. Nevertheless, setting up such a marketing scanning system in project business exists as an essential element in strategy. In fact, it can enable suppliers to antici-pate demand and therefore to develop actions allowing them to optimize their response and even to make it evolve towards solutions more favourable to this supplier. It especially aims to develop and maintain a continuous direct or indirect link with company customers or potential customers. To a certain extent, this counteracts the natural discontinuity of transactions in project business.

This approach should enable the company, in the pre-tender phase and subsequently during tender preparation, to set up and update a set of possible projects. The supplier can then choose whether to follow up these possible projects: Is it interesting to *prepare* and then *propose* the offer or not? This will be backed up by the work of *quest marketing*: the quest for information precisely connected to a given project.

BOX 5.4 Finsys' Project Marketing Approach to China.

Finsys is a Finnish company that started to operate in China in the 1980s and has delivered more than a dozen large projects there. The project under scrutiny in this case is the Z project. For this project, the Finsys' intraorganizational actors are the following: Finsys Europe (Marketing, Sales & Sales Support = M&S) and Finsys China.

From Finsys' point of view, the Z project started when an independent agent contacted Finsys China and introduced them to a project and invited them to bid. The agent had conducted the search of potential project suppliers. He had also informed Finsys' competitors. The initiative came from the buyer's side and Finsys was to determine whether to respond to the invitation to bid or not depending on the feasibility of the project.

The buyer was a state-owned firm located in southern China. The agent was a Chinese businessman operating in Hong Kong. He had personal contacts with the buyer's organization. The buyer did not have control or ownership over the agent. The agent worked on a commission basis. The financiers of the Z project consisted of banks and other investors from Hong Kong and China.

Finsys China was the Finsys Group's wholly owned subsidiary in Hong Kong taking care of local marketing, sales and customer services. The employees of Finsys China were mainly Chinese. Finsys China's task was to perform local selling activities, inform Finsys M&S and assist them with inquiries from and preliminary discussions with the agent and Chinese governmental institutions. Finsys M&S gathered the needed information on the customer, financiers, warrantors and governmental institutions in cooperation with Finsys China. A specific M&S team became responsible for the Z project.

The first issues to be looked into were the financing of the project and whether the project had been approved by the Chinese governmental institutions. The purpose was to find out whether the project proposal should be taken seriously or not.

As the financing and other conditions were in order and the project was taken seriously by FINSYS M&S, more technical details were gathered from the buyer through inquiries. A preliminary proposal was prepared based on the information and sent to the buyer through the agent. When this preliminary proposal was accepted by the buyer, Finsys M&S prepared a detailed offer according to the customer's requirements in the bidding phase. Finsys M&S coordinated all parts of the solution. The offer included technical details and a price estimate. The price was based on the competitive situation in the market. Finsys China acted as a middleman handling the local discussion with the agent and the buyer's representatives.

Negotiations started when, the buyer accepted the offer as a basis for further negotiations. Finsys' M&S team, Finsys China, the buyer's negotiators, the agent, the bank's representatives and the warrantor were involved in the negotiations. All negotiations were conducted in China. The agent represented the customer by providing legal and technical consulting. The agent's role seemed to be more to act as a consultant than merely a middleman.

Source: With many thanks to Henrikki Tikkanen.

Everything seems fine for Finsys in this case. But, if we look more in depth, we see that Finsys discovers the project when it is in the middle of the pre-tender phase. Finsys typically is a company that does not have an established clear relational strategy in a targeted milieu in China in order to anticipate projects. Finsys bases its whole action on the fact of having a presence (Finsys China) in China without entering into the more detailed targeted relationships that need to be built, developed or maintained. We can say that the primary phases of the project marketing process are not present in its approach.

However, as soon as a project is detected, Finsys moves very quickly to progress on it. Nevertheless, this progress and the chances of success for Finsys are jeopardized by the fact that this company is in the dark as to who is the real customer, what is the role of the agent, what are the relational positions of the competitors with the key actors, etc. It could be possible that the agent is the master of the game who places Finsys in a position of asymmetry of information. In many cases, we see a company like Finsys putting a lot of effort and giving away information on a project for the sake of getting ahead of a competitor. In fact, the agent may have a privileged relationship with one of Finsys' competitors and he may be trying to get ideas from Finsys' proposal to pass them on to the competitor in order to improve his proposal. When the phase independent of any project opportunity has not been carried out correctly, a supplier such as Finsys places itself in the very bad position of being subject to forces it does not understand and control.

Part II

MARKETING STRATEGY

Chapter 6

FROM CORPORATE STRATEGY TO MARKETING STRATEGY

Our objective here is not to have a complete presentation of strategic methods used in companies selling projects. It is to define the links that exist between company (or corporate) strategy and marketing strategy. Indeed, as these two levels of decision are interdependent, and in certain cases inseparable, many comparisons are often made between the two, while it is also vital to make a distinction between them. To understand this overlap, it is necessary to have a clear vision of the different ways of dividing and aggregating company activity (the business portfolio, the strategic business units, the market segments, the milieus, the customers and the projects), and also how they are used in strategy formulation. Accordingly, we present the three dimensions of strategy:

- Global corporate strategy: highlighting the division into Strategic Business Units (SBUs) and activities portfolio and the link between decisions made at the portfolio level (global level) and the SBU level.
- Strategy within an SBU: from inside a specific unit we shall analyse the different dimensions at work for the taking of marketing decisions.
- The geographical perspective: one of the key marketing decisions concerns the choice of geographical area. Because every country's market can be viewed as a specific milieu, each marketing approach and offer needs to be adapted.

The Corporate Strategy

Company activity involves identifying the markets or parts of markets in which it has chosen to operate, and then allocating particular resources designed to meet customer needs within a competitive situation. The different methods of strategic analysis, given their different levels of focus, allow us to understand the diversity in the marketplace. These methods are based on segmentation. The process of segmentation covers all the operations that help recognize the heterogeneity of activities and determine its consequences on the firm's organization and operations. There are several levels of segmentation which correspond to the company recognizing varying degrees of market heterogeneity, which in turn determine the level and nature of involvement that the company adopts; strategic segmentation and marketing segmentation.

Strategic Segmentation and SBU

In our context, strategic segmentation applies to a much broader field, such as an industry or a market, than does marketing segmentation. Abell and Hammond (1979) suggest a commonly accepted method of segmentation according to three axes: types of technology used, the functions (or applications) and the types of customers concerned (Figure 6.1). Thus, we can define an elementary activity (Atamer and Calori, 1993) by the simultaneous overlap of the three variables on the three axes. In practice, elementary activities are often analysed to group together those that are highly similar, implying that they have identical key factors for success.

Using this approach, we arrive at a 'limited' number of homogeneous entities that can be grouped together and which allow the company to dedicate specific resources as required (production unit, organization system, financial resources, etc.). There is a need to allocate certain company assets to each such group, and each of these can be considered an SBU. These SBUs make up the relevant cornerstones of the strategy and are the focus of involvement on the part of the company. However, a company can be involved in many areas of strategic activity that

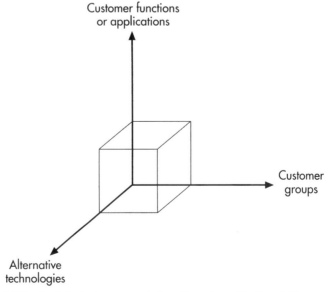

FIGURE 6.1   Method of strategic segmentation (based on Abell and Hammond, 1979).

constitute its activities (or businesses) portfolio; for instance, Siemens' portfolio comprises the following business units: information and communications, automation and control, power, transportation, medical and lighting.

Managing Diversity: Business Portfolio

Most of the methods of analysis of the company portfolio have been designed by large consultancy firms. Widely published and used, they have often been unjustly criticised. They are guides for the decision-making process and should be considered as such. They do not replace the decision maker and are there only to help analyse the competitive fields. In this sense, the methods have proved their worth. Even today, they continue to be the most efficient way to 'decipher' the strategic environment of a company and to help in the formulation of a systematic and reasoned analysis. They lead to simplified and yet acceptable representations of reality. The various methods give something essential to the strategic analyst to simplify the complexity of the real world in order to make a decision possible.

Business portfolio methods such as that of the Boston Consulting Group (BCG), of McKinsey and A. D. Little (ADL) are quite helpful. The idea behind these methods is to get the decision makers to think about the attractiveness of an industry (or a subset of the industry) in which the company operates, and also to assess the assets of the company in relation to the competition in each field of activity. The graphic presentation of the results generally used clearly outlines the choices available. According to its relative position within the portfolio compared with other business units, a generic strategy is recommended for a given SBU: develop, maintain and make profitable vs. partially or totally abandon non-profitable units.

In some cases, it may be useful to combine at least two of the methods when thinking about strategy and even to create one's own method of reflection, if it appears necessary to look for a greater adaptation to the specific characteristics of a trade.

Our presentation could insinuate that we have adopted a top-down strategy logic in which marketing decisions simply result from decisions made at a corporate strategy level. Actually, we assume that an efficient strategic process for a modern company is both the result of a 'top-down' process and a 'bottom-up' process. This is based on experience and our own research into business-to-business environments. Concerning the project marketing field, success on a specific project often greatly influences corporate strategy and even sometimes calls it into question. Our position is based on several observations:

- whatever method is used, a global strategic analysis cannot offer the detail required to make it, on the one hand, 'totally' coherent with the functioning of the markets, customer project characteristics and the rules of the real competitive game, and, on the other hand, internally credible for those in charge. The strategic route chosen for a given SBU can therefore only be considered as a general orientation, simple and definitive over the decided period, but lacking in detail to lead directly to commercial action. The strategic approach has to cover a number of steps to move from global strategic choice to its operational interpretation.

- The missing elements to complete the move from global strategic choice to marketing action cannot only be considered as complements designed to ease operating. These details (e.g. analysis of key actors in a milieu or the extended buying centre on a project) are the result of an analytical process that is distinct from the global strategic analysis. They are the result of a different approach to the activities. Because of this difference, this dual process often leads to differences of opinion about reality and even contradictions. Company strategists saw a homogeneous activity whilst marketers saw heterogeneity. Thus, it is clear that, for the sake of efficiency, these two representations of the market environment be confronted and subsequently lead to an adjustment in global strategy. This can even result in a change in objectives. If this confrontation does not happen, the global strategy becomes a simple exercise of little interest and impact on daily activity because it is judged as ill adapted by the actors involved.

All these elements have led us to adopt a systemic conception of strategy, involving successive iterations between the global analysis and the detailed analysis function by function and, more specifically, the marketing function, in order to clarify choices made by managers and to limit the risk of choice errors. This does not mean one of the strategic processes is wrong (either global or functional), both are useful and legitimate. In our perception of strategy, strategic choice is not a programmed part of the life of a company, but a gradual construction based on interaction and a number of exchanges of opinion and information internally. This does not mean that strategic processes cannot be organized and planned.

SBU Strategy

Marketing thought takes place within a given SBU. As previously mentioned, all decisions are based on the generic strategy which is defined for the activity in accordance with the global characteristics of the activities portfolio and the choices made. We suggest the following model (Figure 6.2) to better understand the various options available for the formulation of marketing strategy. There are three principal dimensions to the model:

- Competencies and resources: together, they allow for both access to the markets and the formulation of offers.
- The market and customer choice: this is obtained through two levels—market segments and clients.
- The offer: this will constitute the bases for tangible content of the exchanges with a specific client for a given project.

To utilize this approach, many successive horizontal and vertical iterations are required. At the upper level, given a specific resources/application overlap, the

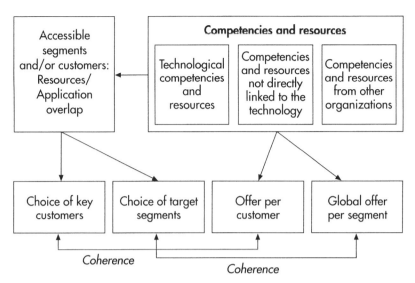

FIGURE 6.2 Choices available for marketing strategy formulation.

company can potentially gain access to accessible market segments and/or accessible customers based on its competencies and resources.

This first level of segmentation, generally based on the definition of the interface of technology and applications, allows the firm to define the technical part of its offering. This is followed by a succession of segmentation exercises, depending both on the degree of market heterogeneity and also on the company's capacity to respond with suitable offerings. The aim is to identify target market segments for the company. For each segment, a global offer per segment is designed, requiring decisions related to the content, the level of performance and the degree of flexibility in order to be able to adapt to different kinds of project. These global offers per segment make up the different bases that then enable the company to adapt to individual project requirements.

When the markets are concentrated, meaning there are few potential customers likely to have projects or when the supplier chooses to follow only some customers, the use of different levels of segmentation may be less relevant. Consequently, the model presented provides a link between company resources and competencies and projects. The marketing approach, therefore, concentrates on management of key customers and adapting the offer to each new customer project. Indeed, experience shows us that companies working on projects can combine the following two approaches:

- They follow certain key customers worldwide and propose solutions that are adapted to each of their projects. They have key account managers who manage customer relationships and find the resources and competencies within their own organization, or externally, to design the offers according to each project. The project is an important episode in the relationship, but one which is largely prepared via the different events taking place within this ongoing relationship.

- They develop actions based on several levels of segmentation leading to segment choice and the design of global offers. In this case, the company must be ready to react when the project comes to light and is detected.

Company Resources and Competencies

The company represents a number of competencies, meaning it can, at best, do better than the competition. These competencies are made up of basic entities or resources that are combined to create the offers (Hamel and Prahalad, 1994). There are two categories of resources, tangible and intangible. Tangible resources are all corporate elements that physically exist and are involved in the offer-creation process such as plant, machines, human resources, capital, trademarks and contracts. Intangible resources are based on information and knowledge, etc. They do not physically exist, but correspond to an accumulation of company production process experiences. Two categories of intangible resources can be distinguished:

- Organizational knowledge resulting from organizational learning: this is a pool of intraorganizational resources developed via experience. It represents group knowledge that exceeds individual knowledge such as technological, managerial and information systems knowledge, etc.
- Marginal intangible resources resulting from the link between the company and the environment: they obviously go beyond the boundaries of the company, unlike organizational knowledge, to include resources (e.g. from inter-company partnerships).

In the project marketing field, intangible resources have an extremely important role to play: capacity to coordinate, integration and mobilization of resources both internally and externally from partner companies, quality of interpersonal relationships within the network of individuals involved and capacity to manage a project. In the project business field, intangible resources play a key role when it comes to coordinating and integrating internal and external tangible resources; for example, competencies of major companies in the building and public works are (Ben Mahmoud-Jouini, 2000):

- the domain;
- the financing;
- project management;
- design;
- functionalities;
- coordination and integration.

We have chosen to classify resources and competencies into three groups:

Resources and Competencies Linked to Technology

This includes both tangible (production technology) and intangible technological resources (Box 6.1). These competencies and resources are often used when defining the technical aspect of the offering; for example, the product functions, the degree of technical integration (components, system, etc.).

BOX 6.1 Resources and Competencies at Alcatel.

Alcatel hot technologies:

- photonic cross-connect;
- submarine networking;
- optoelectronic components;
- advanced optical cable for fibre-optic network;
- optical network intelligence;
- OSS automation;
- switching evolution;
- mobile networks;
- broadland access;
- IP routing;
- multi-protocol label switching;
- quality of service in converged enterprise networks;
- IP telephony;
- customer touch point integration;
- bluetooth.

Source: www.alcatel.com

Resources and Competencies Not Directly Linked to the Technologies

A great many organizational competencies are not directly linked to technology and represent the base for the formalization of offers and differentiation. These competencies are particularly used in the service and the groundwork part of the project offer, where competencies such as human resources are key elements. Here, competencies related to project management, the ability to mobilize talented project managers and those related to the management of customer relationships are included.

Resources and Competencies Found in Other Organizations

These include technical and non-technical resources and competencies to be found in other organizations. During the elaboration of complex offers for a given project, such competencies are brought in. According to the marketing situations frequently encountered with projects, inter-company relations are developed. This cooperation depends on whether the company will 'instantly' find companies offering the needed complementary competencies (short-term perspective and market orientation) or whether it has to prepare in advance by developing close relationships with other companies (long-term and relational perspective). The decision depends on the importance of the competence sought for many projects. It impacts the value of the offer proposed to the client for a given project, the presence or absence of alternatives (scarcity of the competence which could be tapped by the competition) and the amount of training required before being ready to work together. Based on past experience, we can distinguish three situations.

One situation concerns the cases in which the development of long-term and privileged relationships with an offer partner is not necessary in as much as the company can always find the competencies whenever required when it has detected and chosen which project to work on. Later, we shall look at different systems for preparing the offers in collaboration with other companies mainly focused on reactivity and opportunism. These cases occur frequently in, for example, the public works sector, where there is a relatively profuse supplier market. In such a situation, the company makes choices using a short-term logic, project by project.

This type of case can also be found among companies which, because of the products they produce, are reduced to being simple suppliers or find themselves low down in the project pyramid; for example, a manufacturer of specialized steel products for the heavy industrial equipment sector (reactors, industrial boilers, etc.) deals directly with industrial boilermakers who build industrial reactors themselves based on the specifications from an engineering company for a given industrial sector. As there are a number of potential suppliers able to offer very similar ranges of steel, the companies that cannot manage the project themselves (main contractor or contractor for a lot) are unsure as to whether they will be selected. They can seek the support of the customer. In this case, the customer may recommend them for two main reasons. The first reason is that the customer has already worked closely with a supplier, buying standardized products readily available on the supplier market. The customer will count on the price/volume negotiation and recommend this supplier; for example, an industry which buys transformers for its factories will, following an increase in capacity or the construction of a new production site in a given country, seek to keep the same supplier to benefit from their purchasing power.

The second reason is that the client has developed intense relationships with a supplier, which result in a high level of added value. Moreover, the product, or process or service is strategic in the equipment the customer wishes to build. In this case, the contractor confirms the customer's choice. A similar reasoning can be found with the contractor who can also benefit from the price/volume ratio or privileged relationships with certain suppliers he can pass on to the client. These are the push/pull strategies which can be implemented by companies which do not have the capacity to be in the leading position in the project pyramid.

Another situation deals with the development of interorganizational cooperation around a core company that plays a central part in the coalition and has great influence on the directions taken. This type of organization is typified by Airbus, for example, where Aérospatiale (a subsidiary of EADS, European Aerospace Defence System) is the industrial operator and plays this central role. Alliances exist between several major partner companies from different countries. The same goes for military aircraft; Dassault Aviations, a French company and part of the EADS, is the system integrator and has three partners, each supplying different systems (Thalès for radars, Matra for the weapons systems and SNECMA for the reactors).

The last situation concerns the development of interorganizational cooperation with a network organization, without a leader with horizontal, vertical and diagonal coordination between the companies. The relationships between the partner companies are continuous, even if transactions are intermittent. For a given project, skills are grouped together around a leader that can change from one project to another. This type of organization exists in the telecommunications and computer industries.

Alliances exist between IBM and Ariba on e-procurement platforms, between Nortel Networks and IBM, between Nortel Networks and Hewlett-Packard. In these cases, to define the roles of each member, the main industrial groups of the sectors implement charters and programmes. As an example, we present a part of the IBM Business Partner Charter (see Box 6.2). It is interesting to note that companies which direct their strategies towards long-term partnership with key customers operate similarly with their own suppliers. They need to be able to rely on partner expertise according to developments suggested to key customers.

BOX 6.2 IBM Business Partner Charter.

IBM absolutely needs Business Partners. Without you, we won't make our objectives for revenue, for customer satisfaction, for share growth.

Working together, we are stronger than when we work separately. That's why IBM, with you, has created the industry's most extensive Business Partner network. Linking you with other IBM Business Partners in our 'value net' gives us all the ability to deliver broader and better solutions to our customers. By working with Business Partners who provide complementary skills and expertise we also deliver greater client value.

Through our global network we are committed to nurturing our value net of Business Partners. It's just another way we can help you develop new customer relationships and deliver solutions that increase your revenue.

We put our diverse resources to work for you. In IBM's go to market strategy, our sales teams are dedicated to proactively engaging you in opportunities. Because it takes collaboration to address the complex solutions demanded by today's customers, we will work side by side with our Business Partners, so together we can deliver superior client value.

We are committed to helping you optimise your marketing dollars for better business results, so we have created what we believe is the most comprehensive Business Partner support program in the industry: IBM Partner World. Rich with initiatives, co-marketing opportunities, and education to build and sharpen your skills, Partner World provides a framework for consistent growth.

Source: www.IBM.com

The Market Segment and Customer Choices

As mentioned on p. 64, the possession of competencies and resources by a company can condition its capacity to gain access to a part of the market and the customers. In other words, a company should be able to respond to a certain degree of heterogeneity of marketing situations (accessible segments and customers). Marketing approaches will therefore be based on the segmentation and/or choice of customers.

Segmentation is an operation of classification. It aims to provide management with a representation of the markets that is designed to help make choices concerning both how the offer is adapted and the broader market environment. This representation is the result of a process, founded on a simplification of the initial data.

The result depends on the variety and quality of available data. The practical setting up of a detailed segmentation process operates around the three phases (Michel *et al.*, 2002):

- Phase 1: Describe and analyse.
- Phase 2: Understand and explain.
- Phase 3: Make choices.

Phase 1: Describe and Analyse

- Define the objectives of the segmentation. What do we want to know? What are the decisions to be made? Segmentation is a representation of a market as defined by a supplier. Therefore, it depends on its objectives. A new offer from a supplier will not arouse the same level of interest from the customers. This is likely to modify any segmentation based on a former offer. Equally, segmentation can lead to thinking about the outline of a new offer as it helps to find the emerging trends and dynamics which will not be satisfied by the existing product and service.
- Determine the limits of the 'offer–customers–competitors' combination to be segmented. As shown at the beginning of this chapter, marketing segmentation takes place within each SBU in accordance with its characteristics and the implemented strategy type. However, most companies know something about their markets and could therefore begin with smaller areas than the SBU itself. In reality, most companies begin the segmentation with pre-identified subsets. Generally speaking, it is important to give limits to the field of marketing segmentation, just as it is important to define objectives before beginning.
- Identify the criteria that help to describe the markets and customers of the company. This essential phase is often based on intuition and empiricism. A number of individuals within the company receive and interpret information and so create their own view of the market structure. They then base their actions on this view. It is thus important to compare these different market representations and to identify the criteria being used in order to qualify the different actors' behaviour and the global market dynamics. Any segmentation begins with the identification of such criteria from experience and knowledge from inside the company.

Phase 2: Understand and Explain

- Select the determining criteria. Among the criteria above, some are more explanatory than others of the differences in requirements and purchasing behaviour or of the variations in market dynamics. Our aim here is to reduce this mass of information to produce an explanatory diagram that can help with managerial decision making.

- Build the segments. The objective here is to group together types of customers who are in close relation to the discriminating criteria and yet who differ from other customers on the same criteria. Many situations are characterized by a limited number of customers or players. This facilitates the use of a simple approach founded on an 'intelligent' classification of the criteria. The method used is the segmentation tree which classifies criteria through a successive dichotomy. Box 6.3 provides the reader with an example of the segmentation tree method based on Siemens. Rather than overload the diagram, we have chosen not to present it in its entirety. For greater detail, the reader is invited to consult the firm's website.

BOX 6.3 Siemens, Different Levels of Segmentation.

- Information and communications
  - ○ Information and communication mobile (ICM)
    - Consumers
    - Network operators, enterprises
    - Developers
  - ○ Information and communication networks (ICN)
    - Enterprises
    - Carrier
    - Public sector
    - Developers
  - ○ Siemens Business services GmbH&CO (SBC)
- Automation and control
  - ○ Automation and drives (A&D)
  - ○ Industrial solutions and services (I&S)
    - Airfield solutions
    - Cement
    - Diesel power plants
    - E-business
    - Food and beverage
    - Intelligent traffic system
    - IT plants solutions
    - Marine engineering
    - Metals
    - Mining
    - Oil and gas
    - Pulp and paper
    - Siemens industrial services
    - Spare parts for industry
    - Sugar and starch
    - Waste water and drinking water
    - Windfarm

> ○   Siemens production and logistics system AG (PL)
> ○   Siemens building technologies
> ●   Power
> ●   Transportation
> ●   Medical
> ●   Lighting
>
> Source: www.Siemens.com

The segmentation tree method allows the identification and hierarchical classification of the criteria that explain the fact that two customers will not present the same behaviour (requirements, interest, etc.) towards a supplier's proposal. Criteria are classified along a simple criterion (first, second, third, etc.) in order of importance. A first level of segmentation can be defined with the first criterion. If this segmentation does not satisfy the first criterion, the second criterion can be put forward to divide in a finer way the segments of the first level, and so on. This process results in market segments inside which it is possible to identify 'customer–application' ensembles. Practically, only a limited number of segments can be useful. This limits the number of criteria to be used. Therefore, what is important is not the refined character of the segmentation but its usefulness for marketing decisions.

It should be noted that the more detailed the segmentation, the more the company is ready to set up by anticipation an offer strategy and an approach to the market segments. If this is not the case, either because of a lack of information or because the market characteristics are changing, the company has to make up for this using other mechanisms to enable it to acquire greater flexibility and reactivity. These mechanisms will be dealt with in Chapters 8 and 9. However, in some sectors, the time required to develop an offer is often relatively long and needs much forward planning concerning the market characteristics and evolutions. It is thus important to:

●   Acquire better understanding of each segment. We must remember that the resulting segmentation has its origins in a simplification of the information that was gathered during Phase 1. This simplification or reduction of the information helped to build a clear map of the market. Based on a simplification of the initial data, this map does not generally supply us with a very precise description of each segment. A good understanding of the segment therefore needs other qualitative and quantitative data.
●   Quantify each segment. The quantification of the segments often raises many problems specifically in project marketing. It must be remembered that it is essential to be able to quantify the market segments in order to check their operational characteristics, to categorize the possible actions according to their potential profitability, and finally to define company strategy in terms of market share.

Phase 3: Make Choices

- Choice of segments. The market description supplied by the completed segmentation will enable the company to determine the parts of the market on which it wishes to concentrate. It involves taking the company towards market segments where it can best use its resources and competencies, in accordance with customer demands and the competition, and also with the particular type of SBU. A matrix outlining company strengths and segment attractiveness can be used to rank market segments and to define target segments.
- Choice of customers. As previously mentioned, some companies choose to concentrate on the management of key customer relationships. The stakes involved in key account management are extremely high. Therefore, a team often manages them. Without going into the details of key account management, the key criteria for the selection of key accounts are given below:
  —Concerning the status of a key account; this involves explaining the choice of one approach compared with another. This is an important step because in certain companies that sell projects there can be disagreement between the two trends. On the one hand, the desire to concentrate on selected customers and to accept all projects that emerge whatever their importance, as long as they fall within the domain of the company's expertise. On the other hand, a desire to take into account all the projects concerning one specific application with or without geographical limits, whoever the customer.
  —Set up a list of criteria for the selection of the key accounts. These vary from one company to another. Examples are current and potential quantitative criteria (amount and importance of the projects), criteria related to customer structure, purchases, buying process, strategy (technological, geographical development). These criteria allow the degree of compatibility between supplier and customer to be measured.

Once the key accounts have been defined, a specific strategic plan (the account plan) is set up for each one. This plan can be modified according to the specificities of the different units of the key account such as geographic zone, milieu, etc. Thus, the strategic approach for a key account client is both global and local. This means that inside the major axes for development and the global objectives fixed for a given key account customer, there may be different ways of finding answers to its projects.

The Offer

First, an offer includes technical components, service elements and financial components. In project marketing, the offer for a given project is often complex and involves a number of different elements. We shall look at the coherence between an offer as defined above, which can be qualified as a global offer, and an offer designed for a given project. For the supplier, the design of an offer involves:

- Defining as large a scope as possible for the answers to the various project specifications in relation to internal and external resources and competencies.

This means defining the global offer and offer content as well as technical and financial components.

- Adding a certain flexibility to be in a position to make an offer in accordance with the characteristics of each project for a given customer in a given marketing situation. In the adjustment from a global to a specific project offer, a certain number of elements which were not included in the global offer are added according to local specificities and the competition.

Offer definition is based around three main issues:

1   Defining the elements of each component of the global offer both technically and financially: the 'foundation stones'; for example, the electrical installations for a refinery or chemical plant require the use of transformers that can be designed and incorporated in the product range 'beforehand'.
2   Defining as wide a scope as possible, the perimeter of the global offer; just how far (width and depth) can the company go in both dimensions?
3   Integrating packages in the form of solutions for a group of customers with similar problems or a technical problem that is common to several sectors by using the appropriate segmentation. The idea being to take into consideration the fact that, even though, as indicated in the opening pages of this book, each project is different, similarities can exist.

Defining Each of the Elements of the Components of the Global Offer

The use of segmentation, based on the criteria chosen according to the method outlined above, allows defining the different elements in the product and service ranges. We give the example of Alstom transportation, business unit of the international group Alstom. Among the passenger train range, there are six lines of product according to several segmentation criteria: the type of transport (urban, suburban, regional, intercity and long distance), the distances involved, usage, type of metropolis (for the urban transport), the number of passengers (especially variation in passenger numbers):

- Citadis   'the light way vehicle'
- Metropolis 'the metro'
- X'trapolis   'the suburban and commuter train'
- Corodia   'the perfect balance'
- Pendolino   'the perfect balance'
- TGV   'the very high speed train'

Service offer include different types of service whose aim is to supply the client with a given availability of equipment. These include:

- Maintenance.
- Renovation.
- Parts and replacement units. This service offer is organized at four levels of criticality for the client—standard, contract parts, parts plus, premium.

- Asset management.
- Online services.

Clearly, the company will resort to technical needs and utilization criteria to define the technical part of the offer or the core of the offer. It will use more behavioural criteria to define other elements of the offer and the service component (e.g. the capacity to manage alone, or the fact that the customer strategy is to outsource as much as possible and to use external service providers).

The Global Offer and Its Boundaries The global offer brings together all the elements of its different components. This integration can be brought about using two axes:

- The level of integration between the technical offer and the service offer. There is an increasing number of companies which integrate products and services. Their offers evolve from product to product and services to systems.
- The levels of integration between customer and project value chains means that companies venture increasingly further upstream and downstream. This reflects the desire to consider the project in an increasingly wider context and to create greater value for the customer. Moreover, it would appear this type of approach goes hand in hand with the fact that companies are beginning to concentrate more on their core competencies and that delays are getting shorter and shorter. Decisions are now made just in time and suppliers have to be prepared to react almost immediately. This integration allows for greater speed and reduced costs. This is comparable with the manufacturing industry that is based on partnerships and simultaneous engineering. Consequently, offers take on greater depth, design, implementation, maintenance and operation. A construction company can now offer all possible combinations according to the nature of the project: design-installation, corporate financing, design-construction, turnkey, project management and operation and mainten- ance.

As an example, we present Alcatel's All-in-One Service for Network Operators to maintain and develop their telecommunications networks (Box 6.4).

BOX 6.4 Alcatel: All-in-One Alcatel Professional Services for Service Providers.

All-in-One Alcatel Service Providers offer an extensive set of services for network operators that is built around eight domains and, currently, four generic solutions with one goal: 'helping operators to achieve their strategic goals.' The All-in-One Service Portfolio assists them to reduce time to market, cut cost, achieve optimum quality of service and efficient customer care and get increased revenues.

The following set of domains cover all services throughout the life cycle of a project:

- management and business consulting—the objective is to help decision makers in business decisions concerning initial network assessment, market analysis or implementation of a business plan;
- network and service design—the objective is to design future, safe services and network architecture;
- network and service integration—the objective is to ensure that disparate network elements work together (interworking) and that a given network functions with other operators (interoperability);
- network implementation—the objective is to have one leader who coordinates different partners and to deliver a turnkey solution;
- network operation and maintenance—the objective is to ensure smooth performance and quality of the customer (network operator) networks;
- customer administration—the objective is to help the network operators in implementing customer care and billing services;
- skills and resource development concerns training, information and documentation;
- network and service enhancement—Alcatel helps its customers to boost their networks to peak performance and to extract optimal use of installed equipment.

Source: www.Alcatel.com

The reason for presenting the offer in this way is to highlight the global aspect of the offer and to think about new ways of increasing the added value while at the same time taking customer behavioural changes, particularly their outsourcing strategies, into consideration. Also, with this extension come strategic challenges:

- The position of the company in the vertical activity chain.
- The capacity of the company to change its position in the activity chain or to integrate other activities upstream or downstream.

The Production of Pre-assembled Offers: Pseudo-Projects   To avoid presenting their offers as a huge variety of products, services and processes, companies prefer to prepare virtual packages of elements of the offer, called pseudo-projects. These packages are dedicated to groups of customers or to specific technical problems using a segmentation strategy to define their content. The company thereby benefits from the feedback and experience resulting from several identical projects. The objective is twofold:

- To gain as much insight into the predefinition and structure of offers, which can then be completed by other elements or adapted according to the characteristics of a specific project in a specific context. This approach avoids having to re-think the whole offer and also limits its complexity.
- For the company, this means having offers which could be considered prototypes which can then be adapted to the customer's needs and can act as a basis to begin relationships with the customer. This approach could be better implemented by referring to customer projects that have already been realized.

Some companies also develop brand names dedicated to specific pseudo-projects.

In Box 6.5 are two examples that illustrate this approach to the design of pseudo-projects that companies use to identify 'customer solutions'. They come from the telecommunications sector: one from Alcatel concerning customer solutions based on customer applications and the other from Nortel Networks concerning customer solutions for industrial problems. In the Nortel telecom example, differences in the sectors justify the presence of solutions for each sector.

BOX 6.5 Example of Pseudo-Projects.

ALCATEL: customer solutions:

- Access networks
- Multiservice edge and core
- Voice and data convergence
- Value-added services and applications
- Mobile networks
- OSS and network management
- Optical Networking
- All-in-One Alcatel Professional
- Telephone, screenphone modems
- Networking for enterprises

NORTEL NETWORKS: industry solutions:

- Dotcom
- Education
- Government
- Health care
- Managed business solutions
- Financial services
- Hospitality
- Retail
- Transportation

Source: wwwAlcatel.com and www.Nortelnetworks.com

The International Dimension

The international dimension could be dealt with at the same time as segmentation as specific criteria like geographical criteria. Some have chosen this approach (Anderson and Narus, 1999). However, we believe that in the case of project marketing geographical segmentation is more a tool for defining the choices of geographical zone and organization than for defining offer content.

TABLE 6.1 Bases for international project marketing segmentation (based on Albaum *et al.*, 1989, p. 93)

	General market indicators	*Project-specific indicators*
County level	Demographics, socio-economic factors, political factors, culture, technological development, industry structure	Economic and legal constraints, market conditions, project-specific cultural conditions, potential partners
Customer level	Population characteristics, socio-economic factors, company/buyer organization characteristics	Behavioural characteristics, decision making, buying behavioural, parties involved

The process of segmentation in international markets requires an appraisal of the fit between the prospective market, its infrastructure, etc. and a company's ability to handle these circumstances, as well as the fit between the project and the country's needs. This cannot be done purely on marketing grounds such as broader considerations of a company's capabilities and objectives, regulations, networks, actors and needs of the particular country; for example, selling a pulp plant to Vietnam is different than selling a pulp plant to India. Not only does the marketing effort need adaptation but so do the technical specifications, perhaps due to the different raw materials to be used or due to different geographic conditions. Moreover, how new/difficult a market is will also influence the marketing process. International markets (e.g. in regions such as Asia or the Middle East) tend to be more heterogeneous than we believe. The type of government, lifestyle, culture and education level demands specific approaches to building and developing relationships. In such a country as China, where bonding means sharing commonalities, the need to bridge the gap between the supplier and the key actors in the milieu calls for the multiplication of the relational investment. In another country such as the USA where business is business, the Anglo-Saxon attitude, which maintains distance between different parties, calls for a careful and limited relational investment.

Given the resources and capabilities of the selling firm, it has to see whether experience from one market in the region can be applied/used in another market. There are some possibilities of creating meaningful international segments; for example, the level of economic development is a good base for some infrastructural projects such as roads or hospitals. For some projects (e.g. in the food sector) the composition of the agricultural sector, level of technology, buying decision criteria, purchasing power and educational levels are good indicators for segmentation. Country and project characteristics need to be analysed (see Table 6.1). As stressed by Bonaccorsi *et al.* (1996), the key to strategic superiority is the ability to manage, simultaneously, the task of systems integration and the pace of technological advancement. Moreover, the companies have to manage exceptionally severe requirements in both the project and the specific market. The complexities of specific projects can impact on geographical market decisions.

Chapter 7

MARKET APPROACH: SOCIOGRAMS AND PORTFOLIOS

In Chapter 6, we saw how a company defines its offers, based on a number of combinable elements, and how it identifies the markets it wishes to develop. Concerning this second dimension, we analysed the geographical dimension whereby marketing action leads to detection of projects in a specific zone. In Part I, devoted to project business, we identified three very distinct phases of marketing practices: independent of any project, pre-tender and during tender preparation. During these phases, the company seeks to adapt its offer to the client's project with all individuals getting involved in the decision-making process. In this chapter, we shall focus on the explanation surrounding the choice of marketing methods used. In Chapters 8 and 9 we shall analyse each of these methods.

Market as Milieu

The process presented in Chapter 6 was based on successive segmentations (technical, applications, behavioural, geographical, etc.), taking the frequency criterion into consideration. This makes the marketer's task easier, that is, anticipating the offer content (what it could be) and choosing market segments or key account clients. If the supplier is unable to make these choices, it has to constantly adapt and react to the market. The segmentation process is, nonetheless, abstract and conceptual, inasmuch as the aim is to take market heterogeneity and dynamics into consideration and also to make divisions to allow the marketer to create his own representation of the market. This means that several managers who analyse the same market can consider it differently depending on their approach and the categorization they adopt. This representation then leads to the formulation of choices: offers, market segment, geographical zone, etc.

Once the choices concerning a given activity in a given zone have been made, the company's freedom of movement becomes limited since a choice of context has been made. The company enters a milieu which can be defined (Cova *et al.*, 1996) as a socio-spatial entity, geographically bound, in which, through the frequency of socio-economic exchanges, business and non-business actors are intertwined. They share a common representation of business and a set of tacit rules—the 'law of the milieu'. This milieu represents a kind of collective actor who cannot be categorized and specified as with the segmentation approach. Thus, we move towards a vision of the market as a network. The relevant 'independent of any project' entity becomes the milieu. The marketing approach involves understanding this milieu to develop a position for the detection of client projects. There are two methods for this:

- *Sociograms* which allow to understand and adopt the operating methods of the milieu and to identify the most important actors.
- *Portfolios* (of clients or key actors) to define priorities in the distribution of resources.

In the chapters that follow we shall see how. During the independent of any project phase, the allocated resources are mainly relational and basically involve relationships between persons.

Sociograms: The Origin

The idea of representing the actor network surrounding a project has long been used in project marketing. Many practitioners draw up micro-representations of the networks for easier positioning among the web of relationships between the actors surrounding a given project. For them, *'a small diagram is worth more than 1,000 words.'*

More recently, the following points have been added:

1 The idea not to limit this representation of the business arena to the phase tender.
2 A method to make the obtained representations sound, legible and shareable.

Concerning the first point, we have already seen how project marketing has come to consider the independent of any project phase and the accompanying positioning in relations as crucial. For the second point, it is worth looking again, without entering into all the details, at the origins of the method of analysis and representation of networks by sociograms.

A Representation of the Business Arena

Any marketing process is based on a representation of the business arena in which transactions occur. Based on this representation, consciously or not, the company can proceed to make choices and to define action. Consequently, we can wonder which—the market, the industry and now the network—best represents the business arena for a company involved in project business? Is it the market, with a simple, bicephalous form with, on one side, those offers and, on the other, the demands, that represents these actors as aggregated (segments) rather than the relationships between aggregated and non-aggregated actors?

Is it the industry which includes all the actors of the industrial chain and represents the relationships between the aggregated actors according to their involvement in the industry? Or is it the network, which is omnipresent in the socio-economic life of the beginning of the 21st century, that represents relationships between non-aggregated actors? They all partly describe the company business arena, but not completely. Markets, industries, networks, etc.—the list of representations is boundless without a unique grid. However, this ideal grid does not exist.

All the alternative grids are relevant according to whether we are interested in the transactions, clients, competitors, the partners, the clients' clients, market actors, non-market actors, economic relations, technical relations, social relations and so on. Project marketing is based on the representation given by the network, as it is more appropriate to understand what is going on in such activities.

An Idea Derived from 'Hard Sciences'

The theoretical framework of the networks used in project marketing today is the result of a combination of a number of elements taken from different sciences. The notion of network entered the language in the 17th century and evolved in the 18th century. Commonly used in anatomy and medicine (blood circulation, for example), it quickly became accepted in the scientific and technical fields. Its evolution continued with the Industrial Revolution. The 19th century saw the use of the notion of network via technical-economic operationalization; for example, in France major networks were constructed under the Second Empire and at the beginning of the Third Republic such as the postal network, the road and rail networks, the water and canal networks. The communication networks were then dreamt of as the creators of a new universal link. Electrification spread, followed by the creation of the telephone, and then telematic (Internet) networks.

Few sciences ignore the semantic fecundity of the notion of network; ecology and information sciences use it massively. Social sciences continually develop the metaphorical resources of the term, often ambiguously and confusingly. Networks fill the gap left by failing intermediary social bodies; as established institutions begin to fail, individuals turn to the mobile and impalpable. Taken from the information and communication technologies, the notion of network has, since the beginning of the 1980s, entered management and organizational vocabulary, and has been endowed with a positive value by politicians looking to emblazon their discourses. With the wearing immobility of the structure, the evanescence of the group and the totalizing indistinction of the system, the flexible and mobile ideology of the network has arrived at the right time to herald the triumph of pragmatism and the individualization of social ties.

From Network to Network Analysis

For the social sciences, the representation of a social group as a number of networks of connected individuals has its origins in the works of the British anthropologist Radcliffe-Brown, at the start of the century. Indeed, there have been three sociological approaches to the notion of networks (Scott, 2000):

- The German sociometric analysis which led to a number of technical break-throughs (notably the sociograms) by using graph theory.
- All the American research scientists of the 1930s and 1940s, together with the Chicago School, who explored the creation of groups in urban areas.
- The anthropologists in Manchester who analysed the structure, later named network, of communitarian relationships among tribes.

In the 1970s, the INSNA (International Network for Social Network Analysis), which was created at Harvard, took the analysis of networks, which until then had concentrated on interpersonal relationships, into the realm of inter-company relationships (Scott, 2000).

Close to management, the network has been used by innovation sociologists to respond to socio-economic evolution. The notion of network has the advantage of highlighting the major transformation of industrial societies. The economic organization, as a system to coordinate diverse activities, goes beyond the industrial sphere and the realm of the firm. State-funded and semi-public research centres, technical centres, engineering and development centres all become economic actors, just like the authorities. This breakthrough means a new form of coordination, the appearance of a meta-organization that corresponds to what can be called the technico-economic network. The new element is not that the organizational coordination expands at the expense of the market, but that a whole series of actors enter the arena and change the rules (Callon, 1989). The reference is no longer the firm, the research centre or the consumer, but a system of relationships between these different actors, the technico-economic networks which encompass all exchanges.

A Recent Marketing Development

The network concept entered marketing and management vocabulary in an attempt to represent a more complex, interactive and therefore uncertain collective reality than the market could. Before this concept of network came the one of industry or sector, updated by Michael Porter (1980) which led to a description of the links between industrial activities and subsequently those uniting the actors themselves. This evolution in the representation, from markets to sectors, was an attempt to reintegrate the link, the relationship, not only between suppliers and clients, but also distributors and cooperatives and partners. For Porter, the for-mulation of a strategy to face the competition basically implies the creations of links between a firm and its environment. Even if the environment in question is large and includes forces which are both economic and social, the most important field for the firm is the sector, or sectors, in which it competes with other firms.

Clients, suppliers, manufacturers of alternative products, potential entrants to the market are all potential competitors and can, depending on the situation, have a more or less important role to play. Seen in this light, the competition defined above could be described as increased rivalry. Porter's representation is that of opposing forces; the links between actors are considered more as competitive tension than socio-economic relationships. Less a representation of a business scene than a battlefield where all actors try to gain advantage over the others ('competitive advantage').

In the 1980s, the European IMP Group of researchers (Industrial Marketing and Purchasing Group) brought the concept of industrial network to propose an alternative representation of the business arena which goes beyond this warlike reasoning (Mattson, 1985). For the IMP (Hakansson and Snehota, 1989 and Ghauri and Prasad, 1995), no company is likened to an island. Every firm is linked to other firms or organizations belonging to the same network: the actors of the industry, the clients, suppliers, etc. It is also connected with, from outside the industry, the other suppliers of the same client: consultants, standards committees, chambers of commerce, etc. This is easy to accept and to understand when analysing current problems. However, this is not reflected in managerial theory. Generally speaking, the firm is described as a unit with limits and whose performance is decided by internal factors. The environment exists, but is considered as an external factor with its opportunities and constraints. If we continue to imagine the business arena as a network, or network of networks, the firm is defined as an actor, embedded in exchange networks between firms (Ghauri, 1999).

Mapping Relational Positioning

As explained in Chapter 4, the firm has a twofold marketing positioning:

- A functional positioning based on the management of competencies.
- A relational positioning based on the management of relations.

The second is noless important than the first for the success of the firm. Many firms, including the most successful, which have failed dramatically due to over-evaluation of their technological competencies, in relation to their relational competencies, are fully aware of this today. The three major interconnected axes concerning relational positioning in the actors' networks can be presented as follows:

- Knowledge—to really know the network, its actors, the interrelationships, a company has to be part of it. Generally speaking, an outsider only gets a superficial and biased view of the local network.
- Investment—the best way to get to know a network is to enter it. The firm has to invest, knowing there will be no returns for 2 or 3 years (the time needed to establish relationships and to win confidence).
- Time—entering the network is not an isolated event, but rather an episode in the creation of relationships with other actors.

In this relational approach, the principal questions that outline the analysis and representation of a network are the following:

- Who are the actors of the network? What are their characteristics in terms of size, products, experiences, their relationships with other actors, the clients, suppliers, competitors? Are the relationships economic, technical, administrative, legal or social?
- What is the relative position of each actor? What is the role and power of each actor? What are the limits and constraints the network operates on the firm, principally concerning its links with other clients, suppliers and other networks? What possibilities can the potential partners in the network offer the firm (e.g. access to resources which are controlled by others and which could be mobilized)?
- What are the existing links with the actors? What are our direct links? What use are they? Do we have any indirect links with local actors through our partners? Are they useful and do we use them? How can they be mobilized?

The use of the so-called sociogram method can, in a number of cases, answer these questions. It will come in a variety of forms depending on whether the supplier is at the independent of any project, pre-tender or during tender preparation phase.

Portfolios: The Origin

For managers, the allocation of a firm's limited resources between several entities (fields of activity, products, clients, projects, etc.) has always been a major part of their mission. Whatever the hierarchical position, the activities such as a management team running the activities portfolio, the marketing director dealing with a number of market segments, the sales manager responsible for the management of a number of clients and the salesperson establishing his visits to clients, need resources.

In 1952, the pioneering works of Markovitz in this field opened the way for a number of developments in the portfolio concept. Subsequently, the methods designed to help managers in their choices for allocation of resources flourished in the 1960s. These methods are all similar in their approach, first used as a strategy to manage different activities (e.g. the Boston Consulting Group's BCG matrix, Arthur D. Little's and also McKinsey's), then in product range management in the 1970's and more recently in customer relations management.

A Strategic Tool

This involves extracting the key elements for an appreciation and comparison of the possibilities for each strategic activity. For this, the models used in strategy are based on the same two-choice criteria: the attractiveness of the activity and the strengths or competitive advantage of the firm. Thus, the portfolio method uses similar matrix-based representation possibilities. These allow for easy comparison between several elements—strategic activities, products, brands, clients—on two or more dimensions.

A portfolio includes activities that generate massive profit and others that require large investments. Within the portfolio, the profit created by certain activities is used to finance others. The aim is to balance our portfolio so that, at any given time, the assets created by the famous 'cash cows' can be used to develop the 'dilemmas' and to strengthen the 'stars' against fierce competition (for further information, see the BCG matrix in most works devoted to strategy).

More generally, a square, strategic activities portfolio matrix covers four elementary strategies:

- A development strategy in the zones where activity value (attractiveness) and competitiveness (advantage) are both favourable.
- A 'double or quit' strategy in the zones where only the attractiveness of the field of activity is positive.
- A maintenance and stabilization strategy in average attractiveness zones.
- A withdrawal strategy in low attractiveness and low advantage zones. The metaphor of the portfolio works in two ways:
  —first, it refers to the more or less independent elements (folios) whose values can be compared;
  —second, it draws attention to the financial equilibrium of the content.

Although the portfolio method has the obvious advantages of simplicity and globality, there are some drawbacks. First, the very image of the portfolio needs to be taken carefully; it suggests that the content and the strategic activities can be dealt with independently. However, in practice this is rarely the case. In fact, portfolio approaches cannot take the interdependence of the activities into consideration. Moreover, in some cases (e.g. BCG matrices), they only give a relatively simple classification of the activities into four categories which does not enable a clear and precise allocation of resources.

A Relationship Marketing Tool

Despite these reservations, there has been an increase in the use of such methods since the start of the 1980s. This can be explained by a number of factors. One example is the major transformations concerning the functioning of the markets in the last 15 years, which have led companies to focus more on the management of supplier–customer relationships, and particularly the growth in Relationship Marketing (Ghauri 1999). This concern for supplier–customer relationships can also be seen in the management of supplier–customer relationship methods, the calculation and follow-up of customer satisfaction and in the growth of key account management.

Applying the portfolio approach to a firms' clients and/or to a firms' suppliers was first seen at the beginning of the 1980s (Fiocca, 1982; Cunningham and Homse, 1982) following research carried out by the IMP Group. The growth of transactional marketing, based on the optimization of marketing mix towards relationship marketing where the supplier–customer relationship is central, explains this relatively recent attention given to the management of this relationship. This meant we had to wait for the understanding of the importance given to the customer–supplier relationship before the idea of a customer–supplier relationship portfolio could see the light of day.

Today, several elements highlight the importance for the industrial firm to acquire the capacity to spot the differences in status and attractiveness of their clients and to be able to know how to manage the relations:

- Changes in the behaviour of industrial firms, concentrating their efforts on improved supplier–client relationship management considered as a gateway to or the creation of resources.
- The complexity and concentration of the industrial markets.
- A high degree of interdependence between the industrial actors in industrial sectors and networks.

This move towards interdependence between actors, the stability and durability of relationships, has meant that for many industrial firms, most value creation comes from a limited number of clients. As an example, in 1996, the industrial group Alcatel made almost a quarter of its turnover from only six clients, and almost half from 200 clients. This confirms that a limited number of relationships has a determining impact on the global performance of the firm. For the supplier, it is important to detect, choose and individually manage the clients in the portfolio according to the resources to which it can gain access or generate through supplier–client interaction (e.g. volume, the development of innovative techniques, improved image, etc.).

In Chapters 8 and 9, we shall study methods for analysing the milieu and managing supplier–client relationships.

Chapter 8

ANALYSING MILIEUS

The objective of this chapter is to explain how the network of business and non-business actors (the milieu) functions in project marketing. This will enable us to manage the milieu and to make appropriate decisions. We use a case study of Antolini (a construction company) as an example (Cova *et al.*, 1996).

The Firm's Point of View: Case Study of the Antolini Company

The Initial Strategic Approach

In 1986, the construction group HBTP (a token name) covered the entire French territory through local subsidiaries. These local subsidiaries were not created by HBTP but were the result of buying local firms. In order to preserve the local character of its subsidiaries in local markets in which it has an important competitive advantage, HBTP kept the original name of each subsidiary. In the Loiret region (a subdivision of central France), the subsidiary is called Antolini.

In France the main part of HBTP turnover came from local public markets. At that time, a decrease in orders, strong competition, the dominance of price as selection criteria and decreasing profitability characterized this market. Faced with these difficulties, HBTP decided, on one hand, to evaluate its subsidiaries' competencies and, on the other hand, to evaluate accessible private markets. Several segments were isolated such as private hospitals, hotels, industrial and commercial buildings, etc. According to their own competencies and the nature of the local market, each subsidiary targeted some market segments.

From Segment to Milieu

Antolini, presently specialized in local public markets, targeted industrial markets (i.e. the construction of premises for foreign industrial firms willing to develop in

Loiret). Economically, if we adopt a traditional marketing approach, all the firms looking for industrial premises in Loiret constitute the market for HBTP. This demand stems from all the companies in the world that may settle in Loiret and from those French and local industries willing to extend their factories or to transfer their premises to Loiret. This means that it is impossible to calculate or to anticipate the demand, as it may stem from any part of the globe. To do so, Antolini would need a world scanning system to detect projects. Actually, Antolini cannot wait for a foreign company to decide the details of its settlement in Loiret. It would then have no chance to win the order as another company would, presumably, already have won the construction contract. As a reminder, the construction of industrial premises is a private purchase that escapes the advertisement rules of public markets. In general, a call for tender is issued and sent by the foreign company to some construction and engineering firms—often suppliers of the customer country, selected for their reputation or their relational proximity to the buyer.

BOX 8.1 The Loiret milieu.

Loiret is a *département** of the Central region, *préfecture* Orléans. Although Loiret is a rural *département*, it offers many advantages for industry. The geographical interest of its plain, ideally situated on the road to Spain and 1 hour from Paris, has attracted several multinational companies since the end of Word War II such as IBM, 3M or John Deere. In 1973 however, the recession after the first oil crisis plunged the region into a 10-year recession. Mr Colle became Mayor of Orléans in 1980 and decided to revive this region. A liberal and a member of the Republican Party, he developed a new way of running Orléans, the entrepreneurial way. In November 1983, he opened a new division, ADECO (Association for the Economic Development of Orléans) run by Mr Anouilh, a former salesman from THX (a token name). He introduced a policy of communication which involved prospecting foreign companies anxious to set up plants in Europe. As a result, from 1984 Orléans began to attract a considerable number of companies thanks to its own network of international consultants and, in particular, to Mr Desormeaux of RDI, International Research and Development, a consultant in the USA working for several French institutions.

In early 1986, following the general elections, political cohabitation began in France. Jacques Chirac became Prime Minister and appointed Mr Colle to the post of Transport Minister. The activities of Mr Colle and of ADECO therefore benefited from the advantages that came with the Mayor of Orléans' new position. In addition, the mayor–minister was supported in his actions by Mr Sorli, his right-hand man. Meanwhile, the *conseil général*—county council—of the Loiret *département* did not remain idle. At the beginning of the 1980s, Mr Sacreau, the centrist president of the county council himself, used his staff to attract companies from abroad, taking the risk of echoing the message of the municipal teams or even those of the CCI (Chamber of Commerce and Industry). Mr Pinsel, the socialist mayor of

---

* A *département* is a subdivision of France administered by a prefect who is located in the *préfecture*.

Briare, assisted him, among others. In 1984, one year after the launching of ADECO, Mr Sacreau set up, with the support of the county council, ADEL (Agency for the Economic Development of Loiret). He appointed Mr Mouton, a former tax inspector in the *préfecture* of the region, to the position of general delegate of ADEL. While Mr Sacreau ran his county council like a company board, Mr Mouton planned his expenses as if they were investments, 'reasoning in terms of revenue for the *département* as much as expenses for development'. This included the divisions of the *prefecture* which functioned simultaneously, thus making it possible to speed up the administrative work. According to Mr Sacreau: 'consensus is the secret of our success.'

Loiret is a *département* which wastes no time transforming projects into actions. A variety of actions are taken such as converting land at its own expense, buying a factory which was about to close down, elsewhere proposing funds and credits or accepting to pay a high proportion of the infrastructure costs—'actions which are only normal for a rich region and which offer no fiscal advantage,' Mr Mouton indicated. Indeed, companies come to Loiret for two major reasons: the workforce is qualified and stable, which is not the case in the Paris region, and there are no problems with the unions. Unlike other *départements* which are economically underprivileged, Loiret hardly benefits from aid from DATAR (the national agency for territorial development). This agency tends to direct large-scale industrial development towards other zones using financial and fiscal incentives. If the municipality and the county council, that is to say Mr Anouilh and Mr Mouton, work in close collaboration on important international dossiers, Orléans acts independently for activities on a smaller scale. But, overall, the fact that they share a mutual interest and the same political orientation means that they have many collaborative agreements. Loiret needs Orléans power and Orléans needs the economic hinterland of Loiret. This collaboration also includes the CCI and the UPL (the local association of CEOs).

International economic prospecting for new industries is an ambitious task. The ADECO of the municipality of Orléans cannot do it alone and needs all the local partners. However, the ADECO and also the ADEL of the county council must be careful not to be submerged by local industrialists on the lookout for a good deal and, therefore, likely to interfere in the process; they must be kept at a distance during the initial phase of prospects. This does not concern the public infrastructure services like the ANPE (National Employment Agency) and the EDF (*Electricité de France*) which are associated early on, if the project looks viable, but the private sector companies which are only invited at the end of the process.

Source: Cova et al., 1996, pp. 655–658.

In fact, we note that Antolini's marketing practice takes into account a collective actor having its own rules and in which each actor shares certain representations and values. Antolini's marketing manager and his team of sales engineers share the idea that there is a geographically specialized entity gathering all business and non-business actors and conditioning the setting up of industries in Loiret. It is through relationships with some of these actors and through an ongoing learning process enriched with each project that they developed this shared representation.

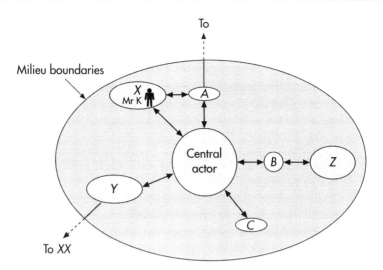

FIGURE 8.1 A model for analysing milieu.

The collective actor formed in this way is called the 'milieu of the setting up of industries in Loiret.' The knowledge of the milieu developed through relational investments enables Antolini to anticipate projects and obtain support on its offers. We can even consider that Antolini has and develops an invaluable informational and prescriptive resource that can be translated into a competitive advantage. Indeed, any foreign company willing to set up in Loiret must actually go through the milieu and obtain the support of some of its actors.

Analysing Milieus: A Method

The method we use for analysing milieus uses sociograms (as explained in Chapter 7) (see Figure 8.1). It is based on some basic principles:

- A milieu is attached to an activity in a clearly defined territory.
- A milieu gathers all business and non-business actors concerned by the activity on this territory.
- A milieu has clear geographical borders, but its actors may have relationships with several actors outside these borders.
- The central actors of the milieu are those who are in close contact with other actors of the milieu.

The method presented here has two dimensions:

- The milieu exists or not (in this case the milieu has not yet emerged and is not structured).
- The company which analyses the milieu is an actor of the milieu or not (in this case the company intends to create a position within the milieu).

Considering this, it is possible to distinguish three cases that require different approaches:

- the firm external to the milieu;
- the firm internal to the milieu;
- the non-existent milieu.

The Firm External to the Milieu

This is the case of Antolini which tries to enter the milieu and establish a position. The milieu in this case can be analysed by means of eight steps.

Step 1: Define the Milieu to Be Analysed

In this case, the milieu or, more precisely, assumed milieu (e.g. 'the construction of premises for foreign industrial firms willing to develop in Loiret') suggests the following:

- a milieu is linked to a market targeted by the supplier firm (activity/territory);
- it is possible to modify the assumed milieu if it is found to be too wide or too narrow either geographically or in terms of activity.

Step 2: Gather Information

By using databanks based on keywords on an activity or a territory, it is possible to find articles and documents dealing with, for example in the case of Antolini, industrial investments in Loiret and more generally on Loiret. In the same vein, it could be possible to look for information about gas in Kazakhstan or on Kazakhstan in general. Actually, when a company does not know a given area, it is necessary to initially take into account institutional actors at micro- or macro-levels (state actors, administration, etc.) and relationships between them even if they have a small influence in the milieu. It is generally easier to find this kind of information. Internet research appears to be a good tool to find information even though it is not the only or the most comprehensive source. Other information sources can be more useful, such as the press, local sales force, agent, key account managers, etc., situated in the same territory, but dealing with other activities.

Step 3: Use of Information

In this step, information is organized at two levels:

- The first level consists of a synthesis of information on the milieu such as list of actors acting in or around the milieu, list of experts writing or communicating on the milieu and so on.
- The second level is an elaboration of a quotation index for the experts and a quotation index for the actors.

TABLE 8.1 Grid to analyse actors of the milieu.

Names Institutions	Role Mission	Structure functioning pattern	Comments Dates, key events Evolution	Names of key individuals	Function	Comments on individuals Potential Evolution

It is the quotation index of experts which is the cornerstone of milieu analysis because it allows the company to quickly gain access to information. It is often easy to identify an expert who knows a milieu well. This expert will be used to understand and map the milieu. This expert is able to propose a representation of the milieu.

Step 4: Interview Key Experts

Once the expert is identified, the company has to contact and to interview him using a semi-structured questionnaire. It is generally easy to contact an expert and he is generally open to speak on his field of expertise. This interview often offers the expert the opportunity to explain and share what he likes. It is generally the case with people such as journalists and experts from public research centres or universities. But consultants do not have the same approach, and it is necessary to define whether the expert should be paid or not and how.

Another question is to define what 'mask' to wear in front of the expert: that of a company, a market research company, etc.? It appears that the best identity is that of a company. The expert is asked:

- to identify the institutional and individual actors, their profiles, their roles, their relationships and the quality of these relationships (see Table 8.1);
- to define and identify other experts using the snowballing technique.

The objective here is to confront different expert representations in order to map the milieu in the same way as in the Delphi approach.

Step 5: Interview Other Experts

The interview can be managed in different ways:

- either, it is considered that a true and rational representation of the milieu exists (in this case, it is possible to use the initial representation elaborated with key experts and to validate or to modify it with other experts);
- or, it is considered that each expert has his own representation (cognitive map) and will present it.

It is important to note that this method is mainly based on expert interviews and not on actor interviews. The reason is that it is difficult for a company that manages the analyses to gain access to actors of the milieu and to question them about their position, their relationships with other actors, etc. This approach is feasible but needs to be managed carefully, because actors in the milieu can consider interviews as weak signals. In fact, the approach using expert interview does not affect the milieu in the same way as interviewing actors.

Step 6: Map the Milieu

Mapping is based on expert interviews. We state that the number and the nature of the relationships a given actor has with other actors can measure the centrality of an actor in the milieu. To evaluate centrality, it is possible to use an actor/actor matrix. We can also use a simple system to qualify the relationship between two actors or a sophisticated one. For instance, we can use a binary scale: $0 = no$ relationship, $1 = existing$ relationship. A more complex evaluation can rely on criteria such as relationship intensity (strong, average, weak), contents of exchanges (administrative, technical, financial, political, social, etc.) and the nature of the relationship (conflict, cooperation, collusion, competition, coexistence). This matrix (Table 8.2) constitutes a good tool to classify actors according to their centrality (central vs. marginal) and to qualify the different links between an actor and the others.

TABLE 8.2 Actors' portfolio matrix.

	Actor 1	Actor 2	Actor 3	Actor 4	Actor 5	Actor 6	Actor 7
Actor 1							
Actor 2							
Actor 3							
Actor 4							
Actor 5							
Actor 6							
Actor 7							

Step 7: Represent the Milieu

The objective is to use a sheet of paper that represents the milieu and to include the highest level of information captured in the previous steps. The representation has to be:

- readable and understandable;
- exhaustive to allow the company to define actions well.

It is, thus, very important to establish graphical rules to map out the milieu (Figure 8.2). Generally, milieu is represented as an oval. In the Antolini case, some actors located in Loiret are within the oval, other actors are not because, although they influence the milieu, they are not located in Loiret. Central actors are positioned in the centre of the oval, marginal actors are on the edge. According to his role, culture and proximity, each actor is represented by a given shape and size. The nature of the relationship between actors is symbolized by arrows (size and orientation) and symbols (e.g. to characterize cooperation or conflict).

We recommend avoiding what is common in marketing: to group together actors who are similar. In traditional market representation, actors are grouped in segments according to their homogeneity and similarity. On the contrary, in project business it is most important to capture individual actors even though they are in the same segment. This is the key to definition of precise and targeted actions.

Step 8: Use of the Representation of the Milieu

Once the representation is mapped out, it is possible to validate it with experts. This representation is the starting point for definition of targeted actions within the milieu. Some companies try to identify how to reach a central actor directly or indirectly and define relational plans. What actor can we target to indirectly gain access to a given actor because it is not possible to contact him directly? What is the best route to create a contact? Building relationships with actors within a milieu is time consuming. This is the reason why companies often have a position in a given milieu before generating economic activity. Some companies use this representation to monitor future market actions.

As we explained in Part I, building a good relational position is not the only factor that automatically leads to success. Building a favourable relational position generally helps a company succeed if the functional position (its offer) is at least equal to its competitors. We don't think that a good relational position allows the company to compensate an unfavourable position on an offer.

In the earlier example, Antolini allocates its resources towards certain actors of the milieu in an effort to develop a relational position and, hence, to be ideally positioned to know forthcoming project opportunities as early as the first contacts between a foreign company and these actors are made. In particular, Antolini has to bypass the barriers raised by ADECO and ADEL. But Antolini is also part of other milieus in which it encounters some of the actors of the milieu who took part in setting up industries in Loiret, such as political actors and some public infra-structure services. The firm can also derive support and benefit from these

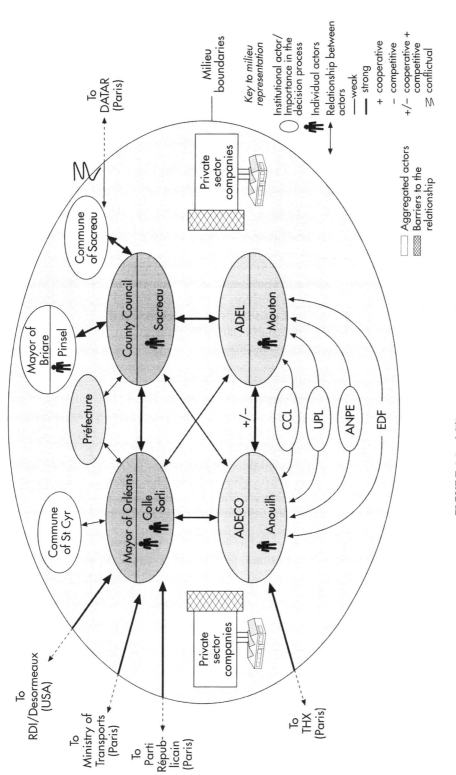

FIGURE 8.2 Milieu representation in Loiret.

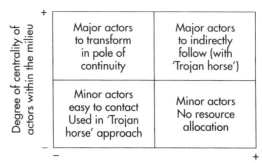

FIGURE 8.3 Actors portfolio matrix.

previous investments in other milieus. More generally, faced with the extreme but traditional situation of project business in which demand is dispersed and unpredictable, Antolini can gain a position prior to any project by considering the milieu as a unit of analysis and thus be prepared when and if a project emerges.

To better structure the approach of actors within the milieu, it is possible to use a classification based on two dimensions:

- degree of centrality of actors within the milieu;
- degree of accessibility to actors by the company.

The combination of these two dimensions leads to a four-box matrix (Figure 8.3) whose objective is to help managers to define specific actions.

Box 1 comprises actors on whom the company is basing its approach to anticipating the existence of projects in a given milieu. The objective is to transform them into a pole of continuity between the company and his potential customers having projects. Marketing actions prior to any project are mainly targeted at these actors. They are allies and potential partners.

Box 2 includes actors who have a key role within the milieu, but the company cannot reach them because of too high a level of investment or for legal reasons. The company does not allocate resources to develop direct relationship but tries to indirectly follow them through other actors (situated in Boxes 1 and 3). These actors can play the role of the so-called 'Trojan horse' to indirectly connect a key actor.

Box 3 includes a group of minor actors who are easy to contact. Maintaining relationships with them allows getting in touch with actors in Box 2. They are used in 'Trojan horse' approaches.

Box 4 constitutes actors who do not need resource allocations.

Step 9: Update the Representation

The representation has to evolve according to new information and new events. This representation is an intermediary vision. In particular, after investing in relationships with different actors, the company will establish a position and win some contracts. Consequently, the nature and the content of information that the company captures is not the same. Some actors' positions, that were previously evaluated, can change because the company learns about the milieu. It is thus necessary to regularly update the representation and, if necessary, to adjust the approach according to the changes.

The Firm Internal to the Milieu

After having invested in relationships with central actors and gained some contracts, Antolini became an actor within the milieu. The analysis is exactly the same because Antolini is not outside the milieu but is a player.

Step 1: Define the Milieu

The milieu still remains 'the construction of premises for foreign industrial firms willing to develop in Loiret.'

Step 2: Interview Internal Experts

In this case, some people within the company, who are knowledgeable about the milieu, can play as internal experts. This step begins with an interview of the salesman in charge of the territory. This person is a key expert when mapping out the milieu. As shown previously, the objective is to identify actors, their role, relationships between actors and the quality of the relationships. Then, a list of people from the company having contacts with actors in the milieu is established. Who is in contact with whom and for what reason? What is the quality of the relationship? A possible (and frequent) limit in this step is the fact that the internal expert often prefers to keep the information and is not willing to share it with others.

Step 3: Interview Other People Involved in the Milieu

Interviews are conducted taking into account their specific knowledge such as technical issues, financial issues, etc. The company can use a focus group managed by the internal expert. In this approach, people involved generally exchange and share information they own.

Step 4: Confront the Representation to an External Expert

The internal expert generally knows people outside the company who well know how the milieu functions (external expert). Making use of this expert allows the company to improve its representation on the milieu and prevents a 'home-made representation'. Sometimes, the external and the internal representation hugely diverge and are incompatible; some actors appear as minor actors to some experts and major to others. This case is often met when a European or US company analyses milieus in Asia or in Africa. Western companies focus on detection of official actors such as companies, administrators and politicians. Moreover, they only consider contractual and official links between them and forget invisible and non-business links that can be dominant in some cultures. This is the case with Chinese families who control networks of small companies in several countries in Asia, or with the Royal Family in Morocco. Friendship, geographical origins (natives from the same village) and family links largely influence the development of relationships within a given milieu.

Step 5: Analyse Interview Content

Same as Step 6 Case 'Firm External to the Milieu' (see above).

Step 6: Represent the Milieu

Same as Step 7 Case 'Firm External to the Milieu' (see above).

Step 7: Use and Upgrade of the Representation of the Milieu

The rigorous representation of the milieu allows us to evaluate past actions and choices and define the limits for future actions. This representation points out the relational deadlock the company faced. The actor who was considered as key 5 years ago may not be central today, but the company did consider him as so. This representation can be used in a long-term perspective in order to evaluate the dynamics of the relational position and the results of relational investments. In some companies the representation can be an opportunity to exchange information between different persons who know about the milieu. People involved share information and build together a relational action plan. In some cases, meetings between people are regular and the group functions as a club.

The Non-existent Milieu

In this case we use the example of the European automatic toll motorway milieu in the mid-1990s (Box 8.2).

In fact, the notion of positioning in a milieu is less interesting for project marketing in the sectors related to emerging and innovative technologies. The absence of past experience makes it difficult to design the business arena in the milieu. It is the projects that bring the actors together that do this; the more projects there are, the more the context becomes similar to a milieu. Little by little, the situation becomes clearer. This is the result of collective experience. Subsequently, when technologically innovative areas, which are difficult to assimilate to existing milieus, are concerned, any analysis becomes delicate; it becomes more like forecasting and locating of actors and establishing the relationships between them.

In 1995, there was no European automatic toll motorway milieu. It needed to be created from various potential actors. The actors were far apart and, like pieces of Lego, could be assembled in a multitude of ways. The only concrete elements were the different colours of the pieces (corresponding to national colours). Moreover, not all the pieces were necessarily there; some might have been at the bottom of the bag! Thus it became impossible for a supplier to act using logic of positioning in this milieu. However, a survey of the participants of the European standardization techniques committees and working groups allowed identification of a few major actors for future projects.

BOX 8.2 Pieces of the European Automatic Toll Motorway Milieu.

In the standardization committees for the European automatic toll motorway network there are:

- the transport ministries representing different countries (particularly Northern Europe);
- the motorway concessionaires and companies (the UK, France and Italy);
- the research departments, consultancies and engineers for all sectors (traffic, roads, management, technology, etc.);
- the communication technology industrialists (hyper-frequencies, infrared, telephone, optics, etc.).
- universities and research centres;
- banks (for the payment systems);
- car and car parts manufacturers;
- traffic control specialists;
- national transport federations.

Such a number of different actors may lead the company to make the assumption of a homothety between the standardization committee and the future milieu. The company's involvement in the working groups allows for an insight into the different actors and a better understanding of their expectations and strategies. Participation in the standardization committees is a key element for an independent of any project marketing approach for the company. It allows establishing standards and norms which correspond to the supplier's key competencies, the creation of associations, the assembling of projects and the development of creative offers.

The call for tenders launched by the UK's Ministry of Transport was an amazing (and maybe unique) case which led to limiting the assumption of homothety. In 1994, the British government began consulting a vast number of companies potentially interested in participating, with others, in the creation of a complete automatic toll motorway network in England. Once the tenders had been received, the British government published a list of all the applicants and sent it to all the candidates. The government was clearly stating its position (unlike the German government's position): it was not looking for individual tests or purchases of the technology, but rather for complete systems. Moreover, the British government demonstrated its desire to play a key role in the development of the milieu; it presented the pieces of Lego to the others and asked for an assembly. It could then choose the best assembly rather than a collection of individual pieces.

Analysis of this document reveals that the actors and participants in the standardization committees (the pieces still in the box), were seeking a part in the development of the milieu. They included:

- anti-fraud specialists;
- surveillance specialists;
- petroleum companies (in the case of motorway services/fuel/smart cards);
- road signs manufacturers;
- payment systems manufacturers (smart cards);
- component manufacturers;
- mobile communications operators (e.g. ATT);
- infrastructure industrialists (concrete, portiques, portals, etc.);
- payment, traffic and transport software manufacturers;
- general contractors (e.g. Bull or IBM) and investors prepared to take the financial risk;
- the global systems providers.

With this list of actors, following the call for tenders, it was impossible to represent a milieu since the vast majority of the hundred or so applicants who belonged to isolated entities. There were very few grouped applicants. There were even a number of applicants that belonged to the same industrial group despite an apparent lack of internal coordination. Moreover, relationships within the standardization committees remained informal and only concerned personal relations that obviously would have no institutional results. In fact, these interpersonal relationships remained strictly nationalistic; the English with the English, the French with the French, etc. Only a few bi-national relationships existed, such as the Franco-Belgian. Hardly any relationships between potential actors could be found, hence the non-existence of a European milieu, just a few small and scattered relations.

Source: Interviews by the authors.

On the other hand, in some national milieus, relationships are clearly identifiable, principally those when calls for tender have already brought partners together. Using the list of actors defined on the basis of the standardization committee's survey and the call for tenders, a list of national actors can be drawn up. Intra-national links can then be identified. Forecasting links between national milieus can then be made based on:

- the personal ties with the standardization committee;
- associations resulting from past calls for tender;
- contacts made during other European programmes.

It is then up to each company to create the European milieu via their actions and presence, while including in the picture the European political actors (Hadjikhani and Ghauri, 2001).

Milieu and Marketing

If we look at the way marketing scanning systems are implemented in project business, we can see that marketing intelligence is essentially based around relationships which have been created, developed and maintained by company members with a number of socio-economic actors operating either directly or indirectly in the milieu that companies operate in (Dubini and Aldrich, 1991).

These contacts are not just the result of the work of the marketers, but all the members of the company. The managers' personal networks, in fact all members of staff, have a part to play in the company's marketing process. The term 'extended staff' is even used to designate staff relations (friends, groups, family, etc.) who also participate in the marketing intelligence. Thus, for the catering contracts in offshore platforms in Africa, a large catering company's intelligence system gathered information from the wives of men working on new personal and company projects. In fact, the system of project marketing intelligence is based on a relational investment in the milieu that it offers the management of the intelligence networks of individuals for the company.

Mutual Debt and Interpersonal Relationship

The study of personal employee networks in project business raises the question as to whether relations in the milieu can come in different forms: from the interested contact to the uninterested purely social relationship. Inter-individual relationships in a professional context are controlled less by an opportunism for short-term egoistic interest than by confidence for a mutuality of long-term interest. The basis of a long-term business relationship between two individuals is less the 'reciprocity' (give and take) than the equality of the spin-offs resulting from a common effort (redistribution of profit) which can be called mutual interest or 'mutuality of interest'. In this case (as for that of actor opportunism), the social ties between two individuals serve the economic link which brought them together, the social tie being purely instrumental.

However, to stop here would be to forget that in business there are a number of cases where the economic link serves the social link (Caillé and Godbout, 1992). The most obvious example, which can be seen everywhere, is the case of the shared professional project which we design (invent even!) to respond to a purely functional need or simply to be with our friends more often. Also, without going as far as the formal project, how much professional information circulates each day for the safeguard of social ties? The inter-individual relationship is therefore not controlled by some functional and utilitarian demand, but rather by itself. In this case, the episodes of the relationship are more exchanges than gifts, just like the countless and daily favours we do to those we love and with whom we wish to remain close.

These regular gifts nourish the idea of debt which exists between two individuals, working both ways; this is what is known as 'mutual debt'; that is, the opposite of the 'give and take reciprocity' in as much as the debt does not have to be settled. If one party wishes to reduce or even break the social tie, that party should settle his debt and reinstate the give and take situation. We can therefore draw up a continuum of the systems of inter-individual business relationships based on the balance between utility and syntony, from the discreet transaction to mutual debt, via reciprocity and mutuality of interest. Equally, there are not only pure systems, sometimes the utility and syntony are closely related, one conditioning the other. A business relationship which was initiated under the system of reciprocity can become one of mutual debt, just as a relationship based on mutual debt can turn into a mutual reciprocity. A friendly business relationship can swing between moments of utility and moments of syntony.

BOX 8.3 Mutual Debt in the Business World!

With the following case, based on the aerospace industry, we shall try to demonstrate how the concept of mutual debt can throw a different light on the exchanges between individuals involved in business relationships.

A German aerospace manufacturer was competing against his UK counterpart for the supply of an important part for a new Italian aircraft. A short while before the Farnborough Air Show, the German marketing department learnt from the Italian purchasing director that the UK supplier was to be chosen because of its better offer. Following this announcement, the German marketing department accepted defeat. However, during the inauguration of the Farnborough Air Show, the director of the German company had the opportunity to dine with the Italian boss, someone he had known for a number of years. The Italian company belonged to the Europaero Group, in which the German director used to have an important position before changing jobs (10 years ago). The German boss had fought long and hard to have the Italians in the group, alongside the Germans, British and French. That evening, the Italian boss passed on some information to his German counterpart and friend who had not asked for anything: 'This is the price to offer if you want to beat the British.' The following day, the marketing department of the German firm quickly made another offer, and, before the show was over, the contract was signed between the Germans and the Italians.

There are three ways to interpret this:

- A first utilitarian interpretation, using the notion of give and take reciprocity, shows how the Italian boss, 10 years on, returns the favour. This is a good example of reciprocity between two individuals who trust each other.
- A second utilitarian interpretation could even find elements of an agreement or even corruption.
- A third, non-utilitarian interpretation, using the concept of mutual debt, shows that the Italian boss, who gets to see his German counterpart less frequently than in the past (new position, from Europaero to industry), uses the opportunity of a long-term economic exchange to recreate the social ties. He is not looking to settle his debt, but rather to start the mutual debt system up again, which, at the same time, may lead to more frequent social exchanges.

Source: Interviews by the authors.

More commonly, such situations are relatively rare, and business relationships are more likely to comprise: daily conversations sharing gifts to continue the mutual debt process (without ever settling it, so the social ties continue), information, availability (time is not important!), little pleasures in life (good food, etc.).

Sometimes, during these conversations, something important for a project activity might be said, but this is not the goal of the relationship.

However, relationships, controlled more by mutual debt than by interest, can sometimes lead to important contracts and major success for companies interested in a leading position in a milieu. The success of a leading French company in the energy sector in Poland can partly be explained by the company's position in relation to the leading actor of the milieu in question: *Solidarność*. Indeed, members of Solidarily hold most of the key positions in the Polish electrical industry. When it was first created at the beginning of the 1980s, the union sought support from major Western trade unions. The CFDT (a French union), a division of the leading French company, responded and the CFDT spokesman at the time is now the top negotiator of the international division for the Polish sector.

Personal Intelligence Networks

There are two schools of thought about the reasons behind personal relationships and networks in a milieu (Belk and Coon, 1993). The first, utilitarian, considers reciprocity and mutual interest as the basis to all relationships. It believes that a simple diagnosis of the relationships within the milieu followed by an evaluation of the entrance process to the milieu leads to a form of marketing intelligence. The manager can then choose his target relationships. He will examine each relationship to see which level is the most interesting and can enable him to initiate a relationship allowing him to gain information concerning a specific project or to influence decisions concerning a specific project. In this situation, both parties are aware they are beginning a relationship which could be mutually interesting in the short term with potential for the mid/long term based on a mutuality of interests. This type of approach is fairly common in sectors such as the construction industry or public works, where the mutuality of interests can sometimes lead to agreements which can sometimes appear unfair!

BOX 8.4 How to Move Up in the Network in Germany.

This is an example of the utilitarian approach from the German energy sector. The director of a subsidiary of a multinational company has defined the objectives for the development of local relationships for the short and mid-term. The relationships have become targets for himself and his 30 colleagues. He has defined his tactics to move up in the network; in other words, to create a relationship with X in the Y organization which is not very interesting but will allow access to Z in the W organization which is a key target. To help his colleagues, he has created a sort of platform for meetings, a series of conferences on current themes, and has invited the targets. His staff were also present at the conferences which allowed them to make initial contact with their targets. The series of conferences correspond to what the Americans call *human networkshops* and in Europe lawyers and other such professionals, call 'utilitarian diners'.

The second school of thought, non-utilitarian, sees the problem of the creation and management of personal networks as more complex. They consider the very notion of network management as contradictory; the very strength of an individual relationships network being based on elements which are neither planned nor managed.

In other words, they can be effective because they are not organized for utilitarian reasons (collecting information, influence, etc.) but for the sake of friendship. The social ties are vital and sacred in this approach. For some top engineers, it is strictly out of the question to use their relationships to obtain information concerning a project. This is particularly the case in the aerospace and energy sectors.

If we continue with this train of thought, marketing intelligence is based principally on networks of interpersonal relationships which could not be organized without a risk of destroying them, which leads us to think about the impossibility of managing relational investment (Caillé and Godbout, 1992). As a solution, some propose that the person who is (or who will be) in a relationship with actors of the milieu does not intentionally manage his action to remain in the non-utilitarian dimension of the relationship. However, it is up to the manager 'to use' the person by 'exposing' him to help develop a network. There could therefore be a double structure in a company with people dominated by a non-utilitarian logic (the givers) who work on relationships and social ties and those dominated by a utilitarian logic (the 'takers') who work on easing and directing the relationships of the former.

In reality, the same people often swing between the two approaches, utilitarian and non-utilitarian. An engineer can go from a state of latent consciousness of what he is doing (in the relationship to pass on information) to a state of unconsciousness, generally during a one-to-one occasion, especially when he is spontaneous, enjoying himself and enjoying the relationship. He can then have a clear conscience since what he does spontaneously and in a non-utilitarian way could be useful for him. He has created a form of debt with the other person, a debt which will strengthen their social ties and thereby guarantee a source of information and influence.

These engineers and other marketers are key elements in the animation of the networks; they give a lot of themselves, creating an atmosphere of confidence the others almost contagiously feel they need to return.

Chapter 9

MANAGING CUSTOMER RELATIONSHIPS

The specificities of the project marketing field that we described in Part I seem to reduce the usefulness of the method of supplier/customer relationship portfolio (see Box 9.1). Actually, this kind of approach is limited by the basic nature of projects. In many cases, due to the low frequency of projects it is impossible to maintain direct economic and technical relationships with the customer. In the approaches traditionally used in project marketing, it is stated that the unit of analysis is the project, not the customer. Each project is unique and needs a specific approach. In this type of approach, the supplier is focused on his project portfolio, not on the customer portfolio. The project portfolio allows the supplier to allocate technical and commercial resources according to the nature of different projects.

Recently, however, companies tend to combine both approaches centred on a single project and on the management of the customer relationship between two projects. The objective is to capitalize on investments realized by the supplier during past projects with a given customer. Actually, the existence of social contact between individuals within the two organizations allows the supplier to detect future projects and sometimes to create projects with the customer. Therefore, methods to manage the portfolio of customer relationships have been developed and are similar to those used in industrial product marketing.

BOX 9.1 Portfolio of Supplier–customer Relationships: the Ardus Case.

Ardus is a company in the energy industry. Recently, Ardus learnt about some difficulties which reduced its resource level. To increase its profitability, Ardus chose to bet on a relational approach for its customers even though all its competitors in this industry generally preferred to focus on each project. Ardus set up a five-step method:

1. prospecting and scanning customers;
2. scoring and ranking customers;
3. targeting customers;
4. setting up partnerships with targeted customers;
5. managing customer relationships.

Step 2 concerning scoring of customers is key. It aims at reducing Ardus's risks when allocating resources proportionate to the customer value, which comprises direct value according to the projects that the customer intends to develop in a short-term perspective, contribution of the customer to the medium- and long-term Ardus strategy, indirect value when some adaptations and developments done with a particular customer are used to improve relationships with other customers.

The selection of customers includes criteria such as (Figure 9.1):

- customer value;
- the customer's willingness to engage in a cooperative relationship with Ardus;
- Ardus's competitive position in the customer account.

Ardus systematically refuses to act as a subcontractor if it is not possible to bring real added value to the customer. Ardus is generally involved in a partnership with the customer from the conception phase and is committed to results.

This approach seems to be cautious but it allows Ardus to limit risks inherent in project marketing. This approach does not allow Ardus to bid on huge and complex projects.

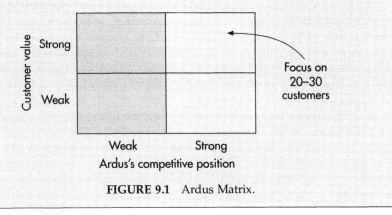

FIGURE 9.1   Ardus Matrix.

So, in project marketing, we can find, in certain industries, long-lasting relationships between the supplier and the customer. The frequency of contacts between companies and individuals which take place during several projects leads to reinforcing the relationship. There is no systematic approach to create and develop a relational position between projects. The relationship develops by muddling through. The portfolio approach that we suggest can help these companies to manage relationships with customers using a more strategic orientation.

This approach can be refined in order to better adapt to the specific situations met in project marketing. In this case, actors in the milieu play an important role and influence the supplier/customer relationship and the projects. As compared with methods used in traditional business-to-business marketing which are focused on supplier/customer relationships, in the case of project marketing the network in which the customer relationship is embedded is taken into account.

Developing a Portfolio of Customer Relationships

It is possible to divide the process of building and managing the portfolio of customer relationships in project marketing into three main stages:

1 The definition of the relevant unit analysed.
2 The dimension of analysis.
3 The allocation of resources.

First Stage: The Definition of the Unit Analysed

The first stage is to define the relevant customer relationship unit to be taken into account, since it influences the nature of the decisions that will be taken in the following stages. However, nearly all the different methods proposed in the literature for managing a portfolio of customer relationships pose formidable problems for the user: Which unit of the organization is to be ranked? Do we analyse the supplier relationship with the decision-making unit, with customer sites, or with entire industrial groups, or only with certain subsidiary companies of these groups? In fact, this first stage rests upon the 'zoom strength' with which a supplier chooses to analyse his customers.

In order to define the relevant customer unit, we suggest (Salle *et al.*, 2000) an approach articulated around a combination of four main questions.

1. At what level in the supplier's organization is the client's analysis conducted?

The person in charge of the customer portfolio analysis will have his own representation of the relevant customer unit to be considered, according to his position in his own company's structure. This contingency may be explained by a series of factors. Examples are the nature of the objectives given to the individual in charge of the analysis, the lead time necessary to achieve these objectives and the level of available resources. Thus, in a number of large companies, we can distinguish, as a general rule, two organizational levels responsible for relationships with customers: a regional level which is dedicated to the establishments belonging to industrial groups present in the geographical zone in question and a central level which is responsible for the coordination of all of the supplier's actions regarding key accounts.

If the regional level is a profit centre, the regional marketing and sales team will concentrate its efforts on the most attractive regional customers. In other words, the team will look at the customers that will allow it to achieve its objectives. These choices may well be made to the detriment of customers who are, in fact, establishments belonging to industrial groups considered to be key accounts at central level, but which do not present the same degree of attractiveness on a regional level. Hence, according to the point of view of the supplier (regional or central), the customer unit does not retain the same meaning.

2. What are the characteristics of the customer's buying decision-making process relative to the supplier's offer?

The objective is to highlight the relevance of this or that customer unit by taking into account client procedures for the coordination of the buying departments or, on the contrary, the relative autonomy accorded to different customer establishments with regard to buying decisions.

3. What are the details of the relationship between the supplier and the customer?

With certain supplier–customer relationships, one of the two organizations may hold a dominant position whilst the other has only limited latitude for individual choice. The organization with the most power may impose its own management methods on the relationship and this, in a way, determines what will become the relevant customer or supplier unit.

4. What are the strategic orientations of a supplier with regard to the customer?

The choice of the customer unit may be done according to the strategy that the supplier wishes to implement with regard to a specific customer; for example, if one of the areas of development of a supplier has better coverage with respect to a particular customer (an industrial group), it may be wise to obtain a global and integrated view of him and to consider all of the potential buying decision-making centres as constituting only one customer unit, obtaining a detailed view at a later stage if necessary.

Second Stage: The Dimensions of the Analysis

The objective of this stage is to determine which dimensions will enable a pertinent ranking of the customer units. The choice of dimensions largely depends on the use of this method and the nature of decisions which are taken (basically, management of customer relationships). As a consequence, the chosen dimensions have to allow the supplier to define a hierarchy between customers and investment priorities.

Since matrices are used to visualize portfolios, the methods presented in the related business literature (Campbell and Cunningham, 1983; Fiocca, 1982; Yorke and Droussiotis, 1994) all use two dimensions which associate several criteria:

- on one hand, customer attractiveness towards a given supplier;
- on the other hand, an appreciation of the nature and dynamics of supplier–customer relationships. Some scholars suggest using dimensions such as 'Vulnerability of the relationship', 'Supplier position in the supplier/

customer relationship', 'Possibility of development in the supplier/customer relationship'.

BOX 9.2 Portfolio of Customer Relationships: the Kanpont Case.

Kanpont is a subsidiary company that belongs to an industrial group operation in the construction and public works sector. The public authorities and administrative organizations represent the majority of its turnover. These customers invest, according to a greater or lesser frequency, in the acquisition of public assets or programmes of varying nature: hospitals, sports centres, bridges, urban development, road works and collective housing. For many customers, the high levels of investment may lead to a continuity in their relationship with Kanpont, even if each project has its own characteristics. Kanpont, therefore, manages a customer relationships portfolio. These relationships are special in that they are influenced by an important number of actors who operate within the specific environment of Kanpont: financial organizations, architects, engineers, politicians, etc. The customer portfolio management approach takes into account two specific points: (1) the existence of continuous customer relationships and (2) the influence of the milieu.

The 'dynamics of the relationship' translates into Kanpont's the relative position. Its evaluation is based on three groups of criteria:

- Kanpont's position in the relationship with its customer. Diversity of contacts, the ease of people access within the customer organization, the hierarchical level of these people within the customer organization, the quality of these contacts, the degree of mutual trust (based on an appreciation of previous contacts with the customer), understanding of the professional stakes of the individuals implicated.
- Kanpont's position with respect to the key actors operating within the customer's milieu. A preliminary stage consists of evaluating the nature and the degree of influence of these key actors. Kanpont's position is evaluated by taking into account the degree and the quality of contacts with these key actors.
- The competitors' respective positions. They are evaluated on the basis of two factors: the relationship the competitor has with the customer (degree and quality of the contacts) and with the milieu (degree and quality of the contacts with respect to the key actors).

The 'attractiveness of the customer' is usually evaluated according to two groups of criteria:

- Quantitative criteria—customer investment budget, size of operations, recurrence of operations, profit margin according to the nature of the works.
- Qualitative criteria—nature of the operations to be undertaken according to Kanpont's skills, customer loyalty (measured by the number of contracts won by Kanpont/the total number of contracts awarded during a set period in time), the number of references, the geographical location of the customer.

Source: Interviews by the authors.

1. Customer Attractiveness   This can be defined as 'the coherence between his characteristics and the supplier strategy'. Taking the supplier point of view, the question is: 'What is a "good" customer?' Actually, according to supplier characteristics, attractiveness will be different; for instance, on one hand, a company having a very flexible production process, able to deal with small-size tailor-made projects based locally, and, on the other hand, a company that focuses on large projects including standardized heavy equipment will not have the same definition of what is a good customer because their strategies are basically different.

We can draw two main consequences:

- First, there is no unique and universal method. Each company has to define and implement its own method in order to manage its supplier/customer relationship portfolio.
- Second, the key point is to have a clear and shared vision of the main axes of the marketing strategy within the company.

However, if customer attractiveness cannot be defined using a standardized method, we can suggest some criteria to facilitate the choices:

- Quantitative criteria linked to the importance of the customer such as turnover, sale volume, profitability, etc.
- Criteria related to the opportunities for the supplier to develop his position with regards to his customer. Here the objective is to evaluate whether customer characteristics allow the supplier to expect a quantitative development. These opportunities both come from the dynamism of the customer in his markets and the growth of these markets.
- Criteria describing the coherence between the respective strategies of the customer and the supplier. The customer relationship is the place in which marketing strategy is effectively implemented, particularly through adaptations, joint developments, innovation. It is thus very important for the supplier to target customers allowing this kind of collaboration. It is necessary to take into account criteria that enable us to describe this coherence between the respective strategies of the customer and the supplier—the more the coherence, the more the customer attractiveness. For instance, this coherence can be evaluated using criteria such as: the customer is in a target segment for the supplier, the similarity of technological evolution, customer ability to forecast (according to his production technology, a supplier would prefer anticipated production planning), continuity in customer projects, etc.

2. The Vulnerability of the Supplier in the Customer Relationship   This can be defined as the uncertainty of the position of the supplier within the relationship compared with that of its competitors. Four categories of criteria are taken into account:

- Position and actions of the competitors—the nature and importance of means that are allocated by competitors to a given supplier/customer relationship in order to modify their position (entry strategy or growth strategy) have strong consequences on the vulnerability of the supplier. It is thus important to understand what kind of competitor actions lead to a certain level of vulnerability. This vulnerability can change according to customer behaviour, the nature of the markets and relationships between actors within the milieu. In some cases, small and regular actions could have more impact than strong and limited actions; in other cases, the contrary will happen. As a consequence, suppliers should be alert to all events and weak signals which emerge within the customer relationship, together with events and incidents that take place in the milieu in which the client is embedded. The supplier should also pay specific attention to the relationships between the customer and key actors in the milieu which may affect the customer relationship.

- Criteria related to the nature of supplier/customer relationship—two main factors influence the nature of the supplier/customer relationship: (1) commitment between the two organizations and the connected actors, (2) the quality of the relationships. Vulnerability largely depends on marketing situations. We can evaluate commitment by the nature and the level of investments made by each organization to work with the other; for example, are these investments weak or strong, reciprocal (the supplier and the customer invest in the relationship), specific or standard? This evaluation allows qualification of existing barriers and the degree of vulnerability. The quality of the supplier/ customer relationship can be analysed by checking different elements such as: the existing conflicts and disputes between the two organizations and their related networks, the nature and the impact of these conflicts and disputes. Some kinds of conflict and dispute are concerned with the customer's core activity and can lead to a high degree of vulnerability. Others have little impact on the atmosphere of the relationship.

- Criteria dedicated to the purchasing strategy of the customer and the position of the supplier. The purchasing function has known an important development during the past 10 years. New purchasing methods including more strategy (instead of administration) lead to changes in the management of relationships from the customer point of view. These purchasing strategies have consequences on sourcing, number of suppliers used, the style of negotiation according to nature of the market (e.g. is price, or cost, or value the dominant criterion?). Is the purchasing behaviour characterized by a partnership with the supplier or by opportunism? According to this strategy, the supplier will face different degrees of vulnerability (Cateora and Ghauri, 1999).

- Criteria related to changes inside the customers or supplier's organization. As changes appear between the customer and/or the supplier, and/or milieu and/or the supplier/customer relationship, the degree of vulnerability of the supplier position is modified. These changes can be opportunities or threats. For the supplier, the key point is to identify those events that can affect the relationship. Many events can take place within the relationship and destabilize it; for example, change in purchasing strategy can lead to change in sourcing, audit within the purchasing department leading to benchmark suppliers, organizational changes on the customer or supplier side can influence the role and position of the participants in the decision process. Cultural change following a merger or an acquisition process and technological changes may also influence the relationship (Buckley and Ghauri,

Attractiveness

	Scales	Mark	Weight	Weighted mark
Customer importance	Very high	4	3	6
	High	3		
	Average	2		
	Low	1		
Possibilities of development of the supplier	Very high	4	1	4
	High	3		
	Average	2		
	Low	1		

Customer attractiveness | 10/16

Vulnerability of the relationship

	Scales	Mark	Weight	Weighted mark
Customer's openness in the relationship	Very favourable	1	1	3
	Favourable	2		
	Unfavourable	3		
	Very unfavourable	4		
Customer's buying strategy	Very favourable	1	1	3
	Favourable	2		
	Unfavourable	3		
	Very unfavourable	4		
Nature of competitor's actions	Very favourable	1	1	2
	Favourable	2		
	Unfavourable	3		
	Very unfavourable	4		

Vulnerability of the relationship | 8/12

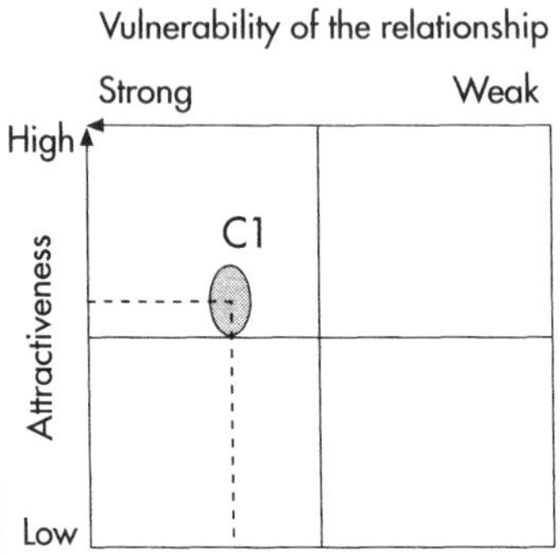

FIGURE 9.2 Positioning of a customer in the portfolio matrix of a supplier.

2002). All these events should be considered as weak signals that the supplier and, particularly, salespeople continuously have to take on board in order to prevent vulnerability of the supplier position in the supplier/customer relationship.

Having defined criteria that qualify attractiveness and vulnerability, the next step consists in determining how to measure and weigh each criterion. This step is not a simple definition of measurement scales. Basically, it specifies the suppliers strategic choices and orientations. A firm whose strategy is oriented toward profitability will give a stronger weight to these criteria when comparing customer attractiveness. Another firm whose main objective is to grow will probably choose to increase criteria such as present and potential turnover. Because huge differences exist between companies' strategic choices, clearly universal scales do not exist. These choices are crucial because they influence the classification of the customers in the portfolio and the nature of resource allocation (Figure 9.2).

Third Stage: The Allocation of Resources

The two dimensions (attractiveness and relationship vulnerability) are used to build the portfolio matrix of supplier/customer relationships. All customers are

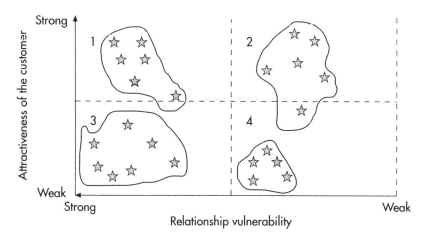

FIGURE 9.3 Example of customer portfolio.

positioned in this matrix. Choices will be different according to the position in the matrix (Figure 9.3).

Target customers are in Cells 1 and 2. They represent high stakes and need to be carefully managed. They receive the higher level of resources from the supplier. As stated by one marketing manager:

> *It is fundamental to carefully follow these target customers because they are also potential customers targeted by competitors.*

1　The supplier has to highly invest in this customer relationship in order to reduce his vulnerability.
2　In this case the investment aims at maintaining the supplier's position. One key point in this cell is to be reactive in order to capture opportunities, such as new developments, that appear.

Customers situated in Cells 3 and 4 have less influence on the supplier evolution. Generally, these customers are the most numerous in the portfolio and the supplier invests less, compared with customers in Cells 1 and 2.

3　Actions managed by the supplier are very selective with targeted objectives. When the investment is too high compared with forecast profitability and if the relationship quality cannot be restored, the supplier can adopt a retrenchment strategy.
4　These customers need a low investment. The supplier actions aim at maintaining the relationship.

For customers in Cells 3 and 4 in the matrix, several options are open such as: cost reduction because of decrease in number of salesforce visits, use of intermediaries such as agents and creation of subsidiaries with cheaper costs and higher reactivity (Figure 9.4).

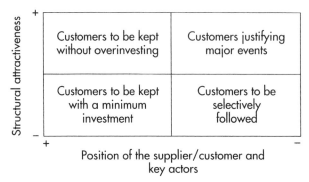

FIGURE 9.4   Relational strategies in the customer portfolio.

By investing human, technical and commercial resources, the supplier tries to reduce his vulnerability in the customer relationship and to restore or/and to improve his position in the matrix. The supplier's actions largely depend on the evaluation of each criterion that makes up the two chosen dimensions. However, the supplier does not control all the elements that are taken into account in the method, and especially those that make up the customer attractiveness dimension. On the other hand, the supplier's actions that aim at reducing the vulnerability of his position in the customer relationships are easier to find and manage. One objective for salespeople is to get the supplier's position to evolve in the matrix from the left to the right side and, more generally, to reduce the global vulnerability of the supplier. To do this, they need to combine relevant actions in the three different phases: independent of any project, prior to the tender and during tender preparation.

Note that evolution to the right side of the matrix is often limited by salespeople who generally prefer to overinvest and manage relationships with 'good customers' instead of allocating time and resources where the vulnerability is high.

Managing the Customer Relationship in the Independent-of-any-project Stage

After targeting customers and defining resource allocations, it is not easy to rationally implement actions and avoid scattering resources.

In most business-to-business marketing situations, the relationship therefore 'goes without saying'. It results both from the frequency of economic transactions between the client and the supplier and from their wish to forge a lasting relationship based on trust, rather than depend on the market and on opportunism (Ford *et al.*, 1998). This mutuality of interests between the two parties makes it possible to create, over time, an atmosphere which is favourable to maintaining the relationship; that is to say, an emotional superstructure which has a favourable influence on the activities between the two parties.

However, in the area of project marketing or system selling, the relationship 'does not go without saying'. Companies which sell project-to-order must in fact cope with great discontinuity in the economic relationship with their customers (Tikkanen, 1998). Contrary to the case of components, operating supplies, raw materials or business services, the purchasing of a project by a given customer may not be repeated until a few years have elapsed since the previous purchase, a fact which limits the capacity of the supplier to maintain the relationship. This type of situation constitutes a major drawback in so far as, in order to be able to anticipate the response to a client's project, the supplier must be in a position to have the necessary information at hand relatively quickly. Access to this information is made possible by maintaining the relationship with the client, directly or indirectly, during the latent period between the two projects. International project marketing raises the crucial question of 'how to manage the relationship left after the project's completion' (Hadjikhani, 1996, p. 319) which could be broadened to 'how to manage the relationship outside of any project opportunity'.

In today's project business, apart from some episodes such as luncheons or playing golf, actions intended to maintain the atmosphere of the extra-business relationship are made up of a host of factors which are often misunderstood, sometimes considered anecdotal, such as giving small gifts, or stem from some obscure network logic such as kinship, sharing a hometown and dialect or going to school together. Consequently, the question of 'how to operate relationships'—going beyond the simplistic recipes of golf and luncheon—can then be formulated in the following way: 'Is there a structure for organizing actions taking place in the context of extra-business relationships which makes it possible to control and support a part of these actions'?

This question can be complemented by the following one which is a constant problem area in the capital equipment industry: 'Is there a way of meeting the client or an important actor when there is no project on the horizon and therefore no shared interest in such a meeting'? Indeed, many practitioners consider it is counterproductive and even negative to mobilize the time of an individual when there is no objective or rational reason for this meeting. With no mutually fruitful exchanges in sight, we are simply wasting the individual's time and, consequently, our own relational position is weakened through a lack of mutual interest.

As stated in Part I, there are four ways for the supplier to limit the discontinuity of economic relationships in project marketing:

- *Mixed activities:* The discontinuity is reduced by broadening the perspective; that is to say, by focusing on a client with a big account capable of having several different projects on the go over a given period, rather than focusing on each project considered individually and independently. This approach is conducted by combining both an offer of products and services, thereby gaining access to the purchasing centre of each project and the maintaining contact with the decision makers within the client's central services. Contacts at these levels of the hierarchy give early access to information on the client's future projects and, in some cases, make it possible to work out solutions with elements common to several projects. So this combination makes it possible to maintain economic contact with the client, bearing in mind the limitation that all or part of the investments specifically committed to each project are not reusable on another project.

- *After-sales and pre-sales services:* Discontinuity is limited by the setting up of a customer services system which makes it possible to maintain contact with him. This post-project management phase can be the bridge to a long-term relationship, as in the case of consulting engineering firms where guarantees, follow-up visits, maintenance contracts and surveys are key elements to ensure customer satisfaction and loyalty. At other times, this approach is limited by the fact that usually persons in charge of logistics and maintenance are not the same (and not at the same level!) as persons in charge of projects.
- *Intermediaries:* The continuity of the relationship with the client is maintained indirectly by the intermediary of a business actor (an agent or engineering company) or of a non-business actor with a strong relational position in the client's milieu. This is the logic of the milieu which tries to maintain the link through the poles of continuity constituted by the parties' stakeholders common to several projects and several clients.
- *Friendships:* Continuity is the result of interpersonal contacts which have evolved from the economic to the social and have become links of friendship whether or not they stem from an ethnic or communitarian logic. Mutual trust and personal friendships between persons of both organizations allow confidential information to be exchanged. Personal friendships appear to be a valuable way for a supplier to deal with a buyer's uncertainties and problems and to reduce his own uncertainties. But, not all interpersonal contacts serve clear organizational objectives and some exist purely for private social reasons. Social relationships can lead to ties of obligation that can benefit the companies concerned. They can also work against the interests of those companies (Ford *et al.*, 1998, p. 161). Consequently, a company that wishes to monitor and control personal friendships faces a real problem: they are unmanageable.

BOX 9.3 The National Bound.

Speed, an important company dealing with telecom systems, identified Cilar, a Swiss firm, as a key account. The key account manager in charge of Speed succeeded in creating a project group whose objective was to redefine Cilar technical standards based on experience cumulated during several previous projects. This group, managed by the Key Account Manager (KAM), includes several specialist—a specialist in telecom and a design engineer, both from Cilar, and a Czech engineer from the Swiss subsidiary of Speed. Knowing that the Cilar design engineer was born in the Czech Republic, the Speed KAM accelerated the matching process of the two companies by associating two Czech nationals. The Swiss Speed subsidiary had previously realized a limited turnover with Cilar. This chance gave Speed the opportunity to enhance the supplier/customer relationship based on interpersonal contacts. The two engineers met each other and developed a good level of closeness. By means of this channel, the KAM got to know that three projects were about to appear in some months time.

Source: Interviews by the authors.

Bearing in mind the fact that a long and costly investment is necessary to build up a relationship, it is easy to understand that maintaining it 'outside business' or 'extra business' is a crucial aspect of the international marketing approach of companies selling projects-to-order. State-of-the-art literature in international project marketing highlights the lack of a structural framework, making it possible to give meaning to the actions of social interactions outside business and to reply to the concerns of the practitioners. Thus, it appears to be a useful approach to borrow an analysis grid from social sciences in order to find a relevant and useful framework.

Insights into the Ritual Construct

In sociology, it has been known for a long time that ritual is a means by which social phenomena mark and ensure their permanence. Indeed, for human sciences, all social relations need rituals in order to develop and persist, and all social groups need rituals to assert and reassert their existence and the adherence of their members:

- ritual renews and invigorates adhesion to beliefs;
- ritual has a psychologically smoothing function;
- ritual helps integration of the individual in the group.

The functions of belief, of uncertainty reduction or of social integration are, therefore, three facets of ritual. A ritual is an ordered sequence of behaviour which is more rigid and predictable than in ordinary action. It is a meaningful but scarcely conscious procedure of dramatized roles, of values and finalities, of real and symbolic means, of communication through coded systems (Bell, 1992). Every ritual has its recurrent temporalities, its models marked by history and its divisions of space to serve as a setting. The force of the ritual can be measured in part by the emotion which rises, an emotion favoured by the attention it wins from the actors of the ceremony, from the onlookers, from the participants involved in this type of communication.

Rituals can be classified in four main categories all of which refer to time:

- 'Initiation' rituals or rites of passage (like the ragging of first-year students).
- 'Calendar' rituals or commemorative rituals (like Bonfire Night).
- 'Cyclical' rituals (like the Monday morning get-together in the office).
- 'Occasional' rituals (rituals for special occasions like a marriage).

Note that the functioning of macro-rituals is based on some principles:

- meeting (every ritual implies a situation in which the actors are congregated together);
- delegation (all the members are not necessarily present; it is enough for some to perform the ritual behaviour as representatives of the community);
- shared emotion which solidifies the link.

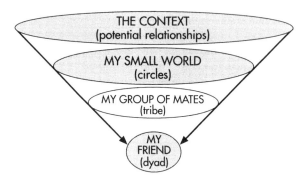

FIGURE 9.5 Levels of socialization.

However, the way rituals work is never clearly expressed and expressible because, although ritual procedures are certainly significant, often actors are not aware of the ritual nature of these procedures.

A Conceptual Framework for the Management of Extra-business Relationships

Based on the previous investigation of the ritual concept and, especially, on the classification of rituals into four categories (initiation, calendar, cyclical, occasional), it is possible to build a comprehensive framework for all the actions taken to manage the extra-business relationship in international project marketing.

This background articulates different levels of socialization that we can characterize in the following way (see Figure 9.5):

- The 'circles' or small worlds in which the buyer and the seller may have the opportunity (not necessarily experience) of meeting each other. The more or less virtual link that exists between a large number of actors of a sector in a geographical zone; for example, the circle of nuclear energy in North America with its great gatherings like the Annual Conference in Tucson.
- The 'tribe' or group of intimate actors of the buyer and of the supplier; that is to say, the link between the supplier and several of his clients and between these same clients. It is the logic of the clan or the club that can be found also from the client's side; for example, in the case of a nuclear company, the supplier's tribe is obviously visible through the holding of big events such as the party organized for the passage of a factory to ISO 9002. Many national and foreign clients are invited to share the good news around the supplier in these special moments.
- The 'dyad' or dyadic relationship between a buyer and a supplier; for example, supplier's factory visit by a client is a typical example of a dyadic event.

On the basis of the existence of four categories of rituals to be put into play at three different levels of socialization between a buyer and a supplier, we are able to elaborate (Cova and Salle, 2000) a conceptual framework which may provide a

Levels of socialization

	Dyads	Tribes	Circles
Initiation rituals			
Calendar rituals			
Cyclical rituals			
Occasional rituals			

Categories of ritualization (left axis label)

FIGURE 9.6   Ritualization/Socialization grid.

useful way of understanding and reorganizing the episodes of the extra-business relationship that are used to limit the discontinuity of this relationship (Figure 9.6).

Today's rites, which are in a phase of considerable expansion, include several characteristics that make them actual events of our times. They correspond to more relaxed and even stranger behaviours than those required for religious rituals, and they are to be found in sports, politics and, obviously, business. Accepted and shared, they are vectors of new forms of identity that the socio-economic actors are trying to build (Segalen, 1998). That is clearly what the companies dealing with projects are trying to set up with extra-business rituals which are rituals of integration designed to support the process of identity building of people in client, supplier and stakeholders organizations. Through the participation in certain rituals at different levels of socialization, they build and develop the identity of their organizations (and their personal identity). At the same time, the supplier is limiting client relationship discontinuity.

We propose an investigation of extra-business rituals in project marketing. We choose a case in the aerospace industry between a French supplier and an Italian customer.

Box 9.4 Managing Rituals in the Aerospace Industry.

BM is a French company, established in the Parisian suburbs, which specializes in the manufacture and sale of landing gear assemblies to aircraft manufacturers. It sells limited series of this equipment to the main European aircraft manufacturers (such as Airbus, Dassault, Eurocopter) and worldwide (e.g. Embraer in Brazil). The design of the gear is specific to each aircraft type and may vary widely in specification, most obviously in size and complexity. BM maintains the ability to offer a complete engineered and designed landing gear for any type of aircraft. European clients award design-and-build contracts for landing gears and have not developed their own product technology in-house. In contrast, US aircraft manufacturers, and especially Boeing, have held the product technology to design landing gears. The long time needed for the development of new aircraft means that BM may be involved in programmes with European manufacturers at least 5 years before service introduction.

The business engineers act more as area managers in charge of detecting and of winning invitations to tender for the aircraft manufacturer. Nothing is specifically organized in BM to manage the buyer/seller relationship outside a project opportunity, whose average duration, as seen before, is around 5 years. Between two projects and apart from the tail-ends of projects and other after-sales actions, the relationship with the clients and the company exists mainly through regular events (every 2 years) such as the Le Bourget Airshow, the Farnborough Airshow or the Singapore Airshow where the whole profession meets for feasts in chalets at the side of the runway—to watch flight demonstrations—rather than in the stands. Some business engineers interviewed admitted that, at Le Bourget Airshow, they sometimes had three lunches on the same day—with the inevitable *foie gras*, lobster and vintage wine—in order to make the most of the meeting possibilities of the Show. These lunch meetings are generally held on a dyadic basis.

AL is an Italian aircraft and helicopter manufacturer selling to air forces around the world. The extra-business relationship with AL is made up of a host of different episodes including airshows. The story of the relationship between BM and AL is 28 years old involving three different projects. The last project awarded by AL to BM is 9 years old and there is no potential project on the horizon in AL. Apart from the exceptional *rendez-vous* that can be linked to presentation of new technology, the BM business engineer in charge of the Italian zone does not miss the opportunity to greet his contacts in AL when he goes there (Milan and its suburbs) for some days on other business, either alone or accompanied by his local partner. More generally, this dyadic relationship follows the same pattern every year: the business engineer goes to Lago to visit his client at AL every year at the end of November, thus commemorating the founding visit made years ago. This visit does not have to be arranged by the BM sales engineer; on the contrary, if the BM sales engineer does not organize this visit, it is his AL counterpart who gives him a reminder in order to know exactly when he plans to come. On the other hand, BM rarely uses the pretext of technical innovation to be presented to AL as the reason for the meeting.

More often, AL is invited by BM to come and visit a factory or a plant; this is a pretext for getting together again, having lunch and discussing the future. These visits can be on a one-to-one or collective basis; a group of actors from Italy, including AL and the Italian partner of BM, then make the journey together. In addition, some internal events in BM are open to close parties such as AL. It could be a celebration on the occasion of the first American order with the supplier to which some selected clients are invited ('we are successful thanks to you') or a day for the presentation of the results of the inquiry into the crash of a prototype equipped by the supplier to which certain clients are invited ('we're one family; we share the good and the bad'). In the same way, AL invites BM to participate in a working group on the future of the European aerospace industry in Milan on the occasion of a major conference held in Milan; or, AL invites members of BM for a flight on his new G3200. Finally, on a completely different basis, there are annual meetings between pilots which bring together on a European level members of BM and AL who are ex-air force pilots.

Source: Cova and Salle (2000).

The actions of integration between BM and AL are quite visible in this case. They take place on three levels: the relationship of the dyad supplier/client BM/AL; the wider relationship with the group of aeronautics actors who are close to the supplier and the world circle of aeronautics players. In all these actions, we observe an ordered sequence of more rigid and predictable behaviour than in ordinary action (the cold-call which salesmen so dread). According to those interviewed, there are instances of coming together, of delegation and of emotion which are not business-oriented. They can be called rituals and they can be categorized in terms of ritualization and socialization.

In this case, the actions of BM are not supported by the whole panoply of ritual in order to maintain the extra-business relationship (Figure 9.7). The framework clearly shows that BM is not using all possible rituals to limit the discontinuity of the extra-business relationship with AL; for example, there is no cyclical ritual at a tribal level of socialization. An example in another field (energy) in Germany helps us understand how to put such an approach into practice. The manager of a local subsidiary of a multinational company decided certain objectives, in terms of development and maintenance of relationships with targeted local actors. In order to support these extra-business relationships, he set up an encounter platform: a cycle of high-level conferences (cyclical ritual) on hot topics, to which he invited the targeted actors. Collaborators were also invited to listen to

Levels of socialization

		Dyads	Tribes	Circles
Categories of ritualization	Initiation rituals	BM flight on AL G3200	BM first US order	
	Calendar rituals	BM November visit to AL		Pilots meetings
	Cyclical rituals	BM/AL lunch at air shows		Air shows
	Occasional rituals	BM trip on other business	BM crash day + AL conference	

FIGURE 9.7 Ritualization/Socialization grid between BM and AL.

these conferences with the aim of maintaining the tribal relationship around the supplier.

Even though this framework presents some limits, we can propose an answer to the question: 'Is there a way of meeting the customer or an important actor when there is no project on the horizon and therefore no shared interest in the meeting'? Indeed, the maintenance and development of an extra-business atmosphere of trust can be systematized through an approach using ritual (i.e. an action of the supplier aiming to construct a collective potential of support for the extra-business relationship with a client). This collective potential could be based on an audit of ritualization with each targeted client on three levels of socialization (dyad/tribe/circle): Rites of passage? Occasional rituals? Cyclical rituals? Calendar rituals? After this diagnosis, a plan for increasing the management of the extra-business relationship with each client could be set up. One idea, for a company, is to benchmark the management of its extra-business relationships with different clients in order to gain insight into its best ritual practices and into the best way to implement them.

The final aim is to provide a ritual platform that enables us to support the construction, development and maintenance of interpersonal contacts, not to organize them! All people in the supplier's organization (salespeople, technicians, managers, etc.) may use this platform according to their objectives. This platform can encapsulate different types of ritual actions, such as clubs, events and more, to provide a global framework for marketing activities outside any business opportunities. This ritual approach is not to be placed among the promotion tools of the company in order to transfer one-way messages. It is merely a relational tool which aims at supporting—and not controlling—the development of interpersonal links in order to fight the economic discontinuity in the supplier/client relationship.

Part III

IMPLEMENTATION

Chapter 10

SCREENING PROJECTS

Depending on the stage at which a possible project is identified in the customer's decision process, information gathering can vary in difficulty in relation to the commercial sensitivity of information. In many instances, customers are keen to maintain a low level of awareness in the market concerning expansion plans, technological innovations, relocation, etc. Since such information cannot be obtained through routine market research, effective intelligence and networking in the milieu together with customer intimacy provide the only real means of securing project awareness before potential competitors become involved.

Intelligence Systems

Information serves not only to highlight project opportunities but also to allow a supplier to identify his competitive position on a particular project at a point in time and to develop appropriate responses (Marsh, 1989). In addition to its value in anticipating and adapting to demand, the supplier has to assess the supply side of the project (e.g. his position in the project pyramid); for example, how is a supplier to ascertain whether or not he is receiving the same trading terms from a key supplier as those offered to a major competitor?

Given the availability of a wide assortment of project opportunities, suppliers need full and accurate intelligence in order to make informed decisions as to where often extensive resource commitments should be directed (Cova and Hoskins, 1997). In addition to its alignment with the supplier's strategic aims and core offering priorities, a project can be weighted using a 'screening' framework comparing attractiveness with the supplier's competitive position. By adopting this approach, the concept of portfolio management can be applied by suppliers to evaluate project value and set tactical decisions within the context of longer term strategic aims.

At this pre-tender stage, the supplier mobilizes and adapts his internal and external resources, developed in anticipation, to the specificity of each project. Several choices are made: which partner, for which tasks, at which level in the project pyramid? The issue of the project entry mode is raised here. Should the supplier enter alone, grouped, with co-contractors, subcontractors or as a subcontractor? Globally, the project screening process leads to definition of a specific resource mobilization. However, far from being solely the outcome of a matrix decision tool, the choice of project entry mode represents a compromise between the three different action logics at play in a given project: the project logic, the relationship logic and the market as network logic.

Relational investments are the cornerstone of a supplier's intelligence system which must be capable of being continuously updated, in order to distinguish project opportunities and their relational context at an early stage in the definition process (Ward and Chapman, 1988). This calls for information concerning the general structure of each milieu (corporate and individual entities, their profiles and attitudes and any affinities between them), corresponding power structures (roles and levels of influence, the degree of cooperation or conflict between the actors) and the law of the milieu (the implicit standards and norms of behaviour accepted by the parties) to be stored, consolidated and disseminated within the organization.

A supplier's intelligence system in project business must be able to function at two levels:

- The independent of any project level—to identify project opportunities in priority milieus or clients which may be of interest to the company.
- The pre-tender level—to secure relevant project information (decision makers, user groups, influencers, gatekeepers, customer business objectives, budgetary and programme constraints, scope for contractor participation in setting specifications, etc.) in support of efforts to anticipate the rules of the game.

BOX 10.1 France Has Stolen a March on the US in Economic Intelligence.

In a report to the US Congress, the Central Intelligence Agency named the French services, along with the Israelis, as the most active country in launching operations against American interests, both inside and outside the United States. However, the damage to the US interests was being done not in the political, but in the economic sphere.

The ability to intercept secret offers made by US armament firms to Middle East countries has allowed French firms to propose better deals. In 1997, they broke into the lucrative Saudi defence market for the first time by signing a contract for the sale of 12 helicopters built by Eurocopter. The recent CIA report accused the French specifically of launching intelligence operations against US military contractors and high-technology firms. The description of the intelligence gathering of a particular country, identifiable as France, said that the country recruited agents at the European offices of three US computer and electronics firms'.

While continuing with traditional intelligence, in April 1996, Chirac set up a special economic and technological intelligence coordination body, The *Comité pour la Competitivité et la Securité Économique*, inspired by the highly effective Japanese Ministry of International Trade and Industry.

However, France is not the only country to seek such information. In 1994, President Bill Clinton asked the FBI to launch an economic counter-intelligence programme. Former French secret service director Admiral Pierce Lacoste told *The European*:

'It is part of an indirect strategy by the US. They want all the trumps. Initially, their target was Japan. But now it is France, for two main reasons. First, France is seen as one of the most vocal and active countries over the strengthening of the European Union and a single currency; and, second, because this country is organizing a new economic intelligence system.'

Source: Adapted from *The European*, 29 August–4 September 1996.

Some information as to future plans may be acquired by reading statements of policy or strategic intent published in the press or corporate reports. Similarly, a plethora of directories and databases are produced to support the intelligence gathering efforts of suppliers in, for instance, the construction sector. In fact, it often seems that the only businesses which manage to thrive in recessions are publishers, conference organizers and on-line database providers. However, when the information becomes competitively sensitive, the boundaries between legality and morality can become blurred, as has so often been demonstrated by infractions in the Pentagon in the USA.

Project Network Analysis

Network analysis and mapping at the project level (pre-tender and tender preparation phases) is very similar to that carried out at the larger level of the milieu, with the exception that the customer now becomes the dominant central figure and each actor becomes a stakeholder with a particular interest and a potential role in the project. It is only through correctly interpreting the soundness of its relational position, relative to that of competitors, that a contractor can judge what partnerships or alliances may be necessary to ensure that it can effectively influence or adapt to the rules of the game.

The major questions to be answered are (Axelsson and Johanson, 1988):

- Who are the actors involved in the project network? What are their characteristics in terms of size, activities, experiences, but also their relationships to one another, to the client, to potential suppliers, to engineering companies, to other actors. Are there technological, social, administrative, legal or other ties?
- What is the relative position of the actors in the project network? What is the role and power of the respective actors? What limitations does the project network pose to the supplier (e.g. possibilities to relate to other clients, areas, markets, fields of application, etc.)? What possibilities do specific

partners in the network offer to the supplier as, for example, access to a better relational position or a better functional position (resources controlled by others that could or could not be mobilized)?

- What are the supplier's own bonds in the project network? Which direct relationship does it have from the beginning, if any? How useful could this be? Does it have relationships with central actors? How useful could they be? How could they be mobilized? Globally, what is its relational position in the project network?

BOX 10.2 The Catalu Shipyard Case.

The Catalu Shipyard is located on the French Atlantic coast. It employs 40 people with an annual turnover of €5 million. Faced with the slump in orders for fishing vessels, senior management had come to the conclusion that Catalu should specialize in more sophisticated segments of the market; vessels for oceanographic and hydrographic research. On this segment, Catalu has a significant advantage based on its expertise with aluminium (calculations, welding and metalworking). While aluminium requires technical expertise for production, it also has the significant advantage of being much lighter than steel, a key element in boatbuilding. Know-how on the different shapes of vessels (monohull, catamaran) and the ability to make the necessary calculations were an obvious advantage for Catalu; for example, for the same function, a catamaran 30 m long offers more scope than a 50-m long monohull. Therefore, Catalu gained an enviable reputation as a market leader in the production of monohull and mostly catamaran service vessels from 10 to 50 m in length.

A specific sales approach was developed to enable Catalu to gain access to this segment and to discover a previously unknown environment through contact with as many key players as possible. Attention was focused on how to be seen as technologically innovative in the late 1980s, leading to new hull shapes. This technological priority brought Catalu into contact with new key players, and brought home the need to understand and exploit networks such as the IMRFCN (the World Institute for Applied Research in Shipbuilding) and the 'Bassin des Carénes', well known for its know-how and technology in research on ship design. With the support of the Ministry for Industry, Catalu was able to carry out, in cooperation with the 'Bassin des Carénes' a series of six trials on new catamaran hulls, that substantially improved performance and reduced surface resistance by 25%.

The 1989 ATRIMA Conference and the Ircho Contract

Each ATRIMA (Association for International Maritime Aeronautic Research and Technology) conference offers opportunities to research centres and firms to make their expertise better known and understood. In cooperation with its technical partner ('Bassin des Carénes'), Catalu presented a paper on the advantages of solutions linked to professional catamarans for oceanographic surveys.

During this conference Mr Martinez, a leading scientist from Ircho, a research organization that had taken the decision to have an oceanographic survey vessel built, expressed interest in this new technology. Ircho had sent out an offer for tender for a steel monohull survey vessel a few months earlier. The specification had been defined in cooperation with Bating, a research outfit specialized in shipbuilding. The first offer flopped as all the replies came in over budget. Catalu did not take part in the first offer for tender. After the ATRIMA conference, Mr Martinez asked Catalu to supply him with; 'a simplified outline proposal in catamaran form'.

Early in 1992, Ircho launched a second offer for tender that insisted on a catamaran solution. Catalu responded to this second offer for tender with a catamaran survey vessel for Ircho and won the contract. The Neptune project, a 35-m catamaran, was due to be launched in late 1993. Catalu participated in offer tenders from other organizations with success in one case and failure in two others.

The Whorcop Call for Tender

In March 1992, Whorcop also launched an offer for tender for an even larger survey vessel, with a steel monohull. This vessel was destined for oceanographic survey missions organized by the Ministry of Maritime Affairs off the coast of Africa and South America. At the time, Catalu was in touch with the project manager at Whorcop. They could not envisage a catamaran solution, let alone one in aluminium. This tender was a flop as all the responses were over budget.

In March 1993, a second tender was launched. This new form of tender was both a success and a disappointment for Catalu, for bidders were authorized to submit a catamaran solution, only as a variant, as long as they proposed a steel monohull version as the main answer. This document presented the technical specifications of the vessel. It presented the technical requirements for the hull, its accessories, power generation and propulsion, as well as details concerning hydraulic, refrigeration and electrical equipment. Questions of comfort for research personnel were also covered.

Whorcop is a state organization with industrial and commercial activities. They are responsible for research on subjects such as 'the variability and evolution of the natural environment', 'geodynamics and natural risks' and 'living marine resources and their environment'. Two hundred researchers and 80 engineers and technicians represent a wide range of scientific competencies to conduct missions for the state, foreign states or private firms. On many of these missions they enter in competition with foreign state agencies or private firms. Whorcop, like Ircho, is attached both to the Ministry of Research and to the Ministry of Cooperation. The latter is in charge of missions planned along the South American and West African coasts.

When purchasing a new scientific vessel, Whorcop sets up a Buying Committee to design the specifications and establish the tender. Alan Martin, the Programme Manager, heads the Buying Committee and has always been the main decision maker in previous operations. In the case we examine, Whorcop requested the help of an engineering agency, Bating, that worked out most of the specifications. Alan Martin, who was a former captain in the Navy, has been in charge of the Buying Committee for more than 10 years. He knows all the yards able to work to specifications and shows a lot of authority when it comes to sailing and shipping.

The Buying Committee is formed of three subcommittees: Technical, Economic and Legal. Martin is also leading the Technical Subcommittee and they have the final say for all tenders. The seagoing personnel do not participate in any of the subcommittees. Captain Morwall has been appointed to the new ship. He is not known to Catalu.

From what is known of the results of the first tender, it is generally thought that shipyards Steelship and Socrato, two of Catalu's competitors, would be shortlisted. The other yards have neither the necessary expertise nor the image to be successful. However, they still run after tenders because of their desperate search for work. They may tender at rather low prices but they are, nevertheless, unlikely to be considered.

Steelship

This is a yard with a long experience of building ships for survey and surveillance missions. Their expertise is monohull steel ships. They have strong links with Martin at Whorcop, for they have sold several vessels to this organization under Martin's supervision. They also have strong links with Bating who approached them when preparing the specifications for the Whorcop tender. They benefit from strong support from the Ministry of Maritime Affairs at a very high level.

Socrato

They also have a strong knowledge and expertise in survey and surveillance vessels. One of their top management is said to have good contacts with the Ministry of Maritime Affairs and the Ministry of Finance. They presently have excess capacity and they are eagerly approaching local and regional politicians they know very well, in order to be favoured with the Whorcop tender. They threaten lay-offs if they are not successful.

Network analysis (Figure 10.1) of the Whorcop project highlights the weakness of Catalu's relational position on the project when compared with one of its major competitors, Steelship. This could be a reason for not tendering for this project and saving the money to be spent to answer this bid (Cova et al., 2000).

Screening Methods

Having identified a possible project requirement, the supplier must evaluate his potential value to the organization and, thereby, to what extent further effort should be expended to develop the opportunity. The screening, or pre-tender selection, process is the intermediate stage between the anticipatory work that has already been carried out and the intense effort required, at all levels, to either participate in defining the rules of the game or complying with those already established from a position of strength. Indeed, a major decision for a company selling projects-to-order is to define whether to go or not on a specific project. Bidding for a project involves both a huge expense in preparing the answer to the bid and an important mobilization of resources that can be damaging for other company business. Consequently, the so-called screening of

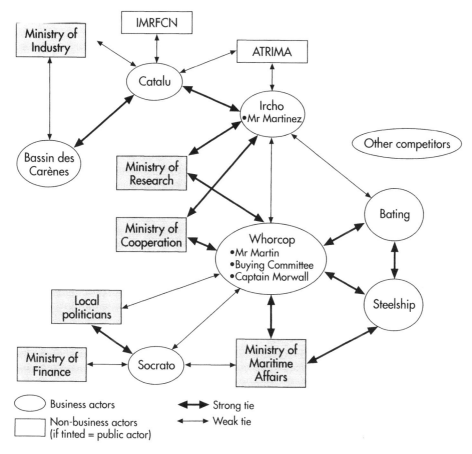

FIGURE 10.1 Project Whorcop network analysis.

projects or pre-bid analysis appears to be a strategic procedure of paramount importance (Paranka, 1971). It aims at solving the go/no-go dilemma experienced by a company faced with any project. It constitutes the basis for designing the marketing action of a company on the project in a bidding or solution fashion.

The main variables used to assess project opportunities are:

- *Attractiveness* of the project to the supplier in terms of alignment with company goals and objectives, the anticipated resource and expertise requirements, the importance of the project to the customer, security of funding, customer attitudes towards the company, risk/reward judgements, likelihood of follow-on projects, opportunity costs, etc. Globally, two major blocks of attractiveness criteria can be used: 'project interest' and 'contribution to the development of the activity'.
- *Competitive strengths* of the supplier in terms of its credibility and past experience, the level of influence among key project stakeholders, the ability to satisfy customer business objectives and/or generate innovative solutions, the availability of knowledgeable staff and strong partners, readiness to

proceed, etc. Globally, two major blocks of competitive strengths criteria can be used: 'functional position' and 'relational position'.

BOX 10.3 Recognizing Political Risks.

Any firm that makes a decision to market its project services abroad should, first, make an assessment of the risks generated by the host country's political environment. Political risk factors can affect the project's cost in terms of labour cost material cost, overhead cost and revenue. The major political source variables that affect any international project are as follows:

- Firm's relationship to the government, agencies, unions, groups and so on. Good relationships with members of the government will protect the interests of the firm and provide information and support.
- Firm's relationship to the power groups (labour unions, business associations, environmental protection groups, radical groups, etc.). This factor is increasingly found in most developed and developing countries. Labour strikes initiated by labour unions and termination of construction operations for environmental reasons by environmental groups are a few examples of the impact of this factor.
- Involvement of local business interests. Considerable political risk can be avoided by involving a high level of participation by host country nationals (e.g. using local suppliers or local subcontractors or having an efficient local partner).
- Impact of regional and external factors. Regional risk factors include terrorism, crime rate and vandalism, which can affect the business on a daily basis. External risk factors include armed or political conflicts between a country and its neighbours, as well as other socio-political disorders.
- Nationalistic attitudes toward the firm. The degree of acceptance that the firm can expect from entities within the host country is reflected in this factor. Examples include anti-foreign sentiment and difficulties due to origin, religion and perceptions.
- Project desirability to the host country. This variable refers to the relative importance of the project to both the government and local power groups. A desirable project may benefit from 'political smoothening' and elimination of barriers.

Source: Adapted from Hashem Al-Tabtabai (2000) 'Modeling the cost of political risk in international construction projects', *Project Management Journal*, **31**(3), 4–14.

Since these variables will change over time together with the project definition, both project attractiveness and competitive strengths may also change, requiring screening to be treated as an ongoing process rather than one calling for a go/no-go decision at a point in time.

The principal aims of the primary screening process are twofold:

- To enable project opportunities to be prioritized and informed decisions to be made as to the allocation of internal resources.
- To determine the optimum mode of entry into the project system and any corresponding external resource requirements.

The screening process is multi-bid in scope and aims at positioning a specific project opportunity in front of other project opportunities in a portfolio of projects which can be represented as a matrix, similarly to what is done for portfolios of clients (Cova *et al.*, 2000).

A screening process for a supplier on a specific project, such as the Whorcop project for the supplier Catalu (see Box 10.2), can go through the following stages (Table 10.1):

1 Assessment of the 'relational position' or 'project network position' of Catalu by analysis of the Whorcop project network and assessment of the level of interaction allowed by Whorcop to Catalu. For example, the project network analysis (Figure 10.1) shows that Catalu holds a weak position (peripheral) in the Whorcop project network which contrasts with the strong position (central) of some of its competitors which are close to the customer and its engineering company. In the same vein, Whorcop is not open to the interaction with Catalu whereas it is open to interact with other suppliers. Consequently, we can assume that the overall relational position of Catalu is weak.

2 Assessment of the 'functional position' of Catalu on the Whorcop project by analysis of the strengths and weaknesses of its competencies in front of the needs expressed by the customer. For example, the functional position appears to be medium/weak in spite of an innovative (maybe too innovative!) technical solution.

3 Assessment of the 'competitive strengths' of Catalu on the Whorcop project, combining its relational and its functional positions. The competitive strengths of Catalu on the Whorcop project can be said to be weak or medium/weak.

4 Assessment of the attractiveness of the Whorcop project for Catalu both in a long-term strategic perspective and in short-term business. The Whorcop project is totally in tune with the Catalu strategy and it will bring business and references. Thus, the Whorcop project is very attractive for Catalu.

Having reached this point, two scenarios are possible:

1 High level of projects portfolio for Catalu. In this situation, the Whorcop project (identified as P4 in the screening matrix) is a real dilemma for the supplier because it is positioned on the borderline between go and no-go projects (see Figure 10.2).

2 Low level of projects portfolio for Catalu. In this situation, there is no dilemma. The Whorcop project (P4) is worthwhile to bid. Catalu has to bid keeping in mind that it has, in one way or another, to increase its chances of success which are already low (Figure 10.3).

TABLE 10.1 Screening of the Whorcop Project by Catalu.

Atractiveness of the Whorcop Project for Catalu	Weight	Rate*	Value
Business perspectives			
Strategic interest of the project	20	10	200
Expected references	20	10	200
Interest of the project			
Profitability	20	5	100
Workload	20	10	200
Control of the incurred risks	20	5	100
	100		800/1,000

Strengths of Catalu on the Whorcop project	Weight	Rate*	Value
Relational position			
With Whorcop and key actors	20	5	100
Degree of opening of the customer	20	0	0
Functional position			
Level of price	20	5	100
References and capabilities	20	5	100
Upstream differentiation/degree of anticipation	20	0	0
	100		300/1,000

* Good = 10, average = 5, weak = 0.

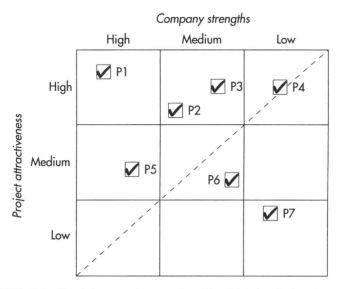

FIGURE 10.2 Catalu's screening matrix with a high level of projects portfolio.

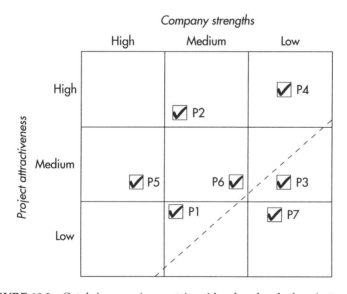

FIGURE 10.3 Catalu's screening matrix with a low level of projects portfolio.

Despite the existence of sophisticated screening methods, some companies use a rather simple way of selecting projects. They base their choice on a sole criterion that could be: size of the project, incurred risk on the project, funding, etc. The incurred risk criterion often leads companies to set up different levels of screening; for example, using the financial risk as a criterion, the following company operating in IT organized a three-layer decision model:

- If the amount of the project is below €150,000, the decision has to be taken as a local level.
- If the amount of the project is between €150,000 and €750,000, it is a joint decision between local and central managers.
- If the amount of the project is above €750,000, a special screening procedure is developed involving major central managers.

In fact, the UK construction company Wimpey (Marsh, 1989) used the screening method to smooth the efforts and investments which are necessary to answer the bid:

- If the chance of winning the bid is below 5%, it doesn't bid.
- If the chance is between 5% and 10%, it bids if preparation costs are low.
- If the chance is between 10% and 20%, it bids if there is no other project on the horizon.
- If the chance is between 20% and 33%, it bids.
- If the chance is above 33%, it fights to the death!

Companies sometimes have difficulty with this screening process in defining stable priorities in project choice for a given period of time. Actually human factors such as intuition, motivation or personal involvement influence the selection of projects. Here is a list of in-company arguments:

> The projects change and evolve over time, at one time they are within the marketing priorities, at another time they are outside the priorities.

> There is always someone in the selling centre to find a good reason to invest in a project and to criticise evaluation criteria.

> Non-priority projects are linked to customers who are themselves linked with other priority customers.

> Unknown to top management, we tendered for projects which had not been selected at the screening stage; when we won the contract everyone complimented us, when we failed everyone turned against us.

In addition, most suppliers claim their project screening process is of the go/no-go type, but flexible enough to vary and balance the different efforts put into each project. More than sophisticated choices concerning markets and competencies, it is often the financial constraints of the yearly budget allocated to project and bid preparation that determine the final selection of projects. Screening is an ongoing process; a project put aside at a given moment in time can become very attractive later; for example, a division of Alcatel discusses, in a project selection committee, previously rejected projects that have evolved favourably for the company.

In some companies that focus primarily on the management of customer relationships using a key account approach, the project screening is at the crossroad of two marketing logics:

- A project-oriented logic which is in tune with what we have described previously (see Chapter 5).

- A customer-oriented logic which searches for all the projects within the customer organization, whatever their size or intrinsic attractiveness.

This is well summarized by the following statement of a key account manager:

> when we manage a key account, it is very difficult to explain to the customer why we invest in a project and why we don't invest in another one. The customer considers that, as a key account customer, we must answer all his queries that are in our field of competencies.

Choosing Entry Mode

Projects are complex transactions which require suppliers to group their competencies into a consortium of firms in order to formulate an offer meeting the customer's specifications. For the suppliers, this gives rise to a multitude of options such as: 'Shall I go alone or in a consortium?', 'With whom can I make a consortium?', 'What will be my contribution within this consortium?', 'Can I bid with several consortia at the same time?', 'In what consortium might I enter?'. This leads to the central question of the mode of entry into the project pyramid which ranges from strategic alliances to deliver fully integrated 'turnkey' solutions to straightforward, single-discipline subcontractor roles. It is evident that a supplier's position in the project pyramid will reflect the degree of responsibility given it to deliver stage-specific objectives and, consequently, the extent to which it is prepared to accept such risk will relate to both its capability to perform the defined scope of work (competitive position) and the attractiveness of the project. As such, the level of entry into the project pyramid (from sole prime contractor to supplier of parts) can be directly related to the bidding strategy. However, at the same time, selection of the level of entry into a specific project goes beyond this single bidding strategy. This decision must be encapsulated in more long-term marketing priorities, such as the development of interorganizational relationships and building up a position in a specific market.

The project screening process is closely associated with the process of choosing a mode of entry into the project system. Some of the more usual roles are:

- sole, main contractor;
- grouped main contractor;
- subproject contractor;
- subcontractor;
- supplier of parts.

The mode of entry into the project pyramid can be directly related to competitive position and project attractiveness and, therefore, plotted on the project portfolio matrix (Cova and Hoskins, 1997), as illustrated in Figure 10.4.

However, it may not be feasible or worthwhile to enter the project life cycle at the outset of the definition stage and, hence, not only are there differing modes of entry but also specific timing of intervention in the project process which determine the scope of work involved. Nevertheless, the identification of worthwhile modes of entry into the project pyramid will, of course, be an iterative

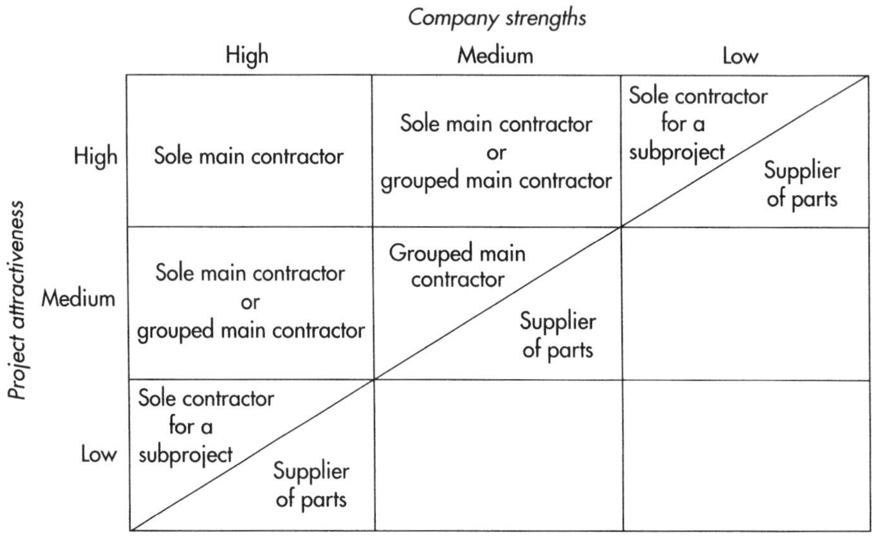

Company strengths

FIGURE 10.4   Matrix of choice of mode of entry.

process based on an assessment of the perceived strength and scope of any offer the supplier feels able to develop.

In project marketing literature, the choice of project entry mode is often linked to the project screening stage; it is approached as a 'by-product'. This deterministic approach to choice of project entry mode can be criticised:

- It takes for granted the one-sided view of project entry mode that aims at an ideal position in the project pyramid, independent of the behaviours and stakes of the other actors of the pyramid. In fact, there has to be interdependency in the decisions taken by the network of actors involved in the project when choosing an entry mode. A processual approach, therefore, is the most appropriate way to tackle the interactions at play during that choice.
- It also takes for granted that all the firms involved can equally access the entry modes listed above, whereas practice reveals major differences in the choice spectrum of firms.
- It looks at this choice as a 'black box', whereas various logics are at play in each organization, each being supported by specific actors who favour a specific choice.

Box 10.4 highlights the many facets involved in the decision about mode of entry into a project.

BOX 10.4 Grinlec Entry in the CP4 Project.

The action takes place in Vietnam at the start of the 1990s. After 40 years of war, then isolation, Vietnam began to open up to the international community. A number of industrial investment projects were set up, particularly in the cement industry sector. The following case concerns the CP4 Cement Works.

Introduction of the main players of the case

- *CVT.* Cemviet is a Vietnam state-run company.
- *Petech.* This is a large international engineering firm. It designs and builds industrial and tertiary plants. It is able to perform each step of the project, from feasibility study to turnkey delivery of plant. Eighty-five per cent of its turnover comes from turnkey plants in a wide range of activities—oil and gas production, refining, petrochemicals—and the rest from the agro-industries, cement, power generation, etc. The major part of its turnover comes from abroad, 20% from Asia. Early in 1990, unlike its competitors, Petech had only completed a relatively low number of cement plants, mostly average sized even though the company included a central core of engineers among its resources who were recruited following the takeover of a company producing turnkey cement works. At the start of the 1990s, Petech decided to renew its efforts in this field, to diversify its activities and also because the international market (new cement plants, expansions and upgrading of existing facilities) offered good opportunities. In the cement industry, Petech competed against other international engineering companies, all of which were able to offer turnkey cement works: FLSchmidt (Denmark) , Kawasaki (Japan) KHD (Germany), Polysius (Germany), UBE Industries (Japan) and also industrial cement groups with integrated engineering departments (e.g. Lafarge, Blue Circle, etc.)
- *Grinlec.* In 1995, Grinlec operated worldwide. For Grinlec, the Asian zone was important. The group specialized in low-, mid- and high-tension electrical equipment for factories and energy transfer. The competition was global and confronts such internationally powerful groups as ABB, AEG, Alsthom, General Electric, Mitsubishi, Schneider, Siemens, etc. Like all its major industrial competitors (ABB, Siemens, etc.), as an engineering company, Petech was one of Grinlec's main customers. Until the 1990s, Grinlec had never sold any electrical equipment for cement plants made by Petech.

Grinlec in Vietnam

For Grinlec, Vietnam has great potential for development. Before the opening up of the economy, Grinlec had a Vietnamese agent in the country. At the start of the year (1990), Grinlec won a €100 million contract to supply an all-important north–south high-tension line. To win, the fight was hard between the major international groups in the sector. They were all looking to enter the market and were prepared to 'make sacrifices'. This deal was the first contract to be offered to a foreign company since Vietnam decided to open its borders. The contract had a huge impact in Vietnam. As a Grinlec manager said 'we became well known, in the local press there were articles about us'. Following the signing of the contract and to begin a marketing campaign, Grinlec created a team made up of one French engineer and three

Vietnamese engineers. Following the deal, Grinlec now has two branches in Vietnam: Ho Chi Minh Ville (ex-Saigon) and Hanoi.

Faced with the double constraint of having to develop infrastructure and the increasing needs of the building industry, the government defined modernization and expansion of the cement industry as one of its priorities. A governmental programme planned the construction of several cement plants. The projects were not linked because they were to be financed differently; by joint venture and Vietnamese investment.

Grinlec has already made a name for itself in the electrical equipment sector for cement works, following 20 years of experience worldwide. To promote its offer, Grinlec worked with both the Vietnamese final client and all the people involved in the cement sector (particularly the engineering companies). At the beginning of the 1990s, Grinlec organized a conference to promote its offer in Vietnam for CVT (the cement works operator) and the engineering companies.

Cement Works Project No. 1 (1991): Cement Plant 1 (CP1)

CVT, the customer, consulted a number of engineering companies. Finally, FLS, a Danish engineering company and a world leader, won. FLS 'naturally' consulted Grinlec for the supply of electrical equipment. There was already a relationship between FLS and Grinlec, having already worked together on a number of projects. At the end of the day, however, Grinlec received no order for the CP1.

Cement Works Project No. 2 (1992): Cement Plant 2 (CP2)

This project was based on a joint venture between CVT and another company. In 1992, several engineering companies were contacted for the CP2 project. Petech decided to invest heavily in the project. At that time, Vietnam was a target country for Petech which had a project for a petrochemical plant with a French petroleum company. The cement works project meant Petech had to continue its progression for $1\frac{1}{2}$ years. Finally, UBE (Japanese engineering company) won the contract. For Petech 'they had better relationships'. For the project, Grinlec received an order from UBE for all the electrical installations (low-, mid- and high-tension) and for the feasibility studies. This was their first opportunity to work with UBE. This was only possible because the client CVT knew Grinlec and was able to recommend it'.

The Abandoned Project: Cement Plant 3 (CP3)

Then, Petech became involved in the initial feasibility studies for a third project for a cement works, led by a French company in association with CVT. The project never got off the ground because the French cement group refused to take it any further.

Cement Works Project No. 3 (1993): Cement Plant 4 (CP4) and the Engineering Firms

In January 1993, CVT launched the CP4 project, a medium-sized cement works worth €100 million, 20% of which corresponded to electrical equipment. The consultation was based on information contained in specifications made by a Japanese engineering firm for CP2. The specifications were Japanese (which are different from European and American ones). The invitation to tender was sent to six engineering firms: FLSchmidt (Denmark), KHD (Germany), Kawasaki (Japan), Petech (France), Polysius (Germany) and UBE (Japan). The invitation to tender included a 1% 'bid bond'.

For an engineering company, the decision to go or not to go for the CP4 project meant taking several different opinions into consideration and the involvement of numerous Petech managers. The manager in charge of the project in Petech advocated that: 'for Petech Cement Division, this represented a huge deal, particularly as the division s annual objectives were €150 million; in other words, a lot. A contract of this size represented about 3 year's work: 1 for the tender, and 2 or 3 until completion ... When there was a bid bond, we looked at it closely. The Director then approved it. Each position was reassessed, and a commercial margin was added. We also looked to see what could be sub-contracted out ... The cost of a bid is around €0.3 million, a number of people had to be present in the country for about 6 months. This was calculated carefully beforehand, and one criterion was the composition of the sector. In some countries, which were dominated by the competition, we no longer even bothered ... OK, let me tell you that to go to Vietnam at that time, believing we could win, was a little mad. Crazy, as we say here. On paper, Polysius were in the strongest position because, for CVT, a Mercedes is better than a Fiat. However, we knew a few things that could alter the situation ... particularly the political and financial dimension ... Why Polysius? In fact, at this time, Vietnam was still fairly shut off. And, as the Vietnamese had a Russian culture, they knew more through reputation about the Germans than the French. The Germans had a technical head start over us'. Despite Polysisus's position as favourite, Petech decided to go for the CP4 project and to make an offer. It should be mentioned that the technology required was not a problem for Petech who had already completed several similar projects throughout the world.

CP4: Engineering Firms Approached Grinlec

To set up their technical offers and establish prices, the engineering companies consulted the electrical equipment suppliers. Some consulted for material only (batch approach), others for material plus studies (package approach). Grinlec was approached by UBE who had already won the CP2. UBE approached Grinlec for a batch ... Following the CP2, which, according to Grinlec, was a good job, relationships between the two companies were good. Grinlec was also approached by FLSchmidt and made a proposal for the electrical equipment. Some time later, the international projects manager at Grinlec was approached by Petech's sales manager who suggested creating a kind of partnership to seek ways of financing the project and to work together until the deal was won (prime contractor in joint venture).

Because of the competitors in the running and their previous experience of the Vietnamese market, Grinlec thought that Petech had little chance of winning the CP4 and that FLS were likely to win. 'At the start of the project, they approached us with the idea of working together. At the time, we thought they had little chance of winning because they hadn't won any cement works contracts for a while. We decided not to say no and were ready to make a proposal, but not to go all the way to striking up a partnership ... because, behind the request, they were obviously going to claim some form of exclusivity. We finally refused their proposal for a partnership. In fact, at the time, we thought FLS would win. FLS were in a strong position ... so we didn't completely shut Petech out, but didn't really leave the door open either ... we helped them a little when they were out there. We told them Grinlec people were available whenever needed. They met, but we could not go the whole way since we were convinced FLS would win. Over there, we helped them like fellow Frenchmen, but it's true we didn't really approach the client all together at any time. Simply because if ever FLS had got wind of it ...' (a Grinlec manager involved in the CP4 project). Basically, Grinlec refused any partnership with Petech, but put in a bid for the electrical equipment for the cement works.

After the first run of proposals, CVT limited the competition to a shortlist of two bidders, FLSchmidt and Petech. Following the refusal of Grinlec, another form of financial arrangement was set up by Petech with French and Japanese money. The Japanese money came from a Japanese trading company. According to a Petech manager, 'we joined up with this trading company because it's a Japanese company and we didn't want to be 100% French. Also, they had an office in Hanoi which could be used as a commercial office, excellent relations and information network. We were able to benefit from their information on a daily basis thanks to their local agents ...'. Finally, Petech won the CP4 bid and Grinlec found itself in big trouble to gain the electrical equipment part of this project.

Choosing Projects

From this case study, we can see Grinlec's decision logics on the CP4 project. Grinlec combines three interdependent perspectives to progress on this project (Figure 10.5):

- *The project logic*. This short-term, opportunistic approach focuses exclusively on winning the project. Adopting this approach would lead Grinlec to play with FLS (by taking into account FLS's favourable position on the project). For

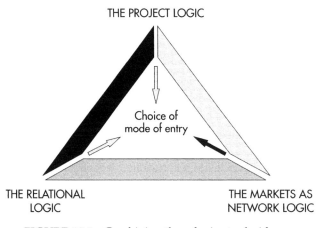

THE PROJECT LOGIC

Choice of mode of entry

THE RELATIONAL
LOGIC

THE MARKETS AS
NETWORK LOGIC

FIGURE 10.5 Combining three logics to decide.

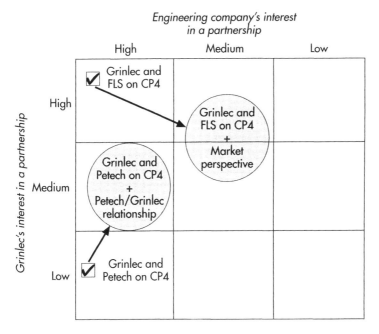

FIGURE 10.6 Reciprocal interest grid on the CP4 project.

Petech, however, integrating Grinlec in its proposal would raise its chances of winning the deal.

- *The relational logic.* This approach takes into account the existing relationship between Grinlec and Petech and would lead to privilege the continuity of the relationship. This would have been of paramount importance if it had been strategically decided that Petech was a key partner for Grinlec.
- *The market as network logic.* The two firms—Petech and Grinlec—also make strategic choices depending on geographical and technical factors. Given these choices, the offer partnership between the two firms on the CP4 project can contribute to the creation or development of the network position of each firm.

According to the logic considered (project/relation/market as network), Grinlec will not make the same choice of partner. A reciprocal interest grid can be used here to assess the relative interest of each company to join the other (Figure 10.6). Grinlec and FLSchmidt both share a strong mutual interest to form a partnership on the CP4 project. This is not the case between Grinlec and Petech if we only focus on the project opportunity; Petech has a strong interest while Grinlec has not. However, considering the relational and market as network logic leads to a rather different choice.

The CP4 case confirms that one of the key issues in project marketing lies in having the capacity to develop proposals and offers once a customer project has been identified. In order to assemble external resources, being functional and/or relational, in temporary network configurations (a project), firms combine different approaches which vary along the three major project marketing time frames: independent of any project, pre-tender, tender preparation.

Independent of Any Project

Apart from the continuous management of key partners (see Chapter 6), the screening process consists, for a given firm, in identifying possible partners and in establishing a relationship that could lead to cooperation on a given project. When the relationship already exists, it consists in perpetuating the contact so as to avoid falling into a 'sleeping relationship' that would be difficult to activate on a specific project. Given the necessary investment to initiate and maintain such relationships, this can only be achieved with a limited number of partners (i.e. those having the required expertise to add value to the proposal made to a customer on a given project). In some companies, these firms, managed as a portfolio of partners, are referred to as 'major partners'. The problem raised and illustrated in this case lies in the fact that some of these major partners do not have identical positions, relative to the geographical areas concerned and the technologies used. Therefore, several partners can be used in parallel, but with specific geographical or technological allocations.

Pre-tender Phase

In this phase, a project has been detected. In fact, projects provide the opportunity for mobilizing part of the milieu and making it committed to a visible and temporary organization which will evolve as the project unfolds. The partnership approaches in a project also vary according to the existence of previous investment in partner relationships independently of any project (virtual network or milieu). In this phase, it is easier for a firm to work with firms with which it is already involved rather than to seek unknowns. If prior investment has been made, this consists in mobilizing the partners identified in the previous phase (independently of any project) as soon as the project is identified. If no prior investment has been made, this consists in identifying and mobilizing external resources as soon as a customer project is identified with a view to develop the proposal. In this case, the relationship can perpetuate and lead either to other common projects or only to a single project. Therefore, the partnerships negotiated on a single project can be either one shot or give rise to common projects depending on the feedback made by the two organizations concerned. This pre-relational stage thus represents a high level of uncertainty for both organizations.

Tender Preparation

The customer has already launched the call for tender. At this stage, the company has to coordinate the key external resources (major partners) that have been mobilized. It is unlikely that the few key external resources that have not already been mobilized by competitors can be activated (unavailability). Only non-key external resources for product supplies or subcontracting purposes can be identified and mobilized before being coordinated.

Chapter 11

PROACTIVE CO-DEVELOPMENT

In terms of offer and demand, the field of project business may represent an extreme case of business-to-business marketing which is radically different from the traditional model of business-to-consumer marketing. The client buying projects is generally the initiator of the project; he has carried out a feasibility study, written specifications, defined a budget and launched a call for tender. He is the protagonist of his project. On the other hand, the project supplier (e.g. the bidder) is naturally placed in the position of submission; he is the stooge. He does not have a basic offer but rather an array of competencies to mobilize once a demand is identified. He has no price strategy but he submits price proposals at the client's request (Cova and Crespin-Mazet, 1997).

However, the reality of project business is far subtler. In many cases, the client faced with increasingly diversified and specialized fields of expertise cannot always precisely define his problem, his need and thus his specifications. He needs help from experts who can be intermediaries such as consultants or engineering firms, but also suppliers who best master the overall complexity of a given technological field. The client's specifications are not always binding, room is left for original technical or financial solutions. Usually, the suppliers winning the bid collaborate very early with the client and find the best solution to the client's problem, best instead of simply complying with the client's need expressed in the specifications. Such a supplier refuses to be a stooge and to react to the stimulus of the call for bidding in a behaviourist way. He tries to make the client's demand his own and to jointly construct it with the client in the course of their interaction. The strategy of these project suppliers is to try to influence the project before the call for bidding is issued so as to avoid the reactive position of a stooge. The interaction with the client and the members of his local network—the *milieu*—takes place long before the call for tender and forms the basis of the marketing strategies of project suppliers trying to anticipate projects.

Project marketing has evolved over the last 20 years from a submission approach, to a construction approach, positioning the firm as an expert on the client's problem. It works less on a latent or pre-defined need than on the readiness of the client and his milieu members to interact with the supplier. More generally, current marketing strategies in project business mostly aim at constructing or deconstructing the demand with the client, relying in particular on the very long definition, implementation and completion process of the project (3 years on average). More than the preparation of the answer to the bid, it is the construction of the demand (i.e. of the call for bidding and its specifications) that come across as central to project marketing tactics. The logic is that of a search for increased control and power in an activity that structurally positions the supplier in a situation of information asymmetry, dependence and submission. Marketing tactics and construction of demand are largely intertwined during the project. The phenomenon of offer and demand co-construction can thus be viewed as a marketing tactic to build the rules of the game.

Construction and Customer Solution

The marketing tactics of joint construction aim at becoming actively involved in shaping the competitive arena. These constructive approaches are based on the idea that it is often possible to participate in the construction of the rules of the game instead of simply accepting them.

It can therefore be seen that project marketing (Figure 11.1) extends well beyond the tactical considerations associated with competitive bidding to an activity, which can be illustrated in terms of the tactical options available to a supplier at the three key stages of project development.

Independent of Any Project

'Independent of any project' is when a specific requirement has yet to be firmly established by the client, inducing the supplier to create the competitive arena in conjunction with other potential participants. This is a proactive approach where the aim is to create the demand. At this stage, the supplier tries to develop a

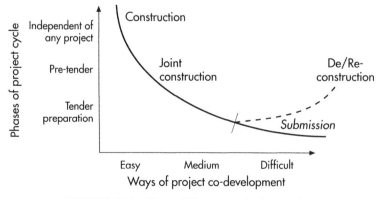

FIGURE 11.1 Three different marketing tactics.

relational position in the network (milieu) made up of relationships between business and non-business actors at different levels, who are potential stake-holders on coming projects.

Pre-tender

'Pre-tender' is when the supplier aims to write the rules of the game in conjunction with the customer and other influential actors. This is an interactive approach which seeks to influence the detailed specifications and procurement strategy. At this stage, the supplier tries to secure its relational position in the network of actors around the coming project (project network).

Tender Preparation

'Tender preparation' is when the supplier seeks to have the established rules of the game rewritten in order to compete on more favourable terms and to avoid the purely submissive approach. This is a reactive approach which is used when the supplier discovers the project at the point when the call for tender is issued. At this stage, the supplier tries to mobilize all its relationships in the network of actors inside and around the buyer.

These tactics of building the rules of the game are closely related to the approach known as 'solution selling'. The concept of solution selling, together with the concept of system selling, has declined and been rediscovered at different times all around the world. In system selling, the seller provides, through a combination of products and services, fulfilment of a more extended customer need than is the case in product selling (Henke, 2000). Systems selling means that the seller offers a combination of hardware products and software (including problem solution, services, etc.) which together form an integrated system able to carry out a total function or set of functions in the buying organ-ization (Mattsson, 1973 and Ghauri, 1983).

Consultative Selling

In the 1980s, a new stream tried to embed system selling in a broader context, based on a deep analysis of the customer's business context. This is the so-called consultative selling (Hanan, 1995). It says to a salesman, 'you are no longer a vendor out to sell a product to a customer, you are a consultant out to help your customer's business grow.' The idea is not only to combine products and services but also to add consultancy activity and expertise to re-engineer the customer's process. In consultative selling, the ability to listen and to build up an understanding of the customer's business is a more important selling skill than persuasion. Empathy and customer's expertise take precedence over product knowledge and technical expertise. Therefore, consultative selling—the idea of going beyond selling products and services to actually becoming involved in the discovery and redesign of customers' business processes—is paying off for some companies. The idea is to create value for customers in three primary ways:

- in helping customers understand their problems and opportunities in a new or different way;
- in providing better solutions than customers would have discovered themselves;
- in acting as their advocate inside their own company to ensure that resources are allocated to them in a timely way and that solutions meet their particular needs.

In the same way, 'customer intimacy' expresses the idea that the salesman has to be so close to the customer's stakes that he acts as if it were his own business (Wiersema, 1995). The goal is no longer to solve customer's problems. It is to help develop his business. Quite often, the supplier can even be a risk-partner in a project. Customer intimacy is not about increasing customer satisfaction, it is about taking responsibility for customers' results. The salesman is in charge of working out change in process both in his organization and the customer's organization. In the same vein, McKinsey proposes the concept of 'customer integration' as the process industry's smart version of business-to-business marketing. In this approach the main idea is to answer the question, 'what does the immediate customer need in order to be successful in his own market'?

The most fitting term (i.e. the most polysemic) for this kind of conception is surely 'solution selling':

> In solution selling, we are trying to redefine the definition of selling. We would like the business card of sellers we train to read 'buying facilitator'. By facilitating the buying process we allow the buyer to feel in control of the buying (Bosworth, 1995).

Solution selling requires using a consultative sales approach rather than selling product functionalities. Solution selling as proposed by Bosworth started in 1985. It says that sales methods used at Rank Xerox for tangible goods are inadequate for intangible services such as those sold at Xerox Computer Services. This approach is designed for complex product/services that are conceptual or intangible, such as projects. These are difficult to explain, especially because they are partly co-developed with the buyer. They are sold to committees where the different members are guided by different rationalities in the decision-making process (Stremersch et al., 2001). They require a sales process conducted by experts for non-experts.

The intimate customer relationship or customer intimacy that is necessary for construction of the project with the client, as is done in solution selling, can be defined in relation to a dual perspective of the supplier/customer interaction (Figure 11.2):

- The depth of interaction, which indicates both the level of the supplier's involvement and the degree of the customer's willingness to interact (i.e. its agreement to work together with the supplier).
- The breadth of interaction, which indicates the extent of supplier/customer

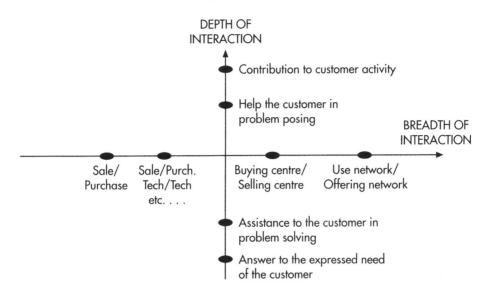

DEPTH OF
INTERACTION

Contribution to customer activity

Help the customer in
problem posing

BREADTH OF
INTERACTION

Sale/   Sale/Purch.   Buying centre/   Use network/
Purchase   Tech/Tech   Selling centre   Offering network
                    etc. . . . .

Assistance to the customer in
problem solving

Answer to the expressed need
of the customer

FIGURE 11.2 Customer intimacy for constructive approaches.

contacts, from simple sale/purchase contacts to complex network/offer contacts involving many functions inside and outside the two companies. The breadth of the interaction appears to be directly linked to the breadth of the offer.

Customer intimacy, which allows consultative and solution selling to develop, has to do with the maximum breadth and depth of interaction (i.e. maximum intensity of interaction in the project process).

This model (customer intimacy) takes into account four levels of depth of interaction that the supplier can put into play in relation to the customer's willingness to interact:

1 The most superficial, it aims at bidding for the project with a compliant offer; in this case the supplier is typically in a product supplier position.
2 A bit deeper, it aims not to stick to the customer's expressed needs, but to propose a variation to the specifications in order to be able to assist the customer in solving his problem; in this case, the supplier positions himself as a solution provider and not only as a mere product supplier.
3 Deep, it aims to help the customer in posing his problem and, consequently, to position the supplier as an expert on the problem of his customer.
4 Very deep, it aims to contribute to the activity of the customer in putting the problem into context; in this case, the supplier is becoming involved in the discovery and redesign of the customer's business processes.

In the same way, four degrees of breadth of interaction have to be considered:

1 The lower, it is limited to day-to-day business such as order acceptance and delivery between salespeople and purchasers.

2   A bit higher, it multiplies dyads in the interaction between the supplier and the customer according to the nature of the problem taken into account, such as quality/quality, logistics/logistics, production/production or quality/purchase, sales/production, etc.
3   High, it associates the buying centre and the selling centre in a coordinated and sometimes dedicated fashion.
4   Very high, it associates the 'enlarged buying centre' of the customer with the 'enlarged selling centre' of the supplier (i.e. the focal network of the customer with the focal network of the supplier).

The crossing of the level of depth of interaction with the degree of breadth of interaction indicates how intense the customer intimacy is and, thus, the content and structure of the offer and demand that will be built jointly.

Constructing Projects

From a constructivistic perspective, the aim is to create the project during the phase independent of any project opportunity. In doing so, the supplier induces a demand by recognizing a project idea corresponding to a problem which remains to be clearly defined by a customer or which might represent an opportunity for an, as yet, unknown customer. The supplier undertakes a speculative commitment to develop the scheme, find or/and create a customer (e.g. by bringing together a group of individual investors). This approach can involve a significant amount of cost and risk. The supplier creates the concept of the project, carries out the feasibility study, gathers the financial package and identifies the actors, all of which could constitute a mixed economy company that will later become its client. All this takes place over a very long time period and associates various actors in a logic of involvement. The project then clearly becomes a technical and social construct initiated by the supplier and raising the interests of the diverse parties involved.

   This approach, which is also referred to in terms of a 'creative offering', is a relatively common practice in the engineering and construction industry as a means of achieving, not least, greater influence, higher margins and more favourable contractual terms. The corporate creed of the North American construction giant, Bechtel (McCartney, 1989), illustrates the point:

> if there is no project, we will create one; if there is no client, we will assemble one; if there is no money, we will get them some.

Although it can take many forms, a creative offer might be best described in terms of a speculative proposal which is presented to a potential customer who has yet to establish clearly defined requirements or, possibly, even a need. The intention is not to sell an inappropriate solution but to reinforce the supplier's credibility and encourage the customer to become engaged in an interactive dialogue at an early stage in the definition process (Lemaire, 1996). The catalyst for this approach can be a 'pseudo-project'. This is a well-defined, but not customized, proposal incorporating the corresponding technical, commercial, financial and relational (partners, suppliers, etc.) components of a potential project. Although such a project is unlikely ever to be implemented, it can be used to provide a flexible framework for constructing the components of a final solution, based on the supplier's own technology and working practices, which are perfectly adapted to the business needs and requirements of the customer.

Suppliers who adopt creative-offering approaches thus evolve progressively towards a position of engineering companies. Sometimes, they give up their industrial activities (product manufacturing) to become service companies. As a consequence, these companies modify their organizations; for instance, ABB created a customer management function and a facility management function and suppressed the product management function. The customer managers are in charge of managing customer intimacy. Facility managers help customer managers to solve problems identified during the course of interaction with customers. They are in charge of integrating products and services coming from the company itself or from other companies. Here the focal company has to include complementary offers coming from companies linked by partnerships and alliances. This integration can be very similar to a consortium, a type of co-selling organization that is frequently involved in project marketing (Smith, 1997).

BOX 11.1 Construction of the Medellín Underground Project.

In 1977, French railway builders from the Francorail Group had been informed by the French Embassy in Bogotá that the Colombian authorities intended to build an underground in the capital. The French, who had just won the contract for the Caracas underground in Venezuela, appeared to be in a good position. A sales approach could be launched with no delay. In early 1978, a delegation went to Bogotá. They discovered that the Colombian administration had an ambitious project of building two undergrounds that would service the four cardinal points of the capital. However, after preliminary contacts, it appeared very soon to the French delegation that, at that time, the financial situation could not enable the raising of necessary funds and credits to set up this ambitious project. However, the local delegate, chosen to back up the French position and whose offices were naturally in Bogotá, was born in Medellín, Colombia, where he had excellent contacts and a local branch office. He was the first one to draw the attention of the French Group to urban transport problems in Medellín.

Medellín is the second largest populated area in Colombia and the capital of the Antioquia province. The city itself has 900,000 inhabitants, but when you include the suburbs it has more than 1,500,000 inhabitants. It has a major university and commercial centre and is located in the valley of a high plateau at 1,480 m. A river flows through the town, alongside which the narrow 914-mm gauge-width railway track stretches from Ciénaga and Santa Marta (harbours on the Caribbean Sea) to Bogotá, used only for goods transport. Originally, another track went through Medellín down to Cali, but after landslides, the track was carried away and was never repaired. To avoid possible flooding and to prepare for 'remodelling' of the town, the river banks have been fitted out with a wide concrete platform strip coating on each bank. Transport in the city was mainly by car, with a dense bus network, leading to spectacular traffic jams at peak hours. The City Council was concerned by this situation and was looking for a solution. The Francorail delegate informed the French Group of this and, at the end of 1978, a delegation visited the site to see what could be done.

Here are the conclusions of their first visit:

1. One of the concrete strips could be used for the track to serve Medellín and its suburbs.
2. Due to the already existing infrastructure, the project costs would be compatible with local financial means.
3. For the project to be successful, it has to be extended to the Antioquia district or the suburbs. It could not remain exclusive to Medellín which only represents two-thirds of the population covered by this new transport system.

Once the delegation got back to Paris, analysis revealed clearly that the Bogotá underground project had no chance of emerging rapidly due to its scope, and the impossibility at that time of raising necessary funds. On the other hand, it seemed possible to set up the Medellín underground project. Thanks to aid from the French Authorities, a free socio-economic study was performed in early 1979 by the French Group, with back up from specialists from Sofrerail (Sofrerail was introduced to add reknown and undeniable neutrality to the Group's action).

This study confirmed the interest in building a railway link for the transport of passengers along the river for the Medellín development scheme. Traffic at peak hours, with a train every 5 min each way, would enable the transport of 15,000 passengers/hour. Moreover, the study advocated revision of the bus routes in harmony with the railway. The project was officially presented to the Medellín District Authorities in late 1979 and received much interest. It was named 'CREATION OF THE MEDELLÍN UNDERGROUND'. It involved a considerable restructuring of the bus routes and was established on the basis of a global transport plan for Medellín and its suburbs. It emphasized the low purchasing costs of materials and equipment, relative to civil engineering costs, so as to get the construction companies, which represented an important pressure group.

In early 1980, a restricted call for tenders was launched in order to confirm costs for implementation of the project. Since the beginning, the local delegate and the French Group only lobbied the Medellín and Antioquia Province decision makers, neglecting those from Bogotá. The French Group was certain that its contacts would push the project through with the means they had available, that they would finance it and ensure that the order be placed before the 1982 elections. It soon appeared, however, that the project needed the support of the Ministry of Transport. This Ministry showed itself to be hostile to giving the contract to the French Group arguing that the call for tenders had been too restricted.

Note here that the project itself was not put into question. On the contrary, the idea was accepted. The French Group had succeeded in creating the Medellín deal. However, knowing that elections would take place in 1982 and that, similar to the US system, a change in the government majority implies replacement of senior civil servants, it was urgent to get things going. In spite of the efforts of the French Group and its various allies, the contract was not signed before the elections. Betancourt and his party won. President Betancourt came originally from Medellín and was very attached to his home town. This was excellent for the project. By the end of April, the decision was taken by the Government to build the Medellín underground.

Source: With special thanks to Jacques Dessinges.

The Medellín Underground case highlights the necessary actions that are required to develop a creative offer approach:

- identification of latent needs that are yet to be expressed by the Columbian actors (traffic problems);
- legitimization by consultants (Sofrerail) of the identified problem;
- mobilization of stakeholders in both the Colombian milieu (local agents) and in the French one (French authorities);
- building up a project network (Medellín city, Antioquia district, local construction companies, etc.);
- translation of the identified problem (traffic in Medellín) into a global solution (including revision of bus routes in the Antioquia district).

The only step that appears to be missing is the development of a relationship with the Ministry of Transport in Bogotá. This may be due to the rather limited view of the potential stakeholders in such a big project or to the action of a competitor who is trying to change the rules of the game.

Creative Offer

Just as in the Medellín Underground case, the creative offer approach to project marketing can be developed along four phases (Figure 11.3):

- identification of latent needs;
- provocative face-to-face;

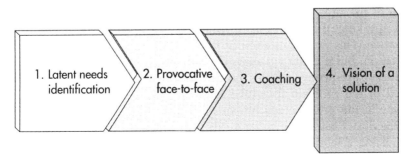

FIGURE 11.3   The four phases of project creative offer.

- coaching;
- vision of a solution.

Identification of the Latent Needs

There is a latent need when a supplier sees, from his perspective and on the basis of his past experience, a situation in the customer's organization that is inefficient or that can lead to a potential problem. This situation is the result of his analysis, but the customer is still unaware of it. The dissatisfaction statement shows that the customer is facing a problem. He merely sees a solution and the problem is perceived as being too complex or too risky. He does not know how to approach the problem that is poorly stated. When a client is able to formulate the vision of a solution, he is not expecting the supplier to solve the problem; he sees himself in the situation of solving it.

The creative offer approach is aimed at leading the customer from the latent pain level to the vision of a solution. The marketer has to be present in the relationship at the very initial step of the process before the problem is formulated; that is to say, he has to be a consultant who spends most of his time making a diagnosis to make sure that all stakeholders share the same vision of the current situation. The first part of his job is about knowing, building and mastering the project network around the targeted person in the client's organization.

Proactive Face-to-face

At the beginning of the process, the supplier starts discussion in an impressionistic way. He uses stories of situations that other companies had to face and that he had to help to solve. He suggests that his customer might be facing similar situations. Quite often, the customer then starts to ask the supplier questions on how he could solve the problematic situations in other business contexts. The supplier will have to translate his stories into the customer business context so that the customer can better understand that the supplier is an expert in this kind of analysis. The job of the supplier is to propose tools of analysis that help the customer understand his business context.

Interpreting the situation from this perspective reveals the problem. Rather than speaking directly about problems, the goal is to shape the customer's own representation of the situation, in order to enable him to express it in his own way. Roughly speaking, this new perspective is the structure of a potentially problematic situation. This first translation of the situation leads the customer to a new interpretation. But it is not yet analysed and shared by the other members of his firm. The new perspective enables the customer to spot variables (potential causes) identified in the problem (potential impact). The customer will not decide to participate in the problem resolution unless it enables him to reach his private goal in the firm. Clearly, the buyer needs the problem to be expressed in a certain manner. Being able to solve it, he would gain social value. Then, when the buyer gets involved in the problem, he feels like the 'ambassador' of the situation. He will be willing to let the problem be recognized by others, so that he can then save the situation by proposing an adequate solution. By identifying the problem, the buyer himself becomes the internal vendor.

Coaching

The supplier, initially only consultant and diagnoser, becomes a coach for his sponsor and mediator, especially when the other partners involved express the problem the same way. After progressive development, several people—the buyer, the technical manager and the financial director—share the same definition of what the problem is. But this constructed vision is still based on different rationalities. The supplier should then propose to coordinate the finding of a solution. In certain cases, other people will take charge of the sale in order to develop various competencies, such as technical support.

Thanks to this process, external couples of problems/solutions have been seen from a different perspective in the client's organization. Adapted to suit the firm, they lead to a new problem/solution couple, which takes the whole of the firm's context into account. The supplier, like a consultant, gets the customer to take over the situation, getting more involved in managing it from the inside.

Vision of a Solution

It is now time for the supplier to elaborate the project which suits the problem he helped to highlight. In the case of an introductory offer, he is the one who structured the criteria of selection, in partnership with the customer. When a firm leads a market study, searching for an answer to a problem and finds one, it means that somebody had already articulated the feeling that the firm had such a need, such a problematical situation. The creative offer approach to project marketing points out that raising a problem from a positive analysing pattern perspective builds up its own solutions. Remember that the cognitive system of a person creates only problems he knows he can solve (Ghauri and Usunier, 1996).

Joint Construction

Here, the aim is to influence the project during the pre-tender phase. The project pre-tender phase is distinguished from the general organizational pre-buying phase by the extreme complexity of the operations which lead to a high level of risk associated with the project situation. As a consequence, the project pre-tender phase is often characterized by an extreme dispersal of the actors into several participating entities coming from both inside and outside the client's organization. The so-called project network, therefore, often includes participants from outside the client's organization such as consultants, banks, engineering firms, government officials, etc. which make up a network of actors around the client. This means that different functions previously fulfilled by the departments of the buying company are now fulfilled by other organizations, which leaves open the question of who is, then, the 'true' customer inside such dispersed and split groups of stakeholders.

The extreme dispersal, antagonism and instability of the project network are globally linked to the fact that a single organization is unable to anticipate all or part of the financial, technical and human exchanges involved, leading it to turn to other organizations. As such, external expertise in the form of consultants, suppliers, etc., which would ordinarily be too costly for any single organization to maintain in-house, together with additional stakeholders such as government departments, trade unions, shareholders, action groups and regulatory bodies, may be involved in the definition and implementation of a project. The following technical, financial and human factors contribute to breaking up and instability on the customer side:

- On a technical level, the project network can be split when an inherent complexity in a tailor-made technical proposal generates a problem of technological evaluation, thereby requiring the assistance of engineering consultants. This assistance may last throughout the whole decision-making process, due to the possible restructuring of project conception during the interactions.
- On a financial level, a great variety of organizations may be employed to finance the project. This helps customers who lack sufficient bargaining power to get funds at the best rates of credit. At the same time, it enables costly projects to be carried out, even if no creditor can afford to finance and to risk venturing alone, through pooled credit organizations or export guarantees.
- On a human level, wide cultural and social gaps often linked to geographical distances imply adaptations and tend to encourage the use of intermediaries, acting as translators in matter of local customs and not only of language.

As for the time factor, the project pre-tender phase could be characterized by very long sequences of interaction before transactions do occur, if they do. It is a long-lasting, negotiated and interactive process in which interpersonal relationships come into play. The structure of the project network evolves during the pre-tender phase, with some partners disappearing from or entering the list of actors, while others will become passive or active as we can see in the following case. The same can be said for the buyer's needs. As a consequence, it is not sufficient to understand the stated needs of the buyer and to be able to supply them; the winning supplier also has to understand how the needs of the buyer can change all along the pre-tender phase and during the whole decision-making process.

BOX 11.2 The World Trucks/Euroelectric Case of Joint Construction.

The story begins in late 1994, when EuroElectric, the Italian giant of electrical equipment, is informed by its Bavarian subsidiary of a project concerning World Trucks' Italian factory (industrial vehicle division of the German World Motors) in Pistoia, close to the city of Florence. World Trucks wants to develop a new automated engine assembly line. This engine line must be conceived to serve not only World Trucks' needs but also those of other European truck manufacturers.

The Pistoia factory is administratively attached to the Italian Division of World Trucks. However, technical and commercial purchasing decisions are centralized at the corporate head office in Bavaria. World Motors' own engineering subsidiary—World Motors Engineering—is often (but not necessarily) called upon to handle the development projects of the various companies of the World Motors Corporation. Concerning the new project in Pistoia, World Trucks Engineering is in charge of coordinating site modernization (i.e. the first part of the project works).

EuroElectric rapidly learns that:

- The electrical diagram of the Pistoia factory, historically equipped by Vanguard, would be completely renewed.
- The electrical part of the project would represent 7 to 8% of the total budget.

In order to efficiently prepare the project, EuroElectric's marketing and sales team meets Mertin Hetter, the man in charge of electricity within the Ecology/Energy Department of World Trucks in Munich. The latter confirms that the project feasibility study has been given to World Motors Engineering, but that competition will still be consulted for the design and implementation of the factory. Immediately after, the marketing and sales team meets with World Motors Engineering's managers in an effort to increase the understanding of their approach and to obtain more information on the project. Based on this meeting, World Motors Engineering's vision of the electrical part of the project can actually be summarized as follows: 'a brick in the total budget'.

At the beginning of 1995, several meetings with Mertin Hetter and World Motors Engineering are organized in Munich for the EuroElectric marketing and sales team which is joined by technical experts. They are able to precisely define the factory energy need and layout. Mertin Hetter is a very bright man, having an extended knowledge on electricity (he belongs to the European norm committee of the CEI) and very open to innovation. His relationships with EuroElectric's team are based on the transfer of technical know-how and enable the progressive creation of atmosphere of mutual trust. It, then, became clearer and clearer that World Trucks' ambition is to turn the Pistoia factory into a reference project, integrating as many technical innovations as possible.

In the meantime, EuroElectric's team meets electrical installers who usually work with World Trucks and World Motors Engineering. In parallel, the German subsidiary of EuroElectric in Munich carries out the important work of information gathering at the customer's head offices and of transmission of this information to the various EuroElectric units involved in the project. EuroElectric thus obtains maximum information about the customer, his habits, purchasing organization, supply management, buyer/seller relationships, etc.

At the end of March 1995, the EuroElectric marketing and sales team started to organize follow-up actions, given that:

- several calls for tender will be issued on the project electrical works;
- both German and Italian suppliers will be contacted;
- World Motors Engineering will be placed in competition with other engineering companies on the project.

The goal of the EuroElectric tactic consists in avoiding World Motors Engineering in order that it can draw up the technical specifications on behalf of the World Trucks electrician. Mertin Hetter is gradually won over to the innovative project presented by EuroElectric. This innovative project allows him to keep his hands on this part of the factory's modernization. This tactic proves to be successful and, in June 1995, World Trucks withdraws the electrical contract and civil works, which was initially awarded to World Motors Engineering. This decision greatly simplifies the procedure for EuroElectric which is thus in a position to participate in the drafting of technical specifications for the several electrical calls for tender.

In spite of this favourable environment, the negotiations with the purchasing department of World Trucks, as is always the case with this client, are very hard for EuroElectric. The Italian supplier is put in competition with Vanguard, the supplier of the original equipment to be replaced, and the Scandinavian giant ABB on the first electrical call for tender. EuroElectric wins this bid and signs the contract by the end of December 1995, and 1996 is dedicated to its implementation.

This first contract makes it possible to reinforce contacts with World Trucks' technical department and, particularly, with the Pistoia electrical department. This project comprises three other phases for which EuroElectric is systematically confronted with competitors but wins all the bids. Total revenues for EuroElectric in the World Trucks project in Pistoia are estimated at €8.5 million. Moreover, EuroElectric has acquired a privileged position both—functional and relational—with respect to other World Truck projects, notably four projects in France.

Source: Interviews by the authors.

In the World Motors case, EuroElectric discovered the project in its pre-tender phase; nothing was fixed. World Trucks had by that time not completed its feasibility study. The scanning system outside any project opportunity allowed EuroElectric to anticipate this project. But EuroElectric was no longer in a position to develop a creative offer approach (see previous section). The project was already created by World Trucks. However, EuroElectric was in a position to jointly build the project with one of the actors of the project network it had selected, namely Mertin Hetter. The idea was to build something which would be mutually beneficial for both parties. Therefore, EuroElectric empowered Mertin Hetter on the project which, in return, gave it the possibility to highly influence the decision-making process. The joint construction approach of EuroElectric aimed to influence the contents of the specifications, the bidding list, the way the bids were launched (number of contracts) in order to decrease the competitive pressure on this project. This approach shows some clear similarities with the construction phase while being encapsulated in the limited framework of a project initiated by the client.

Project De/Reconstruction

From a constructivistic perspective, the aim is to deconstruct and recreate the project during the bidding phase. The supplier, who is in a weak position, starts by deconstructing the demand expressed by the client (and often constructed with a competitor) in terms of perceived risks. He then reconstructs it, directly or indirectly with the client, based on his expertise of the client's problem expressed in terms of incurred risks. It is based on this progressive reconstruction of demand that the supplier can construct his offer at the same rhythm.

BOX 11.3 De/Reconstruction of the Medellín Underground Project.

At the same period, the French Group was approached by Spanish industries who proposed to cooperate so as to secure the order and to share the supplies. The French who has already split the project between the French and Colombian members of the Group decided, after a very tense discussion, to refuse to cooperate with the Spaniards. This decision soon turned out to be very negative. Before becoming President, Betancourt had actually been Ambassador in Madrid where he had built strong links with Spanish top industry, and, among the projects discussed, the Medellín Underground was placed in a high position. Given the advance of the French Group, a Franco-Spanish agreement would have unlocked the project very rapidly. In the opposite case, the Hispano-Colombian game consisted of gaining time so as to turn the situation to their favour. And this is what actually happened.

The Colombian Ministry of Transport, in agreement with the local authorities of Antioquia Province, assigned a project manager. His first task was to give a British engineering firm the mission of critically examining the studies carried out by the French, the Italians and the Spaniards, and to propose a summary project that could serve as a basis for a new call for tender.

At the beginning of 1983, the conclusions of their report were published; the major part of the project should remain the same but it was advised to change the railway gauge to the European width standard (1 m 437 mm) from the existing gauge of 914 mm width. The consequence of this decision was to decrease the equipment cost because of standardization and to increase the infrastructure costs; however, above all, it made the Group's 1980 offer obsolete.

Directly after, an international call for tender was sent to all major world manufacturers. It concerned the supply of 20 electrical trains each carrying two power units and one trailer, the construction of the railway, the laying out of railway markings and the construction of substations for electrical current transformation. The response time was very short and required a remittal of offers by the end of July 1983. In total, 12 proposals were recorded and 11 were declared valid.

At the disclosure of the offers, it appeared that the Spanish Group was associated with the German Siemens, resulting in a fierce competing group. It soon appeared that the battle was limited to the French and the Hispano-Germans. The French were in the best position in terms of price and financing proposals. The Colombian administration declared itself incapable of choosing between the two European groups and appointed a so-called neutral consulting firm to make the decision. Electrowatt Zurich was selected who concluded in favour of the Hispano-German Group, having modified the proposal evaluation grid which gave extra points to the criteria where the Hispano-German Group was best. An inquiry revealed that Electrowatt Zurich was controlled by a subsidiary of Siemens.

Based on the conclusions of Electrowatt Zurich, the Colombian authorities gave the order to the Hispano-German Group. The abuse was so visible that the French Group went to the Financial Court of Bogotá, the highest body in such cases. This was useless and, after 6 months of difficult wrangling, the French action was declared unacceptable. At the end of 1984, the order was awarded to the Hispano-German Group. But, in the middle of 1985 the economic difficulties of the Colombian government increased so dramatically that it declared an adjournment of the payment guarantee it had previously granted on the project. The suppliers stopped their work and production. It was only at the end of 1986 that the contract was reactivated, but with insufficient revaluation clauses.

In 1988, Alsthom (a member of the French Group) took over the Spanish nationalized railway industry, including the firm Ateinsa (a member of the Hispano-German Group). Alsthom found, in the firm's workshops, partially completed railway track destined for the Medellín Underground and gained access to the substantial losses this project represented in the firm's accounts. That is one consolation for the French Group after all their vain efforts between 1978 and 1984!

Source: Thanks to Jacques Dessinges.

In this second part of the Medellín Underground case, it's possible to explain that Francorail did not succeed in signing the contract before the election because the Ministry of Transport acted in favour of the Spanish supplier. In fact, the Spanish supplier who discovered the project a little late did not accept the rules of the game established between Medellín city, Antioquia district and Francorail and introduced a new actor in the project network (e.g. the Ministry of Transport in Bogotá). This actor supported the Spanish in their action of deconstruction and then reconstruction of the project. In other cases, it is possible to have a competitor who is just willing to deconstruct the project in order to have his competitor lose the bid, even if there is no chance to reconstruct the project and win the bid.

The deconstruction/reconstruction approach is based on the notion that all project buying decisions involve perceiving risks, to a greater or lesser extent, by the organizations and individuals involved. Consequently, the project decision-making process and the specifications it produces tend to be driven by these risk perceptions according to the characteristics of the project considered by the customer (Figure 11.4). A thorough analysis of the individual and corporate stakes involved in a project can provide a marketing platform on which to rewrite the rules of the game. The importance attached to individual risks reflects, on one hand, the influence on project feasibility (costs, timing, technical feasibility and impact on customer business activity, etc.). And, on the other, it reflects the characteristics of the buying centre (willingness to innovate, culture, the overt and covert aims of individuals, power and influence, vulnerability of decision makers, etc.). The attitude towards certain risks can be identified during contact with members of the buying centre (what they say, what they do, etc.). Their behaviour should indicate a willingness or otherwise to consider ways of

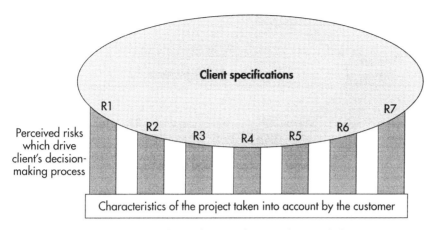

FIGURE 11.4   Risks as drivers of project buying behaviour.

reducing individual or organizational exposure to any potentially adverse technical, financial, commercial and political implications of project decisions.

However, perceived risks in the buying centre may differ significantly from the supplier's assessment of the actual (incurred) risk, based on an evaluation of the client's objectives and the consequences of following a particular project strategy. Not surprisingly, this can arise where both parties do not have access to the same information, conduct a similar degree of analysis or recognize certain key factors and their importance from the same standpoint. Given an appropriate level of expert credibility, a supplier is perfectly placed to exploit the gap between perceived and incurred risk by presenting a solid case for the re-evaluation of a chosen approach. If accepted, the client may then be encouraged to invite the supplier to participate in defining the rules of the game associated with a more effective solution. In this instance, we could describe the marketing action in terms of 'updating a latent demand'; that is to say, the supplier has not simply accepted the expressed requirements, but has taken steps to understand the underlying uncertainty over the project and subsequently compel the client to re-evaluate the demand criteria.

The supplier has a number of options available to him (Figure 11.5):

- Minimize the client's perceived risk in the project it wishes to carry through to a successful conclusion. In this case, the supplier restricts his attention to the client's requirements, as expressed in the specifications and, in such circumstances, the negotiating agenda is invariably set by the client.
- Re-evaluate the priority attached to perceived risks in such a way as to minimize the inherent risk associated with an offer by increasing the importance of those risks associated with competitor proposals or those which are minimized by one's own approach. In this case, the aim of the supplier is to modify the hierarchy of client expectations.
- Impress upon the client those risks judged to be important, but which may not have been perceived in such terms. In these instances, the supplier must be able to put forward risk-reduction measures in the form of a solution.

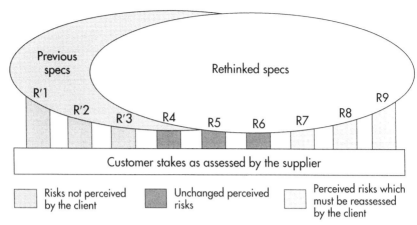

FIGURE 11.5   De/Reconstruction of client specifications.

In the de/reconstruction process, the interaction between the parties may influence, or even recreate, the structure of the decision-making process by identifying a given risk which might be attributed to one of the figures in the buying centre. If the supplier decides to adopt this approach, great care must be taken as to the timing. However, it is out of the question to identify an area of risk, as yet not perceived by the client, and immediately propose a sweeping remedy. The client must be allowed to appreciate the risk, blend it with his representations and begin to redefine the problem in the light of this new information before being able to contemplate the embryo of a solution.

The supplier must therefore encourage a gradual change in the atmosphere of the interaction, which will allow a possible solution, which is oriented towards suppliers' different competencies, to be put forward. In such circumstances, the offer becomes truly differentiated since it is related to a redefinition of the problem in conjunction with and by the client himself. On the other hand, there are many examples of differentiation gimmicks, whereby the introduction of new elements or alternatives has little impact (other than a seductive one) because the client does not have the mindset, an awareness of the issues, the time to take them on board or understand their originality (if there is any) and utility potential.

Chapter 12

FORMULATING THE OFFER

Formulating the project offer is not an isolated task, totally disconnected to any decision taken in anticipation of the project. In fact, the project offer encapsulates into a specific proposal the whole set of decisions taken sometimes long before the appearance of the project (see Chapter 6) in terms of global offer strategy.

Being able to translate its offer into value for the customer is a complex and difficult task in project marketing for the supplier. First, because the client is not an isolated person but a buying centre with different perceptions among its members. Second, because this buying centre is embedded in a network of actors, inside and outside the buying company, who can play an important role in the decision. This so-called 'enlarged' buying centre or project network is both an opportunity for and a threat to all project marketers in the pre-tender phase. Sometimes, the value which would be very important for one of the key players is not directly connected with the project under study.

In this context, the notion of value creation for the client appears to be the critical task on which a supplier's very existence depends. If this notion of value creation is now relatively easy to seize for business-to-consumer marketing and in many business to business situations, it becomes less easy to manage in complex business situations such as that of project activities. In project business, the members of the project network come from different entities within—and sometimes outside—the organization. Each of these entities is likely to have its own rather parochial view of the expected value of the project that often conflicts with those of other entities. It should be interpreted by a supplier as a major opportunity to use various scenarios to influence the project network. Each scenario will depend on the agenda, potential risk and rewards of the members of the project network acting as individuals with sometimes contradictory motives, but linked by the same group dynamic of solving a business problem.

In fact, in any case of project offer, there inevitably remains a good deal of uncertainty surrounding the participants in the 'enlarged' buying centre (who?), their specific requirements in terms of expected value (what?), the timing (when?)

and the manner in which the project will be delivered (how?). Faced with these dilemmas, the supplier experiences difficulties in translating his offer strategy into a valuable project offer for the customer.

The Four Dimensions of an Offer

Traditionally, project-based companies have broken down the project offer into two key dimensions in accordance with the technical, commercial and general parameters of the tender documents (Marsh, 1989):

- the technical/functional offer;
- the financial offer which addresses the financial and contractual conditions imposed by the customer.

Specialists attach great importance to a third-offer dimension (Hadjikhani and Håkansson, 1995) which is often hidden or ignored, the political offer. While playing an important role, it is often difficult to describe. In effect, it rarely corresponds with something expressly mentioned by the customer (except where certain compensation issues or technology transfer is involved) and is not documented. Although implicit, it is readily identified by the customer when reading between the lines of a proposal. It describes the position of the company in the demand milieu and, in particular, within the network of quasi-political figures; for example, in the Spanish building industry there exists a complex network of relationships between contractors and decision makers, at all levels, be they appointed or elected. This huge, informal network operates in accordance with unwritten rules. It has its habits and customs, as in all societies, but the goals sought by its members, more often than not, differ widely in terms of power, public welfare and profit.

It should be noted that, today, most organizations are victims of political myopia. Many politicians do not give sufficient consideration to society as a whole. With the increasing illegitimacy of politicians, their parties, and the rising numbers of associations and other spontaneous, non-political groups, companies also have greater difficulty in putting together a proposal which might bear scrutiny from a societal perspective, from parties who do not belong to the traditional sphere of politics. The global deterioration of standards in public life and those of elected officials has been to the benefit to emerging local, and primarily non-political bodies whose 'hands are clean'. They are now able to play an influential role in projects. As a result, more and more companies are not only concerned about the 'visible project network' (i.e. the socio-economic actors contractually involved in the project: client, engineering company, bank and other institutions), but also the 'hidden project network' (i.e. the socio-economic actors who enter the project on a non-contractual basis: citizens, local associations, international organizations such as Green Peace, opponents, etc.). A supplier who does not grasp this phenomenon and who is only networking visible actors may find himself in the position of having only managed half of the project network (Sahlin-Andersson, 1992).

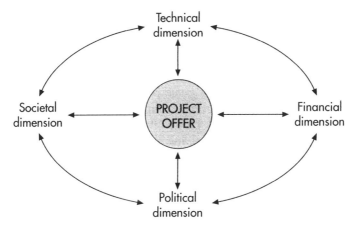

FIGURE 12.1   Project offering four dimensions.

In consequence, we can distinguish between four dimensions of a project offer (Figure 12.1):

- The *technical offer*, incorporating the products/services to be provided (including any technical assistance, after-sales service, training, etc.) and the scope of work to be undertaken.
- The *financial offer*, addressing the financial terms (price, conditions of payment, variation formulae, etc.), contract conditions (guarantees, roles, responsibilities and liabilities), details of any project finance proposals (senior and secondary debt, export guarantees, countertrade, bond issues, build/own/operate and other concession arrangements) and financial arrangements (e.g. BOOT [Built/Owned/Operated Transferred]).
- The *political offer*, including both formal and informal accords between local partners, details of local investments and, generally speaking, all investments made by the supplier within the customer's milieu to improve his political position. In European projects, companies also have to deal with politicians at EU level (Hadjikhani and Ghauri, 2001).
- The *societal offer*, including all action taken by the supplier to improve his position with civilian groups having an interest in—or against—the project (associations, users, inhabitants, etc.). Some suppliers have already placed societal offer high on their agenda and they address environmental and social considerations in the design and implementation of their offers. For two decades now, Bechtel, the famous US engineering company, has incorporated components of what it calls 'sustainable development' into projects around the world (www.bechtel.com); for example, on the Quezon power plant project in the Philippines, Bechtel and its affiliate InterGen worked with non-governmental organizations, local governments and other community leaders to identify actions that would help residents economically, socially and environmentally. The Quezon project's environmental programme included reforesting surrounding hillsides and monitoring the ecology of coral reefs just offshore to protect them from the effects of

industrialization and harmful fishing practices. Royal Dutch Shell has incorporated social responsibility as the most crucial component in their marketing.

In project marketing, companies combine these four components in order to formulate a differentiated offer for a given project. As mentioned earlier, in 'traditional' business-to-business marketing, companies generally use only two components: technical and commercial. Due to the concentration of the buying centre within one organization, the political and the societal offer are rarely used.

The international competition for the huge waste-treatment concession for Marseilles, as summarized in Box 12.1, provides a good example of the incorporation of political and societal dimensions within an offer.

BOX 12.1 Marseilles' Waste-disposal System.

Marseilles boasts Europe's largest opencast tip, just 40 km north of the city in Entressen. In 1994, the European Community decided to finance a project to close the tip and to set up an incineration and waste-recycling system plant. An invitation to bid was launched. Many companies made bids for the design, construction and running of the incineration plant. Entressen had shut down by 2001. The project was worth €150 million.

The city council analysed the bids and shortlisted three:

- La Générale des Eaux and Lyonnaise-Dumez, representing the Sodemith group.
- EdF, Electricité de France, which joined forces with a financing institution, via its subsidiary Pronergie.
- American Waste Management, the US world leader in the industry, which is relying on its partnership with SAE, a local construction company, and the creation of a joint subsidiary Auxiwaste to penetrate the French market.
- The other groups, in relatively weak positions on the Marseilles industrial milieu, were eliminated. These included Bouygues which has never really managed to penetrate the southern French market.

After months of negotiation, the technical and financial bids began to take shape. Auxiwaste proposed original technical solutions to the city councillors with sorting and recovery sites, while the two other competitors proposed more classical and almost identical solutions. In all three cases, they all concentrated on the setting up of a system which would appeal to the Greens and other ecology movements.

However, to stand out from the competition, all the competitors particularly concentrated on elements of the bids which had no direct link with the techniques which were at the heart of the deal, but which rather were directly related with the city council's activities:

- SAE demonstrated a real desire to invest in Marseilles, particularly in the Grand Prado building complex or the Prado-Carénage tunnel. By doing so, it was looking to help the council's urban development projects (Marseilles had got left behind under the previous Mayor). Waste Management guaranteed an:

- ecologically friendly solution for the famous Entressen tip, which could do nothing but satisfy those who could have opposed the project, the Greens.
- The couple Générale des Eaux and Lyonnaise-Dumez was prepared to give serious financial help to get the *Porte d'Aix* building project, or a smaller version, off the ground. The *'Cité de la Biotique'*, the city's biotic centre, may see the light one day thanks to the participation of a subsidiary of the Générale des Eaux. Once again, this would help the Council with its urban development projects and also the Mayor himself, Doctor Vigouroux, with his relationship with a group of local supporters, the Marseilles medical profession. Moreover, both companies proposed the creation of an environmental research centre between the Marseilles Engineering School and the University's Sciences and Technological Engineering Institute which would clearly please another group of Vigouroux supporters, the academic circles.
- Finally, EdF offered to help with the protection of the famous rocky inlets (the *calanques*) much prided by the *Marseillais*, and where it owns land and already organizes social integration programmes for young people from the city's suburbs. In Marseilles, the inhabitants do not say 'the *calanques*' but rather 'our' *calanques*. Recently, there have even been threatening voices saying 'Hands off our *calanques*!'. The inhabitants are afraid of seeing them disappear under the cement of the building contractors, the money of the local business community and the technocratic underhand workings of the city council. Indeed, the latter have even been accused of wanting to use the Land Use Plan to build in places where there has never been anything but pine trees, scraggy oak trees, stunted by the Mistral, and huge white rocks. In the spring of 1992, while the local election was in full swing, an ecologist raised the question during a debate and almost immediately there was a public outcry. An association, 'SOS Calanques', was created. The harbour (the Vieux Port) was ablaze with rumours concerning the limits of the land which can be built on. Not one week goes by without Doctor Vigouroux, a self-proclaimed ecologist, being attacked. It is therefore in his own interest that the members of this association are satisfied! (see Figure 12.2).

Companies must today manage each of the offer dimensions in order to differentiate themselves and their proposals from the competition. Based on the habits and customs in both the milieu of offer and demand and an assessment of the various actors within the milieu of demand, one way of differentiating a proposal is to concentrate on a single dimension given relatively less attention by competitors. In the case of the Marseilles waste treatment contract, while its competitors were prepared to compete on the political dimension, EdF appeared to prefer playing the societal card in the hope of mobilizing those elements of Marseilles society who felt it was more important to conserve the charm of the *'calanques'* than to develop more buildings or a *Cité de la Biotique*. Furthermore, it is not uncommon for companies, as a sweetener for gaining the contract during times of crisis or actual unemployment, to offer employment. All these are effective mechanisms for achieving a differential advantage and a better alignment with emergent parties in the milieu. Some companies do not even

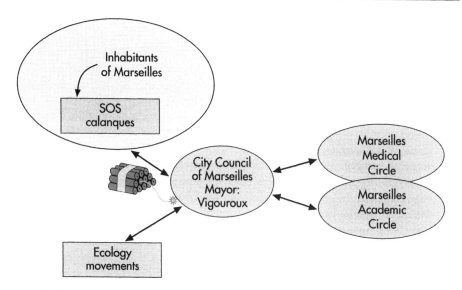

FIGURE 12.2   The project network for Marseilles' waste disposal system.

hesitate to mobilize public opinion against a competing project which is either environmentally unfriendly or unaesthetic to give the impression of being a white knight who will solve the problems of society and those of the politicians grappling with the same public.

The Architecture of the Offer

The four dimensions of the offer have proved to be the basis on which to build the project offer. However, it does not represent a perfect framework for the supplier who experiences difficulties in translating his offer into value for the customer. Recently, the idea of a 'plural architecture' of the project offer has been proposed, based on the way each part of the offer gives support to an actor in the project network (Cova *et al.*, 2000).

Back to the Marseilles' waste disposal case, two interpretations are possible from all the complementary offers that make up the suppliers' bids:

- First, they all offer to support the client's activities (OSC). All offers try to help the City Council (or even the Mayor himself) as far as the protection of the environment is concerned. This is at the heart of the deal with each potential supplier. However, although some services involve simple construction projects, they would nevertheless appear to help the Council even if there is no direct link with the core transaction itself.
- A second possible interpretation is that each competitor tries to establish links in the project network surrounding the Council by offering to some actors (generally non-business actors) something specific, which more or less relates to the heart of the transaction (even if only hinted at). Auxiwaste is looking for the support of, and trying to mobilize, ecologist movements by

OCC = Offer based on supplier's
        core competencies;

OSOCC = Offer supporting OCC;

OSC1 = Offer supporting the client's
         action in relation to supplier's
         core competencies;

OSC2 = Offer supporting the client's
         action with no direct link to
         supplier's core competencies;

OSN = Offer supporting client's
        network.

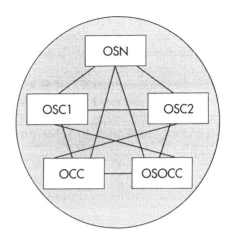

FIGURE 12.3   Project offer architecture.

offering site rehabilitation for Entressen. Somedith is looking for more political support from the Mayor in the medical and academic circles by offering the biotic centre and also financing the creation of an environmental protection research institute. Pronergie is opting for a more societal approach, by hoping to mobilize the inhabitants of Marseilles who seem more concerned by the protection of 'their' *calanques* than the creation of housing projects or a *Cité de la Biotique*. In all three offers, we do not speak of 'gifts' to influence or mobilize such-and-such an actor in the decision process, but rather of complementary offers, or additional services, as part of a package deal. They are neither separate items, nor part and parcel of what can be called total project offers to the decision-making process. This allows for the reconstruction, or reorganization, of the buying centre by recruiting and involving actors who are able to take into consideration the added value created by these different elements of the offers. We can therefore speak of creation of value for these actors, although there is no direct transfer of money, since the City Council will be paying for everything. Therefore, other than the OSC, there are parts of the offers that could be called offers supporting the customer's network (OSN).

The architecture of the offer is somewhat polymorphous, while bringing solutions to the different stakeholders in the project. It consists in 'everything' that can create value for the actors inside and around the client (if it exists as such). This 'everything' can come from anywhere inside and around the supplier: core competencies, peripheral competencies, external resources, etc. The internal hierarchy of competencies no longer stands up in this case. As a consequence, the supplier's offer is not reducible to a core offer (e.g. the product) with added services, as we can see in traditional business-to-business markets. On the contrary, the project offer structures itself around the following architecture which is totally dedicated to help the client and the different stakeholders in their day-to-day activities (see Figure 12.3):

1   The offer based on core competencies (OCC), which consists in bringing into play the supplier's core competencies in order to produce a part of the solution for the client; for example, a machine tool, a water treatment system, a limited batch of components, etc.

2   The offer supporting OCC (OSOCC), which encompasses all the products and services that are needed to use the offer based on the supplier's core competencies. The following items fall into this category: logistics, maintenance and everything dedicated to solve problems which are directly linked with the supplier's core competencies.

3   The offer supporting the client's action in relation to the supplier's core competencies (OSC1); the aim of OSC1 is mainly to solve problems of the client's day-to-day activities; for example, training programmes which increase users' competencies.

4   The offer supporting the client's action with no link to the supplier's core competencies (OSC2); OSC2 broadly aims at improving the position of the client in his markets and with his clients. This type of offer is developing rapidly, especially with suppliers who are organized in key accounts. For them, it is more important to assist the client and to contribute to his strategy than to answer detailed specifications.

5   The offer supporting the client's network (OSN). This does not mean gifts and other 'free meals' to gain the support of an actor inside or around a client, but it does represent an authentic part of the offer which creates value for one or more stakeholders. In the project network, it is not a separate lot but an integral part of a global offer to the enlarged buying centre. The following case of the way in which STX proposed its offer to Poldavia highlights this notion.

BOX 12.2 STX and Poldavia.*

In 1999, the Poldavian armed forces finalized the purchase of intelligent weapons to renew their stock of military equipment. For this, an invitation to bid was sent to three world competitors. Rather than compare the three bids which have not been made public, we shall concentrate on the analysis of one of the competitors, STX. STX is a multinational company from North America and world leader in many defence-related fields. The company made a bid for the Poldavian project, although it had not really anticipated the project as much as its German competitor DDX, which had better relations with the customer. STX's bid was called 'Poldavia and STX: meeting the challenges of the next century together' and was made up of three parts: the customer's challenges, STX solutions, expected customer benefits.

In the introduction to its bid, STX mentioned that the Poldavian armed forces were looking to purchase a new 'multi-function' weapons system and that the Poldavian government also wanted a programme of industrial cooperation to benefit its people on a socio-economic level. Thus, STX offered its weapons systems and the

---

* For reasons of confidentiality, the names used are fictional.

technologies required to meet the country's military and socio-economic challenges.

According to STX, Poldavia faced four principal challenges:

- To provide for national defence by equipping the armed forces (represented by the Poldavian Armed Forces).
- To improve the quality of the environment and reduce air pollution in Poldalski, the capital of Poldavia (represented by the City Council).
- To enhance the quality of education (represented by the Ministry for Education).
- To develop and diversify the country's economy (represented by the Ministry of Finance and Foreign Trade).

STX's proposals were the following:

- STX's *Weapon Enterprise* which corresponds to the Army's requirements and ensures continued relations between the US Army and the Poldavian Armed Forces plus the possibilities for industrial cooperation thanks to STX's worldwide presence and experience (direct offsets with POLDER and PTS coupled with help to improve production and marketing for POLDER and PTS; POLDER and PTS are two aerospace companies in Poldavia).
- The innovative technologies used in the STX hybrid electric bus control system technology for the city of Poldalski.
- STX's expertise as leading service provider to the US Department of Defense for distance learning.
- The STX–HW partnership to promote both Poldavian productivity and its industries via the creation of a hub to stimulate the entire Poldavian economy and to promote Poldavian trade with Eastern Europe and the USA.

According to STX, Poldavia will subsequently obtain lasting benefits from an agreement with them:

- Better defence, at a cost adapted to Poldavia's revenue, linked to the development and growth of Poldavia's defence industry.
- A cleaner environment in Poldalski, thanks to the reduced pollution of its public transport.
- An improved education system and equal opportunities for all at a reduced cost.
- Accentuated economic growth thanks to skilful marketing initiatives.

In the case of STX's offer to Poldavia, the target in the buying decision network was clearly labelled. When we analysed the offer, we clearly saw that at the heart of the offer were weapons, around which everything gravitated:

- A clearly defined group of offers (provided by STX and its local partners) for the country's military–industrial set-up (operational equipment support, equipment adaptation, prices, financial arrangements), known as the *Weapon Enterprise*. STX then accompanied its offer with direct offsets for the two local defence industries PTS's and POLDER. As with most offset agreements, they were accompanied by transfers of technologies to improve PTS's and POLDER's output and sales. Despite this widened offer, STX continued to address the same traditional decision-making body, the Army.

- A more heterogeneous group of offers (provided by STX and its North American partners) for the country's socio-economic benefit were set up which included indirect offsets (with the hub) and other actions to help the customer-country. STX included in the contributions to the country technological skills for pollution-free buses, experience in distance learning and potential investment in the country's economy. In this part of the socio-economic offer, there is both an argument which enhances/justifies the offer for the customer. (This represents the 'soft' part of the offer, it is very communicative, enough to justify the purchase in the eyes of the people, and a 'hard' part which concerns additional service provision by the potential actors in the purchasing decision-making network, other than the Army (Poldaski City Council, Ministry for Education, Ministry for Tourism, etc.) (as illustrated by Figure 12.4).)

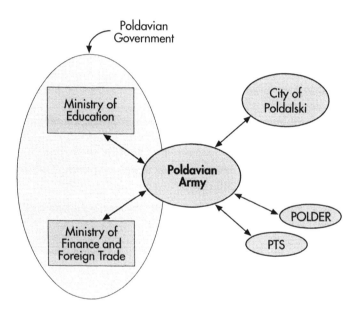

FIGURE 12.4 The project network for Poldavian Weapons Systems.

Once again, OSN is clearly visible. STX tries to help the actors in the Poldavian project network with an additional offer that has no relation to its core competencies. Such additional items are not offered for free; they are paid for, in part, by the principal transaction between STX and the Poldavian military and partly via specific contracts with each of the actors in question. The Study of the STX/Poldavia case:

- Brings to light the distinction, in the OSC, between the offer in relation to the supplier's product (OSC1) and the offer that has no direct relation to the supplier's product but whose aim is to help the customer's activity and market position (OSC2).

- Offers a new distinction between OSC1 or OSC2 and the OSN (the offer supporting the client's network). The latter cannot simply be limited to the purely communicational or relational dimension of project marketing, consigning to a purely classical vision of marketing. Indeed, they are often part of the offer made not to the customer but to a project network, and are either directly or indirectly paid for by the actors concerned. However, they can partly be found in the compensation countertrade part of the offer and, more specifically, as unrelated offsets of the offer (see 'Organizational Implications'), even if this is just part of their role. The unrelated offsets underline the fact that the offer of an offset is an offer to buy (i.e. the selling of customer network products) rather than to sell. Therefore, it is not paid by the buying decision-making network, which is not the case for the other additional offer analysed in this case.

What is known as the project total offer approach—which includes the OCC, OSOCC, OSC and OSN, and has been developed in project marketing and system selling—is typical of a network approach in which the supplier mobilizes and recruits new actors to reorganize the buying centre. The supplier not only seeks to influence, by means of a relational process which can sometimes be construed as the trading of favours, but also tries to directly or indirectly create value. Thus, the supplier seeks out the most suitable buying decision-making network according to his skills and the group's skills. His approach is centred on a coupling between the scope of the additional offer and the decision-making process in the project network.

Organizational Implications

The move from a project offer which supports the core competence (OSOCC) and which supports the customer (OSC1 and OSC2) to an offer which supports the customer's network (OSN) leads to a real break, for example, in marketing approach, company positioning, required employee skills, supplier involvement and responsibility towards the client and competitive situation. This has some consequences for companies.

A Radical Change in Customer Approach

For suppliers, the break between the three levels of project offer (OSOCC, OSC, OSN) reflects a radical change in their perception of the customer. Consequently, suppliers approach their customers differently. This is reflected in the major changes they make to their offers and the suitable organization they adopt. One of the first consequences for the supplier is to move away from the needs stated by the customer to an approach which takes into consideration the customer's strategic challenges in the project. This refocusing means using a different architecture for the project offer as it is concentrated more on customer activity than on supplier competencies. This represents a major paradigmatic change in the vision of how the customer and the market operates. In other words, in the logic of differentiation, companies have developed their offers by adding more and more services directly linked to products in order to help implementation of the product by, and for, the customer. Such an approach has been at the centre of industrial marketing for a long time in order to establish a relationship with a customer by gluing the two actors together. Indeed, we can talk of a paradigmatic change as the supplier, centering on the customer's activity can propose value-adding offers (solutions) which require the integration of partners (subsidiaries or other external organizations). This is the project marketing and solution selling field. There does not exist the same market characteristics nor the same processes as for the marketing of mere industrial products.

The Problem of Managing Technical and Human Resources

In the process of broadening their offer (OCC, OSOCC, OSC, OSN), companies move towards dematerialization of their offer. Companies move away from the focus on technological resources and competencies to one on services and human-resource management. In some cases, the move towards pure services (facility management) is possible. Hence, there occur both cultural problems within a company and the problems of making major changes in managerial practices. The difficulty comes from the need to simultaneously manage, coordinate and mobilize production technologies that are able to produce products on systems with specific technical characteristics and human resources that are able to design, create and offer services of differing complexity and external resources; in other words, both technologies and human resources that are able to create project offer.

Concerning the Organization and How It Functions

Broadening of the offer (from OSOCC to OSC), via moving from the logic of considering the customer's technical needs to one of understanding the customer's challenges, raises the question of how the organization functions. Actually, the situations appear more complex and need approaches adapted to the specificity of each customer. Is it possible to continue traditional marketing and sale organization with product managers, market managers and a geographical sales force? Increasingly, we see that more attention is paid to the customer dimension via teams who are responsible for managing key accounts and whose role is to increase and create maximum customer value. What is the relationship between key account managers (KAM) and the other functions (the part-time marketers), since there is no hierarchical difference between the two? One organizational element, which raises a number of questions within the industrial product companies, concerns the position of units in charge of OSOCC, OSC or OSN. There are two possible cases. In the first case, the unit is a resource to be used for the promotion of core competencies, mainly the products. The service is seen to enhance product differentiation. It is part of the product package and almost inseparable from it. This is the case for OSOCC and OSC1. In the second case, the unit is a profit centre. Usually, the service offers involved are OSC2 and OSN. The question is: What is the role of these offers in the sale of the products? Indeed, divergence can appear between units which are responsible for the product and for OSOCC and those which are responsible for the offer of OSC and OSN. Of course, both types of unit can sell separately or intervene in offer arrangements, together or alone. The problem and risk with this type of situation is the accumulation of profit margin each unit takes, which leads to an extravagant overall market cost for the product services sold.

The Customer's Perception of Interdependence with a Supplier: Loss of Autonomy or Access to More Skills?

The more a company creates value for a customer, by broadening its offer, the greater the interdependence between the two organizations. In fact, the main questions are: Will the customer accept this interdependence? How will he interpret it? The problem is ambiguous in as much as the more the supplier creates value for the customer, via broadening its offer, the more the latter's dependence increases. The customer can interpret such a relationship as either a loss of autonomy, leaving the supplier with the possibility of abusing his position, or an 'insurance policy', guaranteeing the supplier's commitment. These are the limitations of such an approach to industrial marketing offers. Moreover, the customer's acceptance of a certain level of interdependence must lead the supplier to adopt a careful strategy in his choice of customer and his management of supplier–client relationships.

Offset Offer in International Projects*

One major development in international project business over the last 20 years has been the growing importance of a range of trade practices and arrangements, collectively known as 'countertrade'. Countertrade is a form of international exchange in which an import transaction is linked to an export transaction in a reciprocal fashion. There are different types of countertrade agreements (Fletcher, 1996, 1998):

- *Barter* relies on a double coincidence of wants, in the short term, and does not involve money (e.g. Polar, the Swedish record company, sold records to the Soviet Union and was paid in coal).
- *Buy-back* is attractive if the overseas market is closed to licensing or joint ventures. It does require that the firm be prepared to share its technology and also involves long-term relationships. It is attractive if the resulting product received is easy to sell on the world market (e.g. Alfa-Laval

---

* This section is adapted from Ahlström (2000).

delivered a dairy turnkey project to Russia and was paid in products from the dairy plant).

- *Debt* or *switch account* is of interest for a firm that owes or has frozen assets it wants to liquidify (e.g. between socialist countries there are accounts for traded goods that are supposed to balance over time).
- *Counterpurchase* is a long-term proposition, especially when equivalence of accounts are involved. Counterpurchase transactions can involve a number of products, and part of the exchange can be for money (e.g. Scania sold trucks to Pakistan and was paid in money but had later to buy Pakistani products of equivalent value and pay in money).
- *Offsets* generally involve dealing with the military and government, and are linked to the desire to acquire new technology. Offsets refer to agreements where a large system is bought and the seller conducts activities that have a long-term effect on the development of local industry. Long-term relationships are the norm with offsets, which generally involve several partnering companies.

Offset in project business is often called industrial participation, industrial collaboration or business value development. It is considered one of the most important ingredients in the international marketing of big projects and a main reason for choosing a supplier in industries such as aerospace or petroleum industry; for example, in competitive bidding for foreign fighter aircraft contracts, suppliers have every incentive, and are normally required, to create an attractive offset offer as part of their bid. As such, offset is more or less intertwined with other components of the offer in project marketing.

What is an Offset?

Offset has to be regarded as one of the two major forms of countertrade, the other form (i.e. grouping barter, debt, buy-back and counterpurchase) is the more traditional countertrade, generally used by buyers in less developed countries (Fletcher, 1996). The main difference between offset and traditional countertrade is the purpose behind them. In the case of offset, the buyer's purpose is long-term industrial development while, in the case of traditional countertrade, it is more short term and focused on financing the procurement. In fact, offsets are (added) activities that involve transfer of resources to the buying country and are part of the international governmental procurement of a large technical project or system, but not necessary for the use, handling and immediate maintenance of the technical system.

Offsets have their origin in the defence industry. Governments buy defence material to achieve security for their country. To use weapon systems, the buyer needs to be able to use, repair and maintain the material bought. To enhance national independence, the buyer often wants to be able to produce, improve or develop the defence material and, thereby, be less dependent on the supplier. In the early and mid-1970s, a few trend-setting aircraft agreements between US firms and Australia, a group of European countries (for F-16 military aircraft in 1975) and Switzerland (for F-5 military aircraft in 1976) were signed. These contracts included a commitment on the part of the supplier to improve the buyer's exports and local industry, guaranteed by the US government. With these agreements, offset (defence offset or military offset) as a concept was born, and it is nowadays almost always a part of large international defence agreements. Over time, offset has spread into civil industries. Even industrialized countries have, for example, in certain periods required offsets on all government procurements overseas. In large infrastructure projects, such as telecom and the power generation industry, the situation is similar to that in defence, the buyer wanting to learn to handle and maintain the plant or system purchased; local industry participation is required.

Related Offsets

Related offsets or direct offsets are activities that are related to the project sold (e.g. local production of parts of a technical system). Indeed, there is related offset when local content is required. ABB Generation (active in the power generation industry) sold a hydroelectric plant to Taiwan. As a part of the contract, the supplier was required to have parts of the plant produced by local companies. There is also related offset, when a local prime contractor is required. Celsius sold AT4 anti-tank weapons to the USA. Honeywell was chosen as local prime contractor and built the AT4s under licence.

BOX 12.3 Related Offset Offer for the Australian Submarines Contract.

The establishment of an alliance with Australian partners was a prerequisite for successful bidding. In the final round, the Swedish Kockums (represented with its allies by the local joint venture, Australian Submarine Corporation) stood against a German alliance led by Howaldtwerke Deutsche Werft (represented by Australian Marine Systems).

The final submarine system had to be specially developed to be compatible with Australian conditions. The subcontractor systems sold to Kockums/Australian Submarine Corporation were extensive and several offset deals between subcontractors and their Australian counterparts were signed. Consequently, the offset deal has led to an increased business exchange between the two countries.

It is noteworthy that Australia has the most detailed, formalized offset policy, called the 'Australian Industry Involvement Program'. It is a tradition that offset is required in all defence and some civil contracts. What can be accounted for as offset and what activities are encouraged through multiples is very specific. There is an extensive programme to follow up the outcome of offset. In the 1970s, there was a focus on local ability to maintain and support defence material but, since the 1980s, the motive behind offset has turned more and more to industrial development.

The requirements for offset changed, anyway, during the negotiation process, partly due to the extensive political interest. In the request for tender, five of the six submarines were to be built locally. One year later, it was required that all six should be built in Australia. In the contract, the most complicated parts of the five submarines were built in Sweden. The compensation level ended at 70% local content, extended from the original requirement of 60%.

The Submarine/Australia example illustrates a very extensive negotiation phase, where the importance of the related offset deal became more and more crucial. The procurement process was given a high degree of political interest. The federation and active trade unions gave a basis for political interference in the negotiation process. Probably the Swedish offer was the 'best' product, but the contract could never have been won without a competitive related offset offer. Australia bought submarines from Kockums with an offset engagement worth about €1 billion.

Source: Adapted from Ahlström (2000).

Unrelated Offsets

Unrelated offsets or indirect offsets are not directly related to the technical dimension of the project. There exist unrelated offsets in export and trade: Swedish FFV sold ammunition to Austria and had to buy products of equivalent value from Austria. There also exist unrelated offsets in business development: Ericsson sold AXE switchboards to Australia and had among other things to start production and development of other switchboards locally (in Australia) and export a specific share of this local production.

BOX 12.4 Unrelated Offset Offer for the Norwegian Truck Contract.

The Norwegian Ministry of Defence wanted to renew its fleet of all-terrain trucks. A tender was sent to a handful of suppliers who qualified through its dealer network for civilian trucks in the Norwegian market. For the final round, Saab Scania and Mercedes Benz were chosen. Mercedes Benz was expected to have a slight advantage based on an earlier delivery of trucks to the Norwegian Ministry of Defence.

Norway has no written offset policy. However, a practice had emanated from negotiations with international oil companies in the offshore sector and earlier defence procurement. Norway had tried to connect the specific offset deals to bilateral agreements aiming at balancing trade in defence equipment between the countries. But Norway, with a very small defence industry, has not been so successful with this.

Both Saab Scania and Mercedes Benz offered a compensation level of 100%. Saab Scania took the initiative by specifying some offset activities. The largest of these was the offer to establish a production plant for parts for Saab automobiles. It was to be built in Halden, which is close to the Swedish border and in a regional development area. Additionally, Saab Scania offered 30 specified smaller R&D projects (some with letters of intent) including cooperation with Norwegian firms. Saab Scania's procurements in Norway over and above the level of previous years could also be accounted as offset.

The Mercedes Benz offer was considered less developed in detail, and it is reasonable to believe that the differences in the attractiveness of the offset deals was of vital importance for the final choice. In the contract, Saab Scania had a time limit of 7 years to fulfil the offset agreement, but it later argued that these technology-intense development contracts take time to develop and Saab was able to postpone the time limit. Saab Scania sold 1,700 trucks to the Norwegian Ministry of Defence with an offset engagement valued at about €100 million.

Source: Adapted from Ahlström (2000).

FIGURE 12.5 An overview of countertrade forms (adapted from Ahlström, 2000).

Pre-tender phase is crucial not only for conceptualization but also for fulfilment of both related and unrelated offsets. Offset is an integrated part of the total offer, and it is required from the very beginning at registration of interest by the supplier. Some parts of the conceptualization of offset start before the tender phase. Moreover, the fulfilment of offset, for example conducting local investment and subcontracting that can be counted as offset activities, can be described as starting before the main agreement is signed. The buyer or the competition might require this. In many countries, the supplier can do pre-offset in the pre-tender phase and 'bank' offset activities in order to use them as offset fulfilment in future contracts.

In other cases, the buyer requires that offset should be specified in the contract. This implies that the supplier has to make agreements with local partners, write letters of intent, etc. This process can be problematic to manage for the supplier. The supplier has to spur the purchasing department and other functions of the firm into action to find potential business opportunities and subcontractors. Once this process starts, it might result in procurement and other activities. This can then be difficult to coordinate with the tender phase.

Offset is not, at least from the client's perspective, seen as an activity with an end. The idea is to develop commercially sound relationships and local resource bases that will continue after the project is delivered. From the supply side, the company's volume of potential offsets is limited and, therefore, the supplier naturally tries to avoid 'delivering' offset to markets where he does not win the contract.

The Offset Component of the Offer

The four dimensions of the project offer were presented in the preceding section. These are the technical, commercial, political and societal dimensions. Offset is more or less intertwined with other dimensions of the offer. To start with, the borderline between the technical offer and offset components is indistinct. The buyer's remaining capability to test, renovate or modify the technical system, as well as the decision about how many support systems should be placed locally, can be seen as parts of both the technical offer and the offset component. The ability to handle basic maintenance is a part of the technical offer, while the ability to design considerable modifications of the system often is seen as an offset. Requirements for local content when buying a new design might also influence the construction of the technical system. Its design might be dependent on what it is possible to do locally.

The commercial offer extends to the contractual solution regarding offset, including penalties and different degrees of specification of offset. Financially, currency risks and cash flow will differ greatly depending on whether there is local content or a local prime contractor as part of the offset component. Offset is also embedded in the political context. The offset component will, for example, be of higher value if an active 'selling' government supports the supplier by offering cooperation with regard to defence experience or defence technology. This support might also be necessary to transfer defence technology, as part of an offset agreement, to the buying country. This is, at the same time, an example of activities that the supplier can offer as part of the offset component. If large multinational companies are embedded in the local network and support the supplier with local investments, these activities are part of the offset component.

In fact, there is a kind of primary connection between offset and the technical complexity, technical maturity and value of and number of, items in the technical offering. Somewhat simplified, it is quite rational for the buyer to demand related offset when purchasing a completely new design. In a contract for a large number of custom-developed and produced systems, related offset is more suitable on the ground of viable business. Similarly, unrelated offset will be the better choice when a low number of standard-built systems (e.g. trucks) are bought off-the-shelf. There are naturally many levels of new design and customer adaptation between these extremes. In a sense, this gives the buyer a strategic choice, enabling him to decide how proven/newly designed a system to buy, together with what offset to demand; this being based on the buying government's goals for industrial development. Consequently, the following rules apply to the vast majority of offset offers:

- *Offset cannot be treated separately from the other dimensions of the project offer.* The offer in large international governmental procurements is not merely a combination of finance and technical system in a more or less turnkey offer.

The offer also satisfies the agenda of the government buyer and the wishes of many stakeholders, which exceed usage of the technical system.

- *In some markets, offset is sold with the help of a technical system, and not the other way around.* The relative importance of each dimension of the offer is determined in the interaction between the client and the supplier. The buying process with the so-called 'enlarged buying centre' is highly political and the stakeholders' interests need to be satisfied to sell the system. These interests imply that offset will often be the competitive edge, provided that the technical system is sufficient and does not exceed the buyer's budget. The aim to develop the local industry is the reason behind the procurement. Then, offset becomes the main interest.
- *The degree of customization of the technical system and local industry determines the potential for related offset.* The buyer can basically choose between buying a new design with related offset and an off-the-shelf procurement, economically more sound, together with unrelated offset. However, available resources in local industry are also an important condition.

The supplier of the project/system is not, as seen before, just a systems designer selling a project/system and delivering it with the help of subcontractors. The supplier is often rather a consortium of a few large contractors, which is common in infrastructure projects. But in offset situations, an ever larger group of supporting organizations is mobilized:

- *The supporters of the core supplier can be classified into groups of organizations, based on their task in marketing and their part in developing components of the offer.* The groups are the core, the extended core, the subcontractors, the allied companies and other organizations (see Figure 12.6). They are mobilized and managed by the core supplier, the one who designs the project/system and leads the interaction with the client. Many of these supporters can be new, and the relationships not organically grown from mutual use and repetitive exchanges.
- *The extended core.* The core supplier or system designer might cooperate in a strategic alliance (consortium) with one or more partners during conceptualization, negotiations and fulfilment of the offset. These organizations belong to what is called the extended core.
- *The subcontractors.* Existing subcontractors' part of the offer is often important for the competitiveness of the whole project. With this, it follows than an existing subcontractor's part of the related offset offer might be very important. However, it can be problematic for the core to control the existing subcontractors, because a subcontractor might sleep in two beds and because subcontractors might not accept a new role in the selling alliance. Especially, local organizations play both for the home team and the away team. Some actors can, in effect, change sides during the buyer–supplier interaction; for example, local firms cooperating with the core supplier can act as an extended sales organization sitting in the lap of the buyer. They are also value-creators developing (related) offset value in cooperation with the supplier. However, the reason behind the core buyer's trust in local firms is the self-interest of these firms (i.e. they will act in their own interests and make

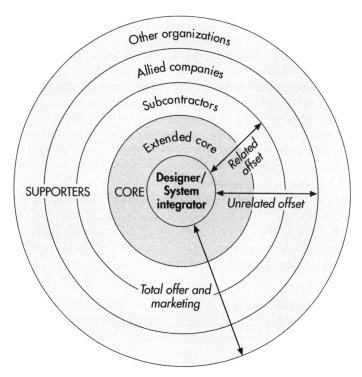

FIGURE 12.6 Core and supporters in the selling side of the offset (adapted from Ahlström, 2000).

sure that the local content and transfer of resources will be as large as possible). Therefore, it is fair to say that these companies play both home and away.

- *Allied companies and other organizations.* For unrelated offset, allied companies are necessary. They are found in the business group, the owner's sphere and the business venture group (including strategic partners and their owners) and also in the form of a middleman (e.g. trading house or offset consultant). The government of the core supplier is the organization which is most important in the marketing process. If the government signs bilateral industrial cooperation agreements, gives development aid, participates in defence cooperation, etc., this will make the core supplier more competitive. Complementary resources controlled by authorities are often part of a country's foreign, industrial and trade policy.

The Submarine/Australia example described earlier can be used to illustrate the myriad of actors involved on the selling side of an offset agreement:

- *Kockums Naval Systems* = systems integrator;
- *ASC* = main contractor;
- *Celsius* = supporting corporation (Kockums owner);
- *Swedish government* = supporting government;
- *German Procurement Office* = offset guarantor;
- *US government* = technology transfer approver;

- *Swedish Marine* = reference customer;
- *Australian companies* = local subcontractors;
- *Saab Instruments* = established subcontractor;
- *Kockums Pacific* = unrelated offset coordinator;
- *Defence Liaison Services* = lobbyist;
- *Trading house* = countertrader;
- *often, one-man firms* = offset consultants.

The mobilization of local partners is of paramount importance in the conceptualization and fulfilment of the offset component of the offer. However, choosing and competing to win the most suitable local firms as partners is not an easy task for the core supplier. First, customer requirements will diminish the supplier's strategic choice of local partners in a number ways. The customer might stipulate a local (existing firm as) prime contractor or require the supplier to be prime contractor. The customer might require that the specific technology is transferred or that specific subcontracts are produced locally. The customer might also (explicitly or implicitly) require distribution of local content among states, local companies or local industries.

Second, there is often competition for local partners among the competing suppliers. This is an important reason for the supplier to be active in a market before the pre-tender phase and to tie up the best local partners. However, the competitive situation makes it difficult for the supplier to be completely open with the potential local partner. It is difficult to give information about a potential contract or cooperation arrangement, which in turn makes it difficult to get prices, calculate costs, etc. A local partner who is less formal and less contract-oriented is, therefore, preferred. There are many changes during the process, and it can be difficult to specify the scope of the work.

The relationship with local partners often includes the transfer of technology. Over time, the interests of local partners might cause changes in the relationship with the core supplier. This, in turn, might cause problems for the core supplier. Here is a list of problems that a core supplier can encounter:

- drawings do not say how things have been done;
- specifications and standards might unexpectedly cause problems;
- there is always a risk of developing a local competitor;
- local partners might turn out to be competitors;
- local partners might think more in the short term than the core supplier;
- local joint ventures and other forms of consortia might be volatile;
- social exchange is even more important than we would expect in technology transfer.

Offset Enlarged Buying Centre

The buying centre is usually seen as multi-organizational and dispersed, with the organizations playing different roles. This also means that different actors represent different and sometimes contrary motives and interests. We have called it the 'enlarged buying centre'. Individuals and, possibly, parts of

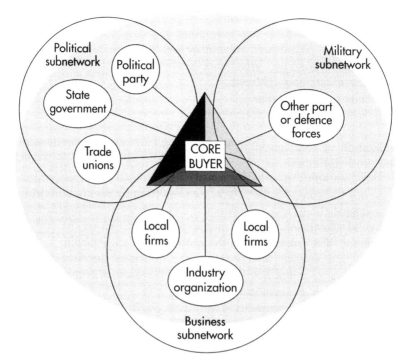

FIGURE 12.7 Core and extended buying centre of the offset (adapted from Ahlström, 2000).

organizations or complete organizations belong to military, industrial and political subnetworks (Figure 12.7).

In most large governmental procurements, there is an organization 'hosting' the formal procurement process; for example, in the Submarine/Australian project, there was the Defence Procurement Agency. This agency is subordinate to the Government and Ministry of Defence. In the same hierarchy, we find other parts of the Australian Ministry of Defence, most importantly the Navy, which is the user organization. Together, these organizations, parts of the same political body, form an inner hierarchy—a core buyer—in the extended buying centre.

Once again, this case allows us to give an overview of the type of actors and roles in an extended buying centre for a contract which includes offset agreements:

- *The Australian government* = decider;
- *The Australian Ministry of Defence* = buyer/initiator;
- *The Australian Navy* = user/initiator;
- *Submarine Project Office* = buyer;
- *Offset Office* = buyer;
- *The Australian Parliament* = approver;
- *The Australian Ministry of Finance* = influencer;
- *The Australian Ministry of Industry* = influencer;
- *Regional state governments* = infuencer;
- *Regional state offices* = value creation/influencer;

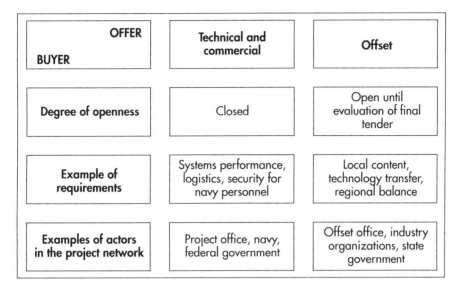

FIGURE 12.8 Two separate processes of interaction (Australian/Submarine case) (adapted from Ahlström, 2000).

- *Local companies* = value creation/influencer;
- *Industrial representatives* = influencer;
- *Union representatives* = influencer;
- *Governing party* = influencer;
- *Political opposition* = influencer.

On the buying side, the pre-tender and tender phases are usually separated into two different interaction processes, one for the technical and commercial dimensions of the offer, and the other for the offset offer. The two separate processes can have different degrees of openness and different actors might be involved. The different actors involved in the two processes constitute different arenas. There can be different norms, rules and argumentation in the two processes (Figure 12.8).

Globally, the implications for the supplier of the requirements of offset on project marketing can be summarized as follows:

- As offset is one of the most important parts in most evaluation processes, it can be used to win a contract. The management and proper analysis of the offset market situation is then vital.
- When there is an existing related industry on the local market, the supplier can expect higher demands for related offset. It is therefore important in these situations for the supplier to see how the potentially new partners could be of use in its international production/ development structure, to make sure that offset proposals can be beneficial for the supplier.
- It is important in the supplier's market analysis to focus on the formality of the buyer offset policy, to judge how dispersed the project network is and how

politicians dominate the project network. These factors might indicate the importance of offset in the total deal.

- It is important to try to influence the important actors in the project network and not to be focused on the buying agency. Depending on the selling strategy, there is probably some actors who can increase the importance of offset activities.
- The ability to mobilize a supporting and subcontractor subnetwork is vital to the development of a competitive offset offer.

Chapter 13

NEGOTIATING PROJECTS

In project marketing, negotiation is one of the most crucial stages. It is widely admitted that the parties face great difficulties in negotiating major projects, and sound proposals which could have been beneficial to both parties have often been disrupted and dropped during this stage. During the last two decades, a lot of research has been done on multinational firms (MNCs) and international marketing. A number of conflicting issues have been identified, but very little research has been done on the negotiation process, the forum where these conflicts can be resolved (Ghauri and Usunier, 1996).

Moreover, in the last few years, the opinion has arisen that European companies are losing their share of international projects due to lack of information and knowledge about the buying organizations from different countries. It has also been observed that these projects mostly involve a number of parties from different fields; for example, international banks such as the World Bank, IMF, EBRD and other organizations as well as politicians at different levels from different countries.

Buyers also face the same kind of difficulty, due to lack of resources and know-how concerning the particular technology, industry and the selling company. Buyers for bigger projects encounter difficulties in evaluating sellers, while they are dependent on a small number of sellers and foreign consultants.

In particular, very little work has been done on international project negotiations. In a typical project, the seller supplies a complete system, components and equipment, and the know-how to handle them. Emerging countries that are updating their infrastructure and technologies are particularly interested in these kinds of project.

In this chapter, we deal with international project negotiations, as they are central issues in project marketing. The chapter particularly deals with third parties' influence on negotiations. As seen before, in many projects governments play a dominant role. The relationship between firms and governments is becoming one of interdependence rather than just dependence. The chapter emphasizes projects in general as well as projects in an international context. Emerging countries are not only markets but also ideal locations for production and outsourcing. The parties have both common and conflicting interests, wish to reach an agreement which is practicable, and seek to solve problems which they fear they may meet in the future.

With the abovementioned background, the purpose of this chapter is to provide an understanding of the negotiation process for projects: How much time it takes? Which issues are important and which contacts are made? How do environmental differences and third parties influence the time, issues and contacts? The main topics discussed in the earlier chapters, such as milieu, tenders, offers and customer relations, are now put in context in negotiations, such as matching, lobbying, informal meetings, etc.

A Model for Project Sales Negotiations

A number of authors working on negotiation have presented different models basically based on the process perspective. They are presented according to their temporal flow: antecedents (goals and background factors), concurrents (process and conditions) and consequents (outcome). These models have some shortcomings; for example, antecedents are assumed, while we suggest that antecedent conditions such as handling of milieu and power relations can be influenced and changed during the process of negotiations. Moreover, there is a lack of understanding of macroeconomic and institutional-level variables that influence individual behaviour. Our model thus relates negotiations to these macro- and meso-levels by introducing the concept of matching.

Existing models on negotiation are thus somewhat general and can be applied to all kinds of negotiation. This chapter, therefore, develops a more specific model for business negotiations in project marketing to depict the dynamism in the process. In our opinion, it covers the essentials of project sales negotiations, in general, and project sales in an international context, in particular, thus taking care of cross-cultural aspects.

The Concept of Matching

We detailed earlier that in project marketing, domestic as well as international, there are several parties involved. Other than people from the buyer and seller side, there is a network of actors involved at three different levels, macro, meso and micro (Ghauri and Holstius, 1996).

At *macro-level* there are often World Bank, development agencies or commercial banks involved. In bigger projects, such as building a power plant, a hospital or a football stadium, there are always other parties who are either financing the project and/or have to approve the project. For the negotiations to run smoothly, the buyers and especially the sellers need to do some networking with these parties. They have to understand the priorities, conditions and requirements set by these parties regarding the bidding process, time constraints and other issues. Most bigger construction companies and companies in heavy industries, such as ABB and Alstom, do have special departments to handle this level of networking. For a company working with project sales, these organizations and actors are very important as they might be involved in many projects with different customers and countries, and, thus, represent the poles of continuity.

In international projects especially in emerging markets (e.g. The Bullet Train Project in Korea or Powerplant in India), these international organizations are not only involved but also play an important role in supplier selection, negotiations and the contract clauses.

BOX 13.1 Home and Host Countries: Different but Similar.

It has become accepted wisdom that companies planning to do business abroad should expect to face problems they do not experience in their home countries. The list of these problems is extensive: dealing with the host country government, minimizing the effect of exchange rate instabilities on company finances, understanding local culture and so on. However, many of the problems that development project management firms (working for the development of third-world countries) encounter abroad seem to be identical to domestic ones. Robert Youker, a former management training specialist at the World Bank compared the domestic and international challenges encountered by development project firms. The following is a list of problems that development project firms should expect both in the international and domestic arena:

- lack of shared perception and agreement on the objectives of the project by staff and stakeholders;
- lack of commitment to the project by the team, management and stakeholders;
- lack of detailed, realistic and current project plans (schedule, budget, procurement);
- unclear lines of authority and responsibility (organization not structured for project management);
- lack of adequate resources;
- poor feedback and control mechanisms for early detection of problems;
- poor or no analysis of major risk factors;
- delays caused by bureaucratic administrative systems (approvals, procurement, personnel, land acquisition and release of funds).

Source: Adapted from Youker (1999).

Matching at *meso-level* refers to the governments or relative departments that influence a particular project. In the case of domestic projects, companies may be used to do networking with relative departments as explained in Chapter 8. In international projects, networking has to be done (arranged) at two governments level, the seller's government and the buyer's government. We have seen several examples where the government of the vendor country 'smoothes the path' for their company. It is a well-known fact that the American government influences/

convinces different governments to buy from American companies. Sales of Boeing planes to Japan or Powerplant to India are just a couple of examples.

For vendors, it is therefore crucial to have good contacts with the relevant government ministries and departments at home and in the country of the project. A visit by the Prime Minister/Minister for Trade and Industry or even by Royals to a country where companies are trying to sell big projects is not unusual and, in fact, has been crucial in acquiring many big contracts. It is, however, the responsibility of the vendor company (companies) to convince the government and to arrange this matching with their counterparts in the buyer's country.

Matching at *micro-level* refers to networking at company level. The vendors need to develop trust and protocol not only with the buying companies, but also with other companies in the project network, such as consultants, subcontractors and agents. These companies may or may not come from the country of the buyer. In one of the cases we studied, for a pulp plant in India, the consultant came from America while the vendor was a Swedish company. The Swedish company in this case had to work more intensively with the consultant than with the buyer. They had to 'convince' the consultant that they had the most suitable technology, price and could adhere to the terms and 'expectations' of the buyer. The consultant helped them not only establish protocol with the buying organization, but also with other government officials in the milieu. The buying organization in this case was a government organization; as a result, they had to do a lot of networking and matching at meso-level, provide assurances and guarantees from their government to the African government, including promises of technology transfer and future cooperation. At this micro-level, the matching process is largely dependent on the type of buying organization—public or private (Table 13.1).

In another case, where a power plant was to be supplied to Nigeria, the vendor had to network with subcontractors and convince them that it would be beneficial for all of them to have a joint strategy and inform each other of their offers, etc. This was quite important, as the subcontractor for civil works (buildings, etc) was a local company in a foreign market, while the supplier of some material was a company from a third country. Through matching at this level, the vendor could, in fact, arrange an 'unofficial' consortium, without the buyer having knowledge of it.

In all business relations, both parties have some objectives when entering into negotiations. In project sales, the seller wants to sell his technology and/or services and the buyer wants to buy the same to satisfy his needs. The variations between parties with respect to objectives and environmental background tend to hinder the progress (process and the outcome) of negotiations. The market position at a particular time, the position of the parties in the market and the number of sellers and buyers also influence the negotiation process (Cateora and Ghauri, 1999).

The existence of both conflict and cooperation is thus the fundamental characteristic of the negotiation process, something to negotiate for and something to negotiate about. The parties have some common interests in finding a problem solution, which suits the supplier's ability and the user's need. At the same time, however, there is a conflict of interest; cost to one of them is income to the other. The perceived distance basically refers to the question of their inability to under-

TABLE 13.1 Negotiating international projects in the private and public sector (based on McCall, 1996, p. 196).

Issues	Public sector	Private sector
Underlying premises	Fair and negotiable price; value for money for general public	Market forces determine what the best offer under the circumstances is
Scope	Approved list of suppliers, tenders; in some cases, open procurement for large projects	Relationships, often open to all suppliers who are proactive
Original contact	Open call for tender; direct approach to select suppliers	Invitation to tender/offer; direct contacts often initiated by sellers
Constraints	Rules, regulations and procedures to follow; unclear authority	Varying national practices; extent of authority to be valued
Issues emphasized	Specifications to follow; formulas for cost and profit	Specifications; delivery time; price and service level
Price criteria	Influenced by policy; often the lowest price	Influenced by the unique advantages of the seller's offer and investment appraisal
Basis of negotiation	Standard form of contract based on tender notice	Sellers often to be matched with buyers' demand, conditions negotiable
Nature of negotiation	Cooperative to competitive, often confrontational at earlier stages; require information gathering to find mutual benefits; often need for closing concessions and adjustments.	Cooperative and to the point, easy transition to identify common grounds; little need for closing concessions or adjustments

stand each other. It is also dependent on inter-country and inter-firm psychic distance between the parties, and on the experience of doing business with each other. The power/dependence relation is one of the basic characteristics of negotiation. It is closely related to objective power relation, which depends on the value of the relationship to the parties and their available alternatives. Expectation is the last aspect of the atmosphere. Two different types of expectation are relevant. First, there are long-term expectations regarding the possibilities and value of future deals. Second, there are the short-term expectations concerning the prospects for the present deal.

The Negotiation Process

The process of international business negotiation presented here is divided into four different stages. A stage of the process refers to a specific part of the

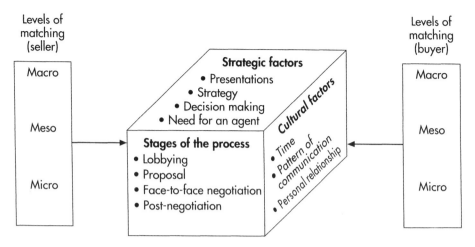

FIGURE 13.1 A model for project sales negotiations (based on Cateora and Ghauri, 1999 and Ghauri and Holstius, 1996).

negotiation process and includes all actions and communications by any party pertaining to negotiations made during that part. Parties communicate with each other to exchange information within each stage. A particular stage ends when parties decide to proceed further on to the next stage or decide to abandon the communication, if they see no point in further negotiations. In the lobbying stage, parties attempt to understand each other's needs and demands, which is done through information gathering and informal meeting. The proposal stage refers to the budget proposal (tender) and the final offer. The negotiation stage refers to face-to-face negotiations and the post-negotiation stage refers to the stage when parties have agreed to most of the issues and are to agree on contract language and format and signing of the contract.

In project sales negotiations, the process has three dimensions. In addition to the four stages, it has a cultural dimension and a strategic dimension. These two dimensions are present in each of the four stages of the process. However, these can play different roles in different stages. This is illustrated by Figure 13.1.

Stage I: Lobbying

This stage begins with the first contact between the parties in which a project is detected and an interest in doing business with each other is shown. All the lobbying and matching activities, analysing the project network, as described earlier are in fact done in this stage. This is done at all three levels—macro, meso and micro. At micro-level, some negotiations take place and tentative promises are made. The dynamism of the process can be observed at this early stage where parties begin to understand one another's needs and evaluate the benefits of entering into the process of negotiation.

The parties gather as much relevant information as possible on each other, the operating environment, the involvement of third parties, influencers, competitors and the infrastructure. Parties need to be aware that their relative power relationship can be altered at any time by such events as the repositioning of competitors, movements in exchange rates or public opinion. As we have defined this negotiation process as being of a problem-solving nature, the main issue here is to define the problem to be solved, the project and what it entails. It is important to define the problem jointly, as it will not only reflect each other's expectations but is also necessary to acquire commitment, on the content of the project, from both parties. The parties should, therefore, truly and openly discuss each other's objectives and expectations in order to achieve a positive problem-solving situation.

Informal meetings take place at all three levels as the parties examine each other's position. Whether the parties continue to the next stage of the negotiation process depends on the perceived level of cooperation or conflict, power or dependence and the expected benefits from the project/deal. The process often ends in failure if excessive conflict is sensed or if a successful future relationship seems doubtful. The parties truly see how they are going to cooperate, examine whether it is realistic to expect to achieve the objectives of both sides and to identify the obstacles that have to be overcome to achieve these objectives.

This stage is often more important than the formal negotiations in international projects. Social, informal relationships developed between negotiators at this stage can be of great help. Trust and confidence gained from these relationships increase the chances of agreement. One method of establishing such contacts is to invite individuals from the other side to visit your office/country in an attempt to develop trust. The prime objective here is to get at each other's priorities. The parties need to understand the interests and fears of the other party.

Stage II: Proposal

After the above, rather informal stage, the vendors prepare the budget proposal or, in the case of a bidding project, a bid. The budget proposal is often discussed back and forth until the vendor gives the final offer for the project. Depending on the lobbying and matching activities, mentioned above, the proposal or the bid may even be discussed informally to arrive at a final offer that matches both parties' expectations and needs. Moreover, the bid or proposal may also be revised or discussed, depending on the relationship between the parties, in relation to competing proposals and other competitor firms involved. It is also very important how the proposal is presented—personally, by mail, etc.

Parties also begin to formulate their strategy for face-to-face negotiation. By strategy, we mean a complete plan regarding problems, the solutions available and preferred choices, relative to the other party's choices and preferences. Parties try to build up their relative power. They compare the alternatives available, make checklists and assign arguments for and against these alternatives. They also decide on possible points of concession and their extent. Negotiation strategy is to be developed not only to handle the opposite party's wishes and demands but also to match or exceed competitor's offers.

Parties try to foresee and take precautions against predictable events. Remittance of funds, taxes and import duties and work permits are just some examples of the rules and regulations of the particular country that must be researched at this stage. An understanding of the infrastructure of the country and the company is also critical at this point. In some countries, especially when the public sector is the buyer, purchasing organizations issue a 'letter of award' (also called letter of

intent/acceptance or memorandum of understanding) after the first stage. Negotiators from Western countries often perceive this letter of award as a grant of
contract. However, this is an incorrect assumption, the letter merely indicates the
other party's intention to negotiate further. Quite often in the case of tenders, the
buyer studies all the tenders received and then sends this letter of award to some
shortlisted (two to four) suppliers, asking them to enter the next stage. This is an
indication that their tender is closer to the buyer's expectations, but needs to be
negotiated.

Parties to business negotiations should have an initial strategy that is dependent
on information attained so far and expectations. Negotiators should list problems
and issues, especially conflicting issues, and form strategies and choices for all
possible solutions they or the other party could suggest. These solutions should be
ranked as preferred, desired, expected and not acceptable. If not acceptable, a
solution that could be acceptable to the other party should be suggested. It is
thus important to have several solutions for each problem or issue. Before
entering the next stage, the vendor should also understand the nature of the
decision-making process of the buyer organization. Do they follow a collective
type of decision-making process, for instance, is there one dominating person who
makes the decision, is the final decision made by a government body/department
or business people?

Having gone through the lobbying stage, the vendor also needs to assess
whether they need an agent, interpreter or a consultant to handle some of the
difficult issues. This might be more important in international contracts as the
vendor might be unfamiliar with the local conditions and cultural aspects. An
agent and/or a consultant could be very useful in such cases. In many cases,
the agent may also be able to gather information on the competitors and their
offer. He might have better contacts with the buying organization and thus will be
able to get more information than a vendor can do himself.

Stage III: Face-to-face Negotiation

The basic issue at this stage is that parties believe that they can work together to
find a solution to a joint problem. The parties should also be aware that each side
views the situation, the matter under discussion, in its own way. Not only that
each side has a different perception of the process but also different expectations
for the outcome. It is therefore important to start face-to-face negotiation with an
open mind and to have several alternatives. At this stage, as the process continues,
parties should evaluate the alternatives presented by the other party and select
those that are compatible with their own expectations. The best way is to
determine criteria for judging the alternatives and then rank in order each alternative, your own as well as those presented by the other party, against these
criteria. Here the parties can even help each other in evaluating these alternatives
and can discuss the criteria for judgement. The main issue is to explore the
differences in preferences and expectations and to come closer to each other. It
is important to grasp the priorities of the other parties, because in that way you
can handle the negotiations more effectively, being flexible on their priorities and
firm on yours.

Experience shows that the negotiation process is controlled by the partner who arranges the agenda, since he can emphasize his own strengths and the other party's weaknesses, thus putting the other party on the defensive. However, the agenda may reveal the preparing party's position in advance and hence permit the other side to prepare its own counter-arguments on conflicting issues. Some negotiators prefer to start negotiations by discussing and agreeing on broad principles for the relationship. Another way to ensure success at this stage is to negotiate the contract step by step—discussing both conflicting issues and those of common interest. In particular, an initial discussion on items of common interest can create an atmosphere of cooperation between parties. The choice of strategy depends on the customer or supplier with whom you are negotiating. It is helpful to anticipate the other party's strategy as early as possible and then to choose a strategy to match or complement it.

It is often suggested that the negotiator should not agree to a settlement at once, even if there is considerable overlap of his position with that of the other party. The negotiator may obtain further concessions by prolonging the negotiation process. A number of studies have revealed that negotiators who directly submit a 'concession' can be at a disadvantage. In view of the diverse cultural and business traditions prevailing in different companies and countries, project sales negotiations inherently involve a discussion of differences. It is very difficult for parties to comprehend or adjust to each other's culture or traditions, but it is important to be aware of these differences. Social contacts developed between parties are far more significant than the technical and economic specifications in many emerging markets. Negotiators from some countries take their time and are very careful not to offend or use strong words and the other party is expected to follow suit.

A balance between firmness and credibility is important in all types of negotiations. It is important to give and take signals of readiness to move from the initial stage without making concessions. Negotiators having prior dealings with each other in normal business relations can easily send and receive signals, but in project sales it is very difficult for those meeting for the first time. Negotiators often send conditional signals such as 'We cannot accept your offer as it stands' or 'We appreciate that your equipment is quite suitable for us but not at the price you mentioned'.

It is also common that the party perceiving greater relative power makes fewer concessions and that the weaker party yields more, often to create a better atmosphere. Maintaining flexibility between parties and issues is of great importance in this stage. These usually occur after both parties have tested the level of commitment and have sent and received signals to move on; for example, the price can be reduced if the party offers better terms of payment. Other elements can be traded off but there may not be a way to evaluate them in accounting terms; for example, entry into a huge protected market may be strategically more important (see Chapter 6) than obtaining handsome profits on the present deal.

Stage IV: Post-negotiation

At this stage, all the terms have been agreed upon. The contract is being drawn up and is ready to be signed. Experience has shown that writing the contract and the language used can be a negotiation process in itself, as meanings and values may differ between the two parties. In several cases involving Western firms and emerging-country parties, the language used and the recording of issues previously agreed on took considerable time. This also happens when parties from two EU countries or even when parties from the same country are negotiating. This stage can lead to renewed face-to-face negotiation. Discussion should be summarized after negotiations to avoid unnecessary delays in the process. The terms agreed on should be read by both parties after concessions are exchanged and discussions held (e.g. by keeping minutes of meetings). This will help test the understanding of the agreement, as parties may have perceived issues or discussions differently. This not only applies to writing and signing the contract but also to its implementation. Trouble may arise later during the implementation of the contract if parties are too eager to reach an agreement and don't pay enough attention to details. The best way to solve this problem is to confirm that both sides thoroughly understand what they have agreed on before leaving the negotiating table. A skilled negotiator will summarize and test understanding: 'Do we understand correctly that if we agree to your terms of payment and repay the credit within 3 years from the date of the contract, you will reduce the price by 7%?'

Cultural Factors

As is apparent from the above discussion, cultural factors play an important role in international projects as well as in domestic negotiations. Different companies and organizations are used to different cultures regarding patterns of communication, treatment of time and formal vs. informal relationships. We have chosen to use the following factors that are most important in this respect.

Time

Time has different meanings and importance in different companies and cultures. While 'time is money' in the Western culture, it has no such value attached to it in many cultures in Asia, Latin America and Africa. This influences the pace of negotiations and the punctuality in meetings. For negotiators, it is important to have advance information on the opposite party's behaviour regarding time. This will help them to plan their time, as well as to have patience and not to get irritated during the process.

BOX 13.2 Time—A Many Cultured Thing.

One of the most serious causes of frustration and friction in cross-cultural business occurs when counterparts are out of sync with each other. Differences in understanding and valuing time often appear with respect to the place of time, its perceived nature and its function. Insights into a culture's view of time may be found in its sayings and proverbs:

- *Time is money*—USA.
- *Those who rush arrive first at the grave*—Spain.
- *The clock did not invent man*—Nigeria.
- *If you wait long enough, even an egg will walk*—Ethiopia.
- *Before the time, it is not yet the time; after the time, it's too late*—France.

Sources: Adapted from Hall and Hall (1990) and Wederspahn (1993–1994).

Most societies/cultures are *monochronic* (M-time) vs. *polychronic* (P-time). Cultures under monochronic time orientation do one thing at a time and tend to adhere to a preset agenda and schedules. If this pattern is disturbed (e.g. the agenda is not followed or things take longer than planned), M-people will point that out and would like to reinstate the agenda/schedule. Meetings in this case are properly planned from start to finish. On the other hand, P-time cultures/people tend to do several things at a time, are flexible and can easily modify agenda/schedule. They do not think that time is 'running away'. To M-time people, these cultures seem quite hectic, unsystematic and too flexible. P-time people are more concerned with people and social aspects than the agenda/schedule. When things take longer, they keep on discussing the issue and do not mind if it takes longer than planned or suggested by the agenda. In negotiations, distinction between and knowledge of P-time vs. M-time is important to avoid irritation and conflict.

According to monochronic time orientation, time has a past, present and future. If can be divided into smaller slots and then different tasks can be allocated to these slots. In this view, time is valuable and can be saved, spent, bought or wasted.

In the context of negotiations, time spent on developing personal relationships, protocols and on entertainment is considered crucial and useful. In some Western cultures (e.g. American) however, business people do not want to 'waste' time on these things and want to go directly to business-related issues:

> The American sense of urgency disadvantages them with respect to less hurried bargaining partners. Negotiators from other countries recognize Americans' time consciousness, achievement orientation and impatience. They know that Americans will make concessions close to their deadline (time consciousness) in order to get a signed contract (achievement orientation) (Ghauri and Usunier, 1996).

In many countries, the concept of preparing agendas for each meeting is not common. People with polychronic time orientation tend to negotiate globally and move from one issue to another and then back; while people with mono-chronic orientation tend to negotiate clauses separately, one thing at a time.

Pattern of Communication

Different cultures have different communication patterns as regards direct vs. indirect and explicit vs. implicit communication. These are related to culture as well as the contextual background of languages. Some languages are traditionally vague, and people from outside find it difficult to communicate with people with such language backgrounds. Indicators such as 'maybe', 'perhaps', 'rather', 'we will consider it' and 'inconvenient' are some examples of ambiguity in international communication and conversation. 'Maybe' and 'inconvenient' can mean impossible in some cultures. In some cultures even 'yes' means 'maybe' and 'perhaps' means 'no'. Some languages (e.g. Arabic and some Asian languages) traditionally contain exaggerations, fantastic metaphors and repetition, which can be misleading for foreigners. It is therefore important to be aware of these aspects and read between the lines. When representatives from two firms/ organizations meet to negotiate a project, their ability to communicate with each other influences the outcome and success of the negotiation. Successful communication, even between two individuals coming from the same culture, can be difficult as people use different contexts to distil words to their specific meanings. Moreover, all of us have selective hearing and different levels of curiosity attached to different things/subject matters. Depending on our background, education, training and environment, both the verbal and non-verbal symbols chosen for communication may not transmit the information as intended. This is particularly difficult when people come from two different cultures. Even if they speak the same language, the interpretations of specific words are less likely to be the same. The political and economic networks create a mismatch between the goals and objectives of the parties involved. The process of decision making differs between organizations and cultures, and can change communication from being decisive to tentative or general in nature.

This is even more important in non-verbal communication. The personal space, handshakes, ways of greeting each other, communication between males and females, signs of irritation, etc. are important aspects of communication patterns, and knowledge of these can improve the negotiation process and effectiveness. What is explicitly said is not necessarily what is implicitly meant. Understanding the non-verbal messages is extremely important in project sales negotiations. This can be done by being observant and through proper listening. Some ambiguous messages can be directly checked by asking questions and observing behaviour.

BOX 13.3 Do Green Computers Remind Americans of John Deere Tractors?

Green, America's favourite colour for suggesting freshness and good health, is often associated with disease in countries with dense green jungles; it is a favourite colour among Arabs but (at a certain time) was forbidden in portions of Indonesia. In Japan, green is a good high-tech colour, but Americans would shy away from green electronic equipment. Black is not universal for mourning: in many Asian countries it is white; it is purple in Brazil, yellow in Mexico and dark red in the Ivory Coast. In America, blue is the most masculine colour, but red is more manly in the UK or France. The most feminine colour in America and the UK is pink, while it is yellow in most of the world. Red is good fortune in China but death in Turkey. In America a candy wrapped in blue or green is probably a mint; in Africa the same candy would be wrapped in red, the colour for cinnamon in America and Europe . . . Lemon scent in the USA and UK suggests freshness; in the Philippines it is associated with illness. In Japan the number 4 is unlucky like the American and European 13; 7 is also unlucky in Ghana, Kenya and Singapore. The owl in India represents bad luck, like black cats in the USA or Europe. In Japan a fox is associated with witches. In China a green hat marks a man with an unfaithful wife. The stork symbolizes maternal death in Singapore, but birth in America and Europe.

Source: Adapted from Copeland and Griggs (1986).

Emphasis on personal relations

Different cultures give different importance to personal relations in negotiations. In many countries, the negotiators are more concerned with the issue at hand and the future relationship between organizations, irrespective of who is representing these firms, while in some cultures the personality of the negotiator is more important than the organization he is representing or the importance of an issue. The emphasis on personal relations can thus be different in different nego-tiations. Negotiators from Spain may have a totally different behaviour than negotiators from Germany or the UK. In project marketing a major concern is to balance relationship and deal-orientation. In this case, the parties normally do not have a long-term business relationship, unlike in most cases, and have to develop trust and a mutually trustworthy relationship. The more the parties trust each other, the easier it is to persuade and to be receptive to each other's messages and agreements. As we know, some cultures put great value/emphasis on personal relationships and friendship. However, it is not just a cultural thing, as our earlier chapters have explained. Analysing and developing protocol with the milieu, 'the law of the milieu', is most important (see Figure 13.2).

Western business people are considered to be more 'task-oriented' and less 'small talk-oriented', while people from Asia, the Middle East and even Southern Europe often are more concerned with first making the personal con-nection before coming to the task.

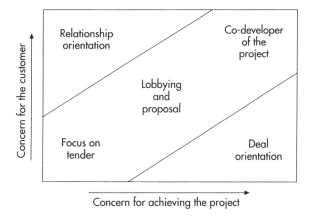

FIGURE 13.2 Relationship vs. deal orientation.

There are clear behavioural aspects in different cultures. As indicated by Hofstede's (1984) study of 69 countries, we can place different countries on different scales. Even countries in Western Europe have clear differences in this respect. In the case of negotiation, it is important to have knowledge of this cultural attribute, as it will help us to understand the behaviour of the other party and to formulate an effective strategy. Knowing whether the opposite party is looking for a collective solution or an individual benefit will help in formulation of arguments and presentations.

BOX 13.4 The USA though the Eyes of Foreign Managers.

The globalization of US markets means that more foreign managers are going to the USA to live. The problem of cultural adaptation and adjustment is no less a problem for them than for Americans going to their countries to live. Here are a few observations from the other side—from foreigners in the USA.

'There are no small eggs in America,' says a Dutchman. There are only jumbo, extra large, large and medium.' This is no country for humility.

'For a foreigner to succeed in the United States . . . he needs to be more aggressive than in his own culture because Americans expect that.'

Young Japanese people have difficulty addressing American superiors in a manner that shows self-confidence and an air of competence. Japanese people simply cannot stand up straight, puff up their chests, look the Americans in the eyes and talk at the same time. Japanese, who are experts at being members of teams, need help in learning to compete, take initiative and develop leadership skills.

Schedules and deadlines are taken very seriously. How quickly one does a job is often as important as how well one does the job.

A Latin American has to refrain from the sort of socializing he would do in Latin countries where rapport comes before deal making. 'Here that is not necessary,' he says. 'You can even do business with someone you do not like.'

Americans say, 'Come on over sometime,' but the foreigner learns—perhaps after an awkward visit—that this is not really an invitation.

'Living alone in the United States is very sad, so much loneliness. Of course, living alone in Japan is also lonely, but in this country we can't speak English so fluently, so it is difficult to find a friend.'

Source: Adapted from Copeland (1986).

Strategic Factors

Negotiation strategy in project marketing refers to a well-thought-through plan and approach. It helps the negotiators connect objectives with operational tools. It specifies the actions and also the expected reactions from the other parties and then actions to handle those reactions. It is a road map that explains where you want to go (with the deal) and how each phase of the process will help you get there.

While negotiating in an international setting, the parties have to prepare thoroughly with respect to how to present things, which type of negotiation strategy should be used and which type of decision-making process is followed by the other party. Whether or not they need an agent or an outside consultant is also a question of strategy.

Presentations

In project marketing, sellers have to, sooner or later, present what they can propose for the particular project. In some cases, it is done in a rather informal setting, while, in others, it is done only in writing (e.g. in closed tender projects). In any case, negotiators have to know whether the presentations to be made are carried out in a formal or informal setting. Whether these are to be made to teams, as in China and Eastern Europe, or to individuals, as in India and the Middle East. The formal vs. informal presentation style is very distinct in many countries. If unprepared, the negotiators can make serious blunders at an early stage of negotiations. It is also important to know whether issues can be presented in groups or whether each issue should be handled individually, and whether presentations should be argumentative or informative, factual and to the point. Moreover, should some or all of the material be translated or not? In some projects, this is crucial. Some countries (e.g. The Netherlands, Sweden, India and Pakistan) are quite comfortable with English, while other countries (e.g. Italy, Greece, China and Russia) might want documents and presentations in their own language.

Negotiation Strategy

A strategy for project negotiation should include (a) the most important priority— basic interest; (b) a list of issues, what is negotiable and what is not; (c) how to convey firmly the above to the other party without offending them or without discussing too much; (d) scheduling of concessions, what to give up when and in exchange of what (Ghauri and Usunier, 1996). While formulating a strategy, it is also important to define common grounds and the overlap between our and the other party's basic interest and priorities. This overlap in priorities should be stressed in the strategy and in negotiations as it will lead to more problem-solving negotiations (integrative) rather than conflict-resolution negotiations (distributive).

At the outset, there are several types of strategy in business negotiations. The most important are tough, soft or intermediate strategies. In tough strategy, a party starts with a rather high initial offer and remains firm on its offer and expects the other party to make the first concession. In soft strategy, a party does not start with a very high initial offer and makes the first concession in the hope that the other party will reciprocate. In intermediate strategy, a party does not start with a very high initial offer and, as soon as an offer is made which is within its realistic expectations, it accepts it. It is important to have information on the opposite party's strategy and to adapt one's own strategy to it and to have a counter-offer ready. Strategy is not only about what we want to achieve and do, it is equally about what we choose not to do. It is therefore important to have a clean understanding about the consequences of not getting this project or getting a project without achieving the basic interest/priority.

Decision making

As for the decision-making process, there are clear behavioural aspects in different organizations and cultures. According to Hofstede's (1984) study of 69 countries, we place different countries on different scales. The countries in Western Europe have very clear differences in this respect. For project negotiations, some knowledge on the other party's overall decision-making pattern is necessary. Do they follow individual or collective decision making? This will also be useful feedback on whether the party is looking for a collective solution or individual/one company benefit.

Some information on the other party's overall decision making pattern is necessary before going into negotiations. Does the party use impulsive or rational decision making? Who makes the decisions? Do the negotiators coming to the table have the power to make final decisions or not? These are issues which are important to know in advance. In many cultures, decision-making is highly influenced by the importance of face-saving and influences the timing of decisions made. Here the role of third parties in a particular decision is of utmost importance and the vendor must have this knowledge.

Need for an agent

It is part of strategy formulation to realize whether or not the firm or negotiators can handle the particular negotiation on their own. What type of cost and benefits can be achieved by employing an agent for a particular negotiation process? Quite often, companies are reluctant to pay apparently heavy fees to agents or consultants for the business they believe they can handle themselves. In our opinion, the more unfamiliar or complicated the other party or the market, the greater is the need for an agent or a consultant. Because in these markets companies do need some assistance. Otherwise, they might risk losing the project. These days, specialized agents and consultants are available for different geographic as well as technology areas. There are enormous efficiencies to be achieved by using their expertise. In some cases, agents are needed to open doors for you so that you can meet the real decision makers. For a project marketer, sometimes it is not easy to identify or locate the decision makers or the powerful influencers. Local agents are helpful not only during the lobbying stage, but also during the face-to-face negotiations. They can help in understanding and interpreting the hidden messages and complexities of cross-cultural communication. But, as seen in the Finsys case (Chapter 6), not all agents are equal, and some of them are even counterproductive for the supplier, if they are not carefully selected.

Planning and Managing Negotiations

Dozens of books have been written about negotiation, many of which I disagree with. I don't believe in negotiating through intimidation, fear, bluffing or dishonest tactics. A good negotiation concludes as a good deal for everyone. Negotiation starts with what you want to accomplish. Then the realities and, sometimes, the complexities enter the picture. Sometimes many points of view and many elements have to be considered, but the deal itself must always be kept in view. Your first step should be to rid yourself of an adversarial position. The reality is that you have a mutual problem, which you are going to solve to your mutual advantage. The intention must be to structure a deal that resolves the problem and gives each of you what you want. It's not always possible, of course. When it can't be done, you are better off making no deal than making a bad deal. A bad deal usually brings a future filled with enormous problems. Negotiating demands recognition of reality on many levels. Only amateurs try to accomplish something that isn't real or possible; it is an attempt that inevitably leads to failure. Amateurs tend to dream; professionals consider the realities of a deal (Nadel, 1987).

In the past, the ability to negotiate was considered innate or instinctive but it is now regarded as a technique, which can be learned. Experimental studies, empirical observations and experience have made it possible to grasp the art of negotiation. This section provides some guidelines for planning and managing the negotiation process in the four stages.

The most important success factor in negotiation is preparation and planning. One may have excellent negotiating skills, persuasive and convincing communication style, a strong market position and relative power, but all these cannot overcome the shortcomings caused by poor preparation. As mentioned in the previous section, the presence of cooperation as well as conflict and the relative power/dependence in international business negotiation demands careful preparation and planning. In the problem-solving approach, this becomes even more important as both parties do truly want to do business with each other. In spite of this cooperative behaviour, negotiation involves trade-off between own and joint interests.

Managing Lobbying Stage

As stressed throughout the book, analysing and developing relationships within the network around a particular project is very important. When negotiating, the selling company needs to establish relationships at three different levels. This demands lobbying at macro-, meso- and micro-levels. As we have discussed the three levels earlier, here we discuss only micro-level lobbying and how the seller should handle this stage with the buyer.

Prepare

Before courting the other party, the seller needs, first, see whether this project is suitable for him or not. This can be in respect to capabilities, resources, other obligations and projects at hand.

The initial points to consider are issues such as implications of the deal, the interests at stake, the 'fit' with organizational objectives and possible economic, political or other restrictions between parties. What will each gain or lose and how important is the deal for them? What alternatives does either side have? These issues must be considered in terms of tangible and intangible motives.

Comparison of one's own and the other party's strengths and weaknesses is quite important. In business negotiations, the other party does not only include the buyer or the party you are negotiating with, but also the competitors who also have an interest in the same business. In most cases, a party's arguments or preferences are influenced by the offers other competitors have made. Many negotiators use professional investigators for this task of getting information on the other parties and the competitors to find their weaknesses. According to one estimate, in the USA and France, billions of dollars are spent annually on industrial spying. In our opinion, the information required to prepare the plan for negotiation need not include such underhand methods. It is quite easy to get a lot of information from the annual accounts of firms and by talking to their executives, customers and suppliers. However, you need to have some sort of scanning activities, as discussed earlier, for forthcoming projects. Lobbying needs to be started at a very early stage, perhaps as a co-constructor/developer of the idea for the project (see Chapter 11). From the beginning you have to identify important parties/actors and develop relationships with them, preferably before they ask you to send a proposal for the project.

BOX 13.5 Dark Glasses: Not Coolness but Prudence.

A psychologist at the University of Chicago discovered that the eye is a very sensitive indicator of how people respond to a situation. When you are interested in something, your pupils dilate; if somebody says something you don't like, they tend to contract. But the Arabs have known about the pupil response for hundreds if not thousands of years.

Arabs may watch the pupils of your eyes to judge your responses to different topics. Because people can't control the response of their eyes, which is a dead giveaway, many Arabs wear dark glasses, even indoors. By watching pupils, Arabs can respond rapidly to mood changes. That's one of the reasons why they use a closer conversational distance than Westerners do. To watch the pupils of each other's eyes, two conversing Arabs would stand twice as close to one another than two Westerners would do.

Pupil watching would be difficult to master for a Westerner because we are taught in the West not to stare: it is too intense, too sexy or too hostile. It also may mean that we are not totally tuned into the situation. Maybe we should all wear dark glasses.

Source: Adapted from Cateora and Ghauri (1999).

In international business relations, buy-back arrangements and other countertrade agreements (see Chapter 12) are becoming more common, and in large international projects buyers are demanding some sort of buy-back. Emerging countries engage in countertrade deals to correct their trade deficits as well as to earn hard currency. It is important to calculate deals in monetary terms when conducting trade in this medium. The seller might end up with goods which cannot be easily marketed in the home country. The countertrade demand can be just a bluff, so that the seller who seeks to avoid the expenses of buy-back may offer a major price discount. The plant's output supplied under the particular contract is part of the payment in some cases. China uses its cheap labour and re-exports products from local plants to the seller's country. Another example is the iron-producing Carajas project in northern Brazil. Most of the production of this complex is exported to Japan to pay for project financing.

Gather Information

Key information needs to be collected prior to you making a proposal and committing yourself. You have to collect information on the costs, rules and regulations of the particular market. Who will be the people involved and their priorities. What is the project network? Is it the government, trade unions or other groups who may be involved in one way or another?

To negotiate effectively, the marketer must gather information on the strengths and weaknesses not only of the opposite party, but also of other related parties such as competitors. By considering the resources and behaviour of competitors, marketers can develop their own options on different issues. There are several strategies by which the seller can pre-empt competitors (e.g. offering credit to the buyer, price reductions or long guarantee periods). Sellers must also allow for alternative solutions to conflicting issues. Question your own position: 'What if they do not accept this?'

Build up Relative Power

Negotiators can determine who has the relative power advantage by gathering information about the other party, considering each party's position and developing different alternatives. They can try to build their own relative power by developing arguments against the elements of power and improving their own position. In the negotiation process, this kind of power may be increased by repeatedly mentioning the weak points of the other party. The uncertainty regarding infrastructure and exchange rates must be handled here. Parties can agree on adjustments in the event of exchange rate variations. The party with greater information automatically acquires more power. The negotiator may have to work as a detective to ascertain the buyer's needs, his strong and weak points and the strong and weak points of competitors. By being active in the negotiation process, an experienced negotiator can build up information in order to gain relative power. This can be done by asking the other party questions. It can also be done by giving conditional answers such as '*If* you agree to pay cash … *then* we can consider looking at our price,' or '*What if* we agree to pay cash *perhaps then* you can lower the price by 5%.'

Managing Face-to-face Negotiation Stage

Negotiation Team

A difficult question arises regarding who should conduct negotiations whenever a deal is to be made in a new market. Who is the most appropriate person to hammer out a particular deal? In fact, persons involved in international business negotiation can do more harm than good if they lack an integrated knowledge of their own firm and the objective of the deal. Whoever is selected for negotiations must have a good grasp of the deal's implications. This is especially true when long-term relationships are being discussed. One way to minimize this risk is to appoint a negotiation team, where the key members are selected from different departments.

It is important for management to realize that the selected person(s) should be replaceable without creating organizational problems. When replacement is necessary, management must be able to escape deadlock. Sometimes negotiations end in an impasse and you may have to start with new players. It is also possible that the selected negotiators and the other party cannot reach a meeting of minds if there is a clash of personal chemistry. It may become necessary to change negotiators in such situations. This discussion gives rise to another question. From which level should the executives for the negotiations be chosen? In most countries, parties expect to negotiate with members of equal status. The managing director from one side expects to negotiate with his counterpart. It is advisable that firms match like with like.

Parties need to consider not only who should represent the company but also the number of negotiators (i.e. whether we opt for individual or team negotiations). Team negotiation affords marketers the opportunity to benefit from the advice and guidance of many participants. It is difficult for a single individual to be adept in all kinds of commercial, technical and legal issues. In bigger projects, there are several issues to be considered, such as the subcontractors, the production capacity and the financial and legal situation. The best way, however, is to conform to the opposite party. If the opposite side is sending a team, then so should we.

Quite often, negotiators believe they have only three options: (i) persuasion, (ii) threat or (iii) concession. In fact, there are many alternative solutions to a problem. Different issues can be combined to produce many alternatives. If the customer demands a 5% concession on price, the other party can ask the customer to pay cash instead of the 1-year credit proposed. In one case, the buyer demanded a 5% concession on the contract price after everything else had been agreed. The seller instead proposed that he was willing to give a 10% rebate on all spare parts to be bought by the buyer during the next 3 years. This offer was accepted gladly by the buyer. One way of creating alternatives is to judge each conflicting issue on a scale from our ideal position to their ideal position. Here we should look for overlaps. Is there any overlap of our and their position? If not, how can we create an overlap? What is their minimum acceptable position? What is our minimum acceptable position? Can we move from there, perhaps give up on this issue and gain in another way which is not so sensitive to the other party, but equally important to us?

Be Understanding

For negotiations to be successful, one party must understand the other party's position. This will help each side interpret and anticipate the other side's reactions to the argument. Anticipating and developing rational reactions to the argument allows each party to formulate new arguments and alternatives. This stimulates flexibility towards conflicting issues. Each party has to recognize the needs of the other, quite apart from gathering information and asking questions to check the other party's position. Being a patient listener will help improve negotiations. We can understand the meaning behind the words by listening attentively. We can create a positive and cooperative atmosphere in the negotiation process by showing the other party that he or she is well understood. However, be careful while listening—it is not what is said, but how it is said that is more important and we should try and read between the lines.

The harder a party tries to show understanding of the opposing viewpoint, the more open it will be to alternative solutions. A universal feeling exists that those who understand are intelligent and sympathetic. Parties feel obliged to reciprocate in these situations. The ability to look at the situation from the other's point of view is one of the most important skills in negotiation. It is important not only to look at things as the other party sees them, but also to understand the other party's point of view and the power of his argument.

Manage the Communication

The information exchanged must be adjusted for easier comprehension by the other party. Technical specifications and other material should be provided in the local language. Not only does this facilitate effective communication but it also demonstrates respect for the local language and environment.

The problems of perception and language barriers often cause difficulties in the negotiation process. This is frustrating and places an added burden on all parties involved in the negotiating process. Different cultures interpret messages differently. An octopus is said to have several arms in the USA. It is said to have several legs in Japan. In Sweden, 'next Sunday' does not mean the coming Sunday but the Sunday after. In India, 'next Sunday' means the coming Sunday. 'Nice weather' means sunshine in Europe. 'Nice weather' means cloudy or rainy weather in Africa and many Asian countries. The exchange of gifts and terms of reciprocity are quite normal in Asia, yet considered close to a bribe in many Western countries. It is important that negotiators adopt appropriate behaviour for each negotiation. The chosen arguments should be tailored to the particular customer. One standard argument cannot be used throughout the world. Barriers to communication also arise from real or perceived differences in expectations, which create conflict instead of cooperation between parties.

In cross-cultural negotiations, *non-verbal communication*, in particular in the expression of emotions and the attitude of a negotiator toward the other party, is sometimes more important than the spoken language. Non-verbal communication can be telling. Liking, disliking, tensions and appraisal of an argument are shown by numerous signs such as blushing, contraction of facial muscles, giggling, strained laughter or just silence. People, sitting down, lean forward when they like what you are saying or are interested in listening, or they sit back on their seat with crossed arms if they do not like the message. Nervousness can manifest itself through non-verbal behaviour, and blinking can be related to feelings of guilt and fear. It is difficult to evaluate non-verbal communication, as it is connected to the subconscious and emotions. Effective communication and understanding of people will assist you in adjusting your arguments to the moods and expectations of the other party. Negotiators may continue to hold out, not because the proposal from the other side is unacceptable, but because they want to avoid feelings of surrender. Sometimes simple rephrasing of the proposal or a different approach to the presentation can alleviate the problem.

What Makes a Good Negotiator?

A number of studies identify the characteristics of a good negotiator. A marketer's personality and social behaviour are of equal importance to social contacts and formal negotiation in many countries.

Depending on their behaviour, negotiators are often grouped into different categories, such as bullies, avoiders or acceptors. Bullies want to threaten, push, demand or attack. Avoiders like to avoid conflicting situations and hide in fear of making a wrong decision or being held responsible. They will normally refer to their superiors for a final decision, 'I have to call my head office ...'. Acceptors always give a very positive answer and say 'Yes' to almost anything, which makes it difficult to realize which 'Yes' is 'Yes' and which 'Yes' is 'Maybe', and whether he will be able to deliver what he is promising or not. The best way to handle these behaviour types is to first identify them and then confront them by drawing a limit, helping them feel safe and by asking them how and when they would be able to do what they are promising. We have to be tactical while confronting these types because, sometimes, they themselves are not aware of their behaviour.

Patience

It is essential to know the negotiators' precise authority. In Eastern Europe and China, one team may negotiate one day, followed by a fresh team the next day. When this process is repeated a number of times, it becomes very difficult for negotiators to establish who is the negotiating party and who has the final authority. One of the characteristics of a good negotiator is the ability to discover the timetable of the other party and allow plenty of time for the negotiation process. It is usually not feasible to expect to fly to a distant country, wrap things up and be home again in a week. Nor is it reasonable to coerce a party that is not ready to reach a decision. Negotiations with emerging market customers take a long time! Patience and time are the greatest assets a project negotiator can have while negotiating with customers from these markets. Some negotiators take their time, discussing all issues and justifying their role through tough negotiations.

Negotiators must be in a position to change their strategies and arguments, as the process of negotiation is highly dynamic. They must be flexible. The other party will often ask questions, probing the seller's weaknesses, just to provoke and obtain more concessions. It is important to keep calm and find out first if the questions asked are relevant and justified. Negotiators can use this in their favour if questions are not justified and the buyer has wrong information. A good negotiator is not just a person who can conclude an apparently good contract for the company or one who can arrive at a contract in a short time; a good negotiator is one whose agreements lead to successful implementation.

Managing Post-negotiation Stage

What Is a Good Outcome?

A good agreement is one which leads to successful implementation. There are many examples of firms getting into trouble because they could not implement the contract conditions of a particular deal. Therefore, in some cases, no agreement may be a better outcome for the firm. A good outcome benefits both parties and does not make either party feel that it has a less advantageous contract. Sometimes, negotiators want to avoid specifying some issues and want to keep them ambiguous. It is important to understand that, on the one hand, ambiguity can lead to reopening of the conflict later on in the implementation stage, and, on the other hand, if we want to specify such issues, it might prolong the negotiation process or prevent an agreement. Sometimes, this ambiguity is unintended, whereas, on other occasions, it is intentionally deployed to speed up the process or to give the impression that the particular issue needs to be renegotiated.

It is normally considered that a good business deal is one which provides financial gains. But what were the objectives of the firm when it decided to enter into negotiations? Was it the present project which was most important or was it future projects? The outcome must be related to the firm's objectives. If the objectives have been met, then it is a good outcome. A successful negotiation is not a question of 'win–lose' but a problem-solving approach to a 'win–win' outcome.

The main purpose of the contract is to avoid misunderstandings and trouble in the future. The agreement should foster relationship development and be flexible enough to deal with expected or unexpected future changes. The language and terminology used in the contract must be simple and clear. It must not be necessary to seek legal help every time the contract is consulted.

Chapter 14

PRACTICAL GUIDELINES

The purpose of this chapter is to provide some practical guidelines for managers about how to organize their marketing efforts. While doing so, we keep in mind the project marketing process and the development of the functional as well as relational position. In addition, we discuss the key issues in different project components such as screening, project development, offer formulation and negotiations.

Many companies working with project marketing follow some type of procedures and guidelines while preparing to formulate an offer for a certain project. We try to provide some guidelines that can help companies to do the same, but more systematically. In the following sections, we present the points that are general in nature but specific to that particular stage in a project. These points must be adapted to specific characteristics of the project, such as the industry, geographical location and specific customers. The appropriateness and depth of coverage will depend also on the company's objectives, milieu and other parties at macro- and meso-levels.

Designing Strategic Priorities

In order to focus the resources of the company on specific targets which will allow anticipation of projects, the marketer needs to define priorities concerning several elements (Chapter 6):

1 Diagnosing company competencies and resources, both internal and external (allies, partners, subsidiaries, agents, etc.). As a result, the company will have a clearer idea of where to focus its actions and what to propose.
2 Targeting market segments relying on the market attractiveness/strength logic.

3 Defining key customers on the basis of ability to manage long-term customer relationships.
4 Designing the global offer for various segments/customers according to the characteristics of each segment or key customer. This design encapsulates three main decisions: (i) components of the offer, (ii) parameters of the offer and (iii) pre-assembled offers.
5 Selecting geographical zones according to country factors and investing in local network intelligence. Here networking needs to be the drive at macro-, meso- and micro-levels.
6 Matching the selection of geographical zones as well as projects with company objectives in the short and long term alike.

Developing a Functional Position

As it is impossible to totally anticipate the project offer, the company has to develop a process of adjustment of its global offer to the specifications of the context (Chapters 6, 10 and 11):

1 Translate the global offer into pseudo-projects dedicated to limited groups of customers or to specific technical problems.
2 Capitalize on internal and external resources and competencies in order to maintain a potential offer.
3 Update the parameters and components of the potential offer according to the interaction with key actors and/or key customers.
4 Screen projects according to the resulting functional position.

Developing a Relational Position 1—Milieu Analysis

The objective is to be in a position to detect projects far upstream though networking with business and non-business actors within the milieu (Chapter 8). The idea is to know about opening projects before your competitors do, so that you can start developing your position in the project 'milieu':

1 Gather information on an activity in a territory, in order to highlight key actors and 'experts'.
2 Interview 'experts' who can provide you with information about institutional and individual actors, their roles, their profiles, their relationships and the quality of these relationships.
3 Map the milieu in order to understand the relational position of the actors, the competitors and your company (sociogram).
4 Establish a relational development plan detailing the resource allocation framework (time, costs, people, etc.) according to the portfolio of actors.

Developing a Relational Position 2—Customer Analysis

The objective is to be in a position to detect the project far upstream through customer intimacy and long-term relationships (Chapter 9):

1 Defining the relevant unit of customer analysis: Is it the entire industrial group or a subunit of this group (a business unit, a site, a subsidiary, etc.)?
2 Selecting the criteria that constitute the two dimensions of customer analysis: 'customer attractiveness' and 'vulnerability of other relationship'.
3 Building the matrix of your portfolio of customers and defining generic strategic orientations for each group of customers.
4 Allocating resources to each customer according to his position within the customer portfolio's matrix.
5 Fighting against discontinuity of the relationship with the customer by combining mixed activities: after-sale and pre-sale services, intermediaries and friendships.
6 Creating a ritual framework to structure the actions devoted to limiting discontinuity of the extra-business relationship.

Screening Projects

The rationale for this section is to provide guidelines on how to manage relationships with key actors and customers in a given milieu. Managing such relationships leads to the early detection of projects. These early detected projects do not all have the same value for the supplier. The screening process allows the supplier to define the level of investment to be made on each project (Chapter 10):

1 Evaluate the attractiveness of a project along two major blocks of criteria; one related to short-term 'project interest', the other related to long-term 'development of the activity'.
2 Assess the strengths of your company in this project along the two components of project competitive position: 'functional position' and 'relational position'.
3 As a project cannot be judged in isolation and needs to be compared with other project opportunities, the screening process implies using a matrix of project portfolios and comparing the attractiveness of projects analytically.
4 According to the position of the project in the matrix in relation to company workload and the cost of tender preparation, the level of involvement of the supplier in this project is decided.
5 Starting from this decision (go/no-go), the project becomes the focus of the marketing approach.

Mode of Entry

Projects are complex transactions which require suppliers to group their competencies into a consortium of firms in order to formulate an offer meeting customer's specifications. This provides the suppliers with a multitude of options by which to enter the project pyramid, from main contractor to supplier of parts (Chapter 10):

1   Assess the choice spectrum available to your company in the project pyramid according to the company's position in the activity chain and the degree of freedom of movement allowed in this chain.
2   According to its position in the project portfolio matrix, the mode of entry is quasi-predetermined if you stick solely to a project-driven approach.
3   The result of the project portfolio matrix must be encapsulated in a wider perspective which also includes relational logic and the market-as-network logic.
4   Compare the ideal position in the project pyramid with the behaviours and stakes of the other actors who join the consortium to make a proposal.

Project Development

The marketing tactics of project development aim at becoming actively involved in shaping the project at three stages: independent of any project to create the project, pre-tender to write the rules of the game in conjunction with the customer and key actors and during tender preparation to deconstruct and recreate the project (Chapter 11):

1   In any case, do not just focus on the expressed needs of the customer but include in your analysis everything that is at stake for the customer.
2   Keeping in mind the latent needs of the customer, you must help him to discover his problems by means of storytelling and metaphors.
3   Identifying the problem, the customer himself becomes the ambassador of the problem. You must, as a consultant, coach him in order to progressively develop the project.
4   Now that the customer is able to express his needs and state his problems accurately, he can articulate his vision of the solution that you support.

Project Offer

Formulating the project offer is not an isolated task but the result of the complete marketing process. In fact, the best offer strategy is the construction of the demand. Consequently, the project offer is largely based on the vision of a solution jointly developed with the customer and his network (Chapter 12):

1   In order to develop a solution for the customer and his network, you must put into play your competencies in four different dimensions: technical, financial, political and societal.
2   In order to build the project offer, you must not start from your competencies

but from the client's vision of a solution and integrate 'everything', internal or external, that creates value for the client and for the actors in his network.

3   In the case of offset requirements, it is important not to treat them separately from the other dimensions of the project offer. The mobilization of local partners is thus of paramount importance in the conceptualization and fulfilment of the offset component of an offer.

4   The ability to mobilize a supporting network of subcontractors and other subnetworks in the buying country is vital for the development of a competitive offset offer.

Negotiating Projects

As all the offer components have been dealt with in earlier sections, here we provide some guidelines for face-to-face negotiations. In most projects, parties from different cultures and countries are involved. That means that the communication process and understanding of each other's interests and behaviours become very important. In project marketing, culture is not the only problem that causes uncertainty, the nature of this business is such that there is discontinuity and parties do not meet each other on a regular basis. We have synthesized the following guidelines from Chapter 13:

1   Formulate an appropriate strategy that fits your objectives and define common as well as conflicting issues. Strategy also means that you need to choose what not to do and what is not acceptable. Quite often, 'no contract' is the best option.

2   Check your offer and prepare alternatives asking yourself, 'What if they do not accept this?' (e.g. the price).

3   Be prepared for some 'tough' negotiations. The best strategy is to match your strategy with the other party's strategy.

4   Control your concessions. Concessions are viewed and interpreted in two opposite ways: as a sign of openness and willingness to cooperate or as a sign of weakness and readiness to yield.

5   Be flexible with the negotiation agenda, especially if the other party does not want to follow it strictly. Interconnect different issues (e.g. price can be reduced if the other party offers better terms of payment).

6   Manage the communication process efficiently, considering language and other cultural differences. Beware of implicit meanings. The best way is to check and verify; for example, 'Do we understand correctly that if we decrease the price by 5%, you will be able to pay the whole amount within 6 months?'

7   Observe non-verbal communication. This can be done by learning something about the other party's culture. By carefully observing body language, you can read the message between the lines. This is particularly important when people are not speaking their native language.

REFERENCES

Abell, D. F. and Hammond, J. S. (1979) *Strategic Marketing Planning: Problems and Analytical Approaches*. Englewood Cliffs, NJ: Prentice-Hall.

Ahlström, M. (2000) 'Offset Management for Large Systems: A Multibusiness Marketing Activity', *Linköping Studies in Management and Economics*, Dissertation No. 44.

Albaum, G., Strandskov, J., Duerr, E. and Dowd, L. (1989) *International Marketing and Export Management*. Wokingham, UK: Addison-Wesley.

Al-Tabtabai, H. (2000) 'Modeling the Cost of Political Risk in International Construction Projects', *Project Management Journal*, **31**(3), 4–14.

Anderson, J. C. and Narus, J. A. (1999). *Business Market Management: Understanding, Creating and Delivering Value*. Englewood Cliffs, NJ: Prentice-Hall.

Atamer, T. and Calori, R. (1993). *Diagnostic et Décisions Stratégiques*. Paris: Dunod.

Axelsson, B. and Johanson, J. (1988) 'Internationalization as Network Processes'. Proceedings of the 4th International Marketing and Purchasing Conference, Manchester, September.

Bansard, D., Cova, B. and Salle, R. (1993) 'Project Marketing: Beyond Competitive Bidding Strategies', *International Business Review*, **2**(2), 125–141.

Baron, D. P. (1995) 'The Nonmarket Strategy System', *Sloan Management Review*, Fall, 75–85.

Belk, R. W. and Coon, G. S. (1993) 'Gift Giving as Agapic Love: An Alternative to the Exchange Paradigm Based on Dating Experience', *Journal of Consumer Research*, **20**, December, 393–417.

Bell, C. (1992) *Ritual Theory, Ritual Practice*. Oxford: Oxford University Press.

Ben Mahmoud-Jouini, S. (2000) 'Comment Passer d'une Démarche Réactive à une Demarche Proactive Fondée sur des Stratégies d'Offre Innovante', in A. Bloch and D. Manceau (eds), *De l'Idée au Marche: Innovation et Lancement de Produit*, pp. 361–380. Paris: Vuibert.

Björkman, I. and Kock, S. (1995) 'Social Relationships and Business Networks: The Case of Western Companies in China', *International Business Review*, **4**(4), 519–535.

Bonaccorsi, A., Pammolli, F. and Tani, S. (1996) 'The Changing Boundaries of System Companies', *International Business Review*, **5**(6), 539–560.

Boston Consulting Group (1970) *The Product Portfolio Concept*. Boston: Boston Consulting Group.

Bosworth, M. T. (1995) *Solution Selling: Creating Buyers in Difficult Selling Markets*. New York: McGraw-Hill.

Boughton, P. (1987) 'The Competitive Bidding: Beyond Probability Models', *Industrial Marketing Management*, **16**, 87–94.

Buckley, P. and Ghauri, P. (eds) (2002) *International Mergers and Acquisitions*. London: ITB Press.

Caillé, A. and Godbout, J. T. (1992) *L'Esprit du Don*. Paris: La Découverte.

Callon, M. (ed.) (1989) *La Science et ses Réseaux: Genèse et Circulation des Faits Scientifiques*. Paris: La Découverte.

Campbell, N. C. G. and Cunningham, M. T. (1983) 'Customer Analysis for Strategy Development in Industrial Markets', *Strategic Management Journal*, **4**, 369–380.

Cateora, P. and Ghauri, P. (1999) *International Marketing: European Edition*, p. 132. London: McGraw-Hill.

Copeland, L. (1986) 'Managing in the Melting Pot', *Across the Board*, June, 52–59.

Copeland, L. and Griggs, L. (1986) *Going International*, p. 63. New York: Plume.

Cova, B. and Crespin-Mazet, F. (1997) 'Joint Construction of Demand: The Dynamic of Supplier-Client Interaction in Project Business', in H. G. Gemunden, T. Ritter and A. Walter (eds), *Relationships and Networks in International Markets*, pp. 343–359. Oxford: Pergamon Press.

Cova, B. and Holstius, K. (1993) 'How to Create Competitive Advantage in Project Business', *Journal of Marketing Management*, **9**, 105–121.

Cova, B. and Hoskins, S. (1997) 'A Twin-Track Networking Approach to Project Marketing', *European Management Journal*, **15**(5), 546–556.

Cova, B. and Salle, R. (2000) 'Rituals in Managing Extrabusiness Relationships in International Project Marketing: A Conceptual Framework', *International Business Review*, **9**, pp. 669-685.

Cova, B., Dontenwill, E. and Salle, R. (2000) 'The Product/Service Couple in Business to Business Marketing: From Service Supporting the Client's Action to Service Supporting Client's Network', Proceedings of the Eric Langeard International Research Seminar in Service Management, La Londe les Maures, June, pp. 188–203.

Cova, B., Mazet, F. and Salle, R. (1994) 'From Competitive Tendering to Strategic Marketing: An Inductive Approach for Theory-Building', *Journal of Strategic Marketing*, **2**, 29–47.

Cova, B., Mazet, F. and Salle, R. (1996) 'Milieu as a Pertinent Unit of Analysis in Project Marketing', *International Business Review*, **5**(6), 647–664.

Cova, B., Salle, R. and Vincent, R. (2000) 'To Bid or Not to Bid: Screening the Whorcop Project', *European Management Journal*, **18**(5), 551–560.

Cunningham, M. T. and Homse, E. (1982) 'An Interaction Approach to Strategy', in H. Håkansson (ed.), *International Marketing and Purchasing of Industrial Goods: An Interaction Approach*. New York: Wiley.

Dessinges, J. (1990) Stratégies d'offre – créatrices de projets, *Revue Française de Marketing*, **127/128**, 83–89.

Dubini, P. and Aldrich, H. E. (1991) 'Personal and Extend Networks are Central to the Entrepreneurial Process', *Journal of Business Venturing*, **6**, 305–313.

Fiocca, R. (1982) 'Account Portfolio Analysis for Strategy Development', *Industrial Marketing Management*, **11**, 53–62.

Fletcher, R. (1996) 'Network Theory and Countertrade Transactions', *International Business Review*, **5**(2), 167–189.

Fletcher, R. (1998) 'A Holistic Approach to Countertrade', *Industrial Marketing Management*, **27**, 511–528.

Ford, D., Gadde, L. E., Håkansson, H., Lundgren, A., Snehota, I., Turnbull, P. and Wilson, D. (1998) *Managing Business Relationships*. Chichester, UK: Wiley.

Ghauri, P. N. (1983) *Negotiating International Package Deals*. Uppsala, Sweden: Almqvist and Wiksell.

Ghauri, P. N. (1988) 'Negotiating with Developing Countries: Two Cases', *Industrial Marketing Management*, **17**(1), 49–53.

Ghauri, P. N. (ed.) (1999) *Advances in International Marketing: International Marketing and Purchasing*. Greenwich, CT: JAI Press.

Ghauri, P. N. and Holstius, K. (1996) 'The Role of Matching in the Foreign Market Entry Process in the Baltic States', *European Journal of Marketing*, **30**(2), 75–88.

Ghauri, P. N. and Prasad, B. (1995) 'A Network Approach to Probing Area's Inter-Firm Linkages', *Advances in International Comparative Management*, **10**, 63–77.

Ghauri, P. and Usunier, J–C. (1996) *International Business Negotiations*. Oxford: Pergamon Press.

Günter, B. and Bonaccorsi, A. (1996) 'Project Marketing and Systems Selling—In Search of Frameworks and Insights', *International Business Review*, **5**(6), 531–537.

Hadjikhani, A. (1996) 'Project Marketing and the Management of Discontinuity', *International Business Review*, **5**(3), 319–336.

Hadjikhani, A. and Ghauri, P. N. (2001) 'The Behaviour of International Firms in Socio-Political Environments in the European Union', *Journal of Business Research*, **52**(3), pp. 263–275.

Hadjikhani, A. and Håkannson, H. (1995) 'Connected Effects Due to Political Actions Against a Business Firm—The Case of Bofors', Proceedings of the 11th Industrial Marketing and Purchasing Conference, Manchester, September.

Håkansson, H. (ed.) (1982) *International Marketing and Purchasing of Industrial Goods: An Interaction Approach*. Chichester, UK: Wiley.

Håkansson, H. and Östberg, C. (1975) 'Industrial Marketing—An Organizational Problem', *Industrial Marketing Management*, **4**(2/3), 113–123.

Håkansson, H. and Snehota, I. (1989) 'No Business Is an Island', *Scandinavian Journal of Management*, **5**(3), 187–200.

Hall, E. T. and Hall, M. R. (1990) *Understanding Cultural Differences*, p. 196. Yarmouth, ME: Intercultural Press.

Hamel, G. and Prahalad, C. K. (1994) *Competing for the Future*. Boston: Harvard Business School Press.

Hanan, M. (1995) *Consultative Selling*. New York: Amacom.

Henke, J. W. Jr (2000). 'Strategic Selling in the Age of Modules and Systems', *Industrial Marketing Management*, **29**, 271–284.

Hofstede, G. (1984) *Cultures Consequences: International Differences in Work-related Values*, Newbury Park, CA: Sage Publications.

Jansson, H. (1989) 'Marketing to Projects in South-East Asia', in S. T. Cavusgil (ed.), *Advances in International Marketing*, **3**, 259–276. Greenwich, CT: JAI Press.

Johnston, W. J. and Lewin, E. L. (1994) *A Review and Integration on Organizational Buying Behavior*, Report No. 94–111, July. WP Marketing Science Institute.

Kotler, P. (1999) *Marketing Management*. Englewood Cliffs, NJ: Prentice-Hall.

Lemaire, J-P. (1996) 'International Projects Changing Pattern: Sales Engineers—Changing Poles', *International Business Review*, **5**(6), 603–629.

Luostarinen, R. and Welch, L. (1990) *International Business Operations*. Helsinki: KY Book Store.

McAfee, R. and McMillan, J. (1986) 'Bidding for Contracts: A Principal Agent Analysis', *Rand Journal of Economics*, **17**(3), 326–338.

McCall, J. B. (1996) 'Negotiating Sales, Export Transactions and Agency Agreements', in P. Ghauri and J-C. Usunier (eds), *International Business Negotiations*, pp. 185–202. Oxford: Elsevier Science.

McCartney, L. (1989) *Friends in High Places. The Bechtel Story: The Most Secret Corporation and How it Engineered the World*. New York: Ballantines.

Markovitz, H. (1952) 'Portfolio Selection', *Journal of Finance*, **7**, pp. 77–91.

Marsh, P. V. D. (1989) *Successful Bidding and Tendering*. London: Gower.

Mattsson, L. G. (1973) 'System Selling as a Strategy on Industrial Markets', *Industrial Marketing Management*, **3**, 107–119.

Mattsson, L. G. (1979) 'Co-operation Between Firms in International Systems Selling', in L. G. Mattsson and F. Wiedersheim-Paul (eds), *Recent Research on the Internationalisation of Business*, Symposia Universitatis Uppsaliensis, pp. 160–170. Uppsala, Sweden: Almqvist and Wiksell.

Mattson, L. G. (1985) 'An Application of Network Approach to Marketing: Defending and Changing Market Position', in N. Dholakia and J. Arndt (eds), *Changing the Course of Marketing: Alternative Paradigms for Widening Marketing Theory, Research in Marketing*. Greenwich, CT: JAI Press.

Michel, D., Naude, P., Salle, R. and Valla, J. P. (2002) *Business to Business Marketing: Strategies and Implementation*. Basingstoke, UK: Palgrave.

Michel, D., Salle, R. and Valla, J. P. (2000) 'Marketing Industriel: Stratégies et Mise en Oeuvré, 2nd edn. Paris: Economica.

Millman, T. (1996) 'Global Key Account Management and System Selling', *International Business Review*, **4**(6), 631–645

Nadel, J. (1987) *Cracking the Global Market*. New York: Amacom.

Paranka, S. (1971) 'Competitive Bidding Strategy: A Procedure for Pre-Bid Analysis', *Business Horizons*, June, 39–43.

Porter, M. (1980) *Competitive Strategy*. New York: The Free Press/Macmillan.

Sahlin-Andersson, K. (1992) 'The Social Construction of Projects. A Case Study of Organizing an Extraordinary Building Project—The Stockholm Globe Arena', *Scandinavian Housing and Planning Research*, **9**, 65–78.

Salle, R. and Silvestre, M. (1992) *Vende à l'industrie: approche stratégigue de la relation business to business*. Paris: Liaisous.

Salle, R., Cova, B. and Pardo, C. (2000) 'Portfolio of Supplier-Customer Relationships', in A. Woodside (ed.), *Advances in Business Marketing and Purchasing*, Vol. 9, pp. 419–442. Greenwich, CT: JAI Press.

Scott, J. (2000) *Social Network Analysis: A Handbook*, 2nd edn. London: Sage Publications.

Segalen, M. (1998) *Rites et rituels contemporains*. Paris: Nathan.

Sjöberg, U. (1993) 'Institutional Relationships: The Missing Link in the Network Approach to Industrial Markets', Proceedings of the 9th International Marketing and Purchasing Conference, Bath, September.

Skaates, M. A. and Tikkanen, H. (2000) 'Focal Relationships and the Environment of Project Marketing', Proceedings of the 16th International Marketing and Purchasing Conference, Bath, September.

Slatter, S. P. (1990) 'Strategic Marketing Variables under Conditions of Competitive Bidding', *Strategic Management Journal*, **11**, 309–317.

Smith, J. B. (1997) 'Selling Alliances: Issues and Insights', *Industrial Marketing Management*, **26**(March), 149–161.

Stremersch, S., Wuyts, S. and Frambach, R. T. (2001) 'The Purchasing of Full-Service Contracts', *Industrial Marketing Management*, **30**, 1–12.

Tikkanen, H. (1998) 'Research on International Project Marketing', in H. Tikkanen (ed.), *Marketing and International Business—Essays in Honour of Professor Karin Holsrius on Her 65th Birthday*, pp. 261–285. Turku, Finland: Turku School of Economics.

United Nations (1983) *Features and Issues in Turnkey Contracts in Developing Countries*, New York: UN Centre on Transnational Corporations.

Ward, S. C. and Chapman, C. B. (1988) 'Developing Competitive Bids: A Framework for Information Processing', *Journal of Operational Research Society*, **39**(2), 123–134.

Wederspahn, G. M. (1993–1994) 'On Trade and Cultures', *Trade and Culture*, Winter, 4–6.

Welch, D., Welch, L., Wilkinson, I. and Young, I. (1996) 'Network Development in International Project Marketing and the Impact of External Facilitation', *International Business Review*, **5**(6), 579–602.

Wiersema, F. (1995) *Customer Intimacy*. New York: Knowledge Exchange.

Yorke, D. A. and Droussiotis, G. (1994) 'The Use of Customer Portfolio Theory: an Empirical Survey', *Journal of Business and Industrial Marketing*, **9**(3), 6–18.

Youker, R. (1999) 'Managing International Development Projects: Lessons Learned', *Project Management Journal*, **30**(2), 6–7.

INDEX

Actors
  business 35–36
  non-business 35–36
  society 17–18
Agents, need for 200
Analysis
  customer 35, 211
  milieu 35, 85–98, 210
  project 35
  see also Project network analysis
Anticipation approach, 44–49
  see also Deterministic approach

Barter 173
Built, Owned, Operated, Transferred
      (BOOT) 33, 50
Business portfolio 59, 61–62
Buy back 173
Buyer benefits 8–9
Buyer, types of 10–11
Buying centres 29–31
Buying process 28–29

Choosing projects 140–142
  market as network logic 141
  project logic 141–142
  relational logic 141
Communication 195–197
Company resources 64
  intangible 64
  technological 64–65
  see also Resources

Components see Project components
Competencies see Company resources
Complexity see Project business
      characteristics
Constructing demand 48–51, 148–151
Constructivistic approach 41–42
  see also Deterministic approach
Consortiums 135
Consultative selling 145–148
Continuity 43–44
Corporate strategy 59–62
Corruption 46–47
Counterpurchase 174
Countertrade 173–184
Cultural factors 194–195
Creative offer 151–152
  see also Offers
Customer attractiveness 108
Customer intimacy 146–147
Customer solution 144–145
Customer relationships 103–105
  concepts of extra-business relations
      116–120
  in-between projects 112–116
  portfolio development 105–112
  ritual construct 115–116
  supplier vulnerability 108–110
Customer uncertainty 24–25

Debt see Switch account
Designing strategic priorities 209–210

Deterministic approach 41–42, 44–48
see also Constructivistic approach
Developing a functional position 210
Developing a relational position 210–211
Discontinuity see Project business
characteristics

European Public Market Code 26

Feasibility study 9–10
Financial commitment see Project business
characteristics
Functional position 36–37

Geographical perspective 75–76

Independent of any project 144
Intelligence systems 123–125
International communication 195–197
International strategic factors 198–199
Invitation-to-tender 25–28, 35
negotiated competitive or closed 26
open to the best offer 26
open to the best price 25
restricted to better offer 26
restricted to better price 26

Joint construction 153–156

Lobbying see Negociation

Mammoth projects 14
Market segment 67
describe and analyse 68
international 75–76
make choices 71
understand and explain 68–70
Market share 37
Marketing scanning 53–54
Matching 186–189
Milieu and marketing 98–102
Mode of entry 135–136, 211–212
Multidimensional projects 14
Mutual debt 99–101
Mutuality of interest 99

Negotiation 185–207, 213
planning and management 200–207
process 189
characteristics of a good
negotiator 206

face-to-face negotiation 192–193
lobbying 190–191, 201
management of 201–207
post-negotiation 193–194
proposal 191–192
teams 203–204
strategy 199
Network analysis see Project network
analysis
Non-business actors 35–36

Offers 71–72, 212–213
definition 72–75
formulation of 161–184
design and architecture of 166–167
financial 163
offset 173–184
political 163
societal 163–164
technical 163
see also Creative offer
Offset 174–184

Package deals 6
see also Project typology
Partial projects 5–6
see also Project typology
Participants, numbers 17
Periods of project marketing 34
Personal intelligence networks 101–102
Political actors 17, 18, 20
Portfolios 82–84
a marketing tool 83–84
a strategic tool 82–83
Presentations 199
Pre-tender 34–35, 45–55, 142, 145
Proactive co-development 143–160
Project business characteristics 13–21
complexity 16–20
financial commitment 21
supplier/customer discontinuity 20–21
uniqueness 13–16
Project buying 25–29
see also Invitation-to-tender
Project components 10–12
Project creation 51
see also Pseudo-projects
see also Constructing demand
Project de/reconstruction 156–160
Project development 212
Project marketing 23–40
Project network analysis 125–128

Project pyramid 30
Project sales model 186–207
Project typology 4–10, 14
Proposal *see* Negotiation
Pre-tender 34, 45
Pseudo-contract 50
Pseudo-network 50
Pseudo-product 50
Pseudo-projects 50–51, 74–75

Relational investment 43
Relational position 36–37
Relationships, building 43–44
Resource allocation 110–112
Resources 51–52
    see also Company resources
Risk 37–38
    see also Project de/reconstruction

Screening 211, 124, 211
    methods 128–135
Society, influence of 17–20
Sociograms 78–82
    analysis 80
    derivation of 79

representing the business arena 78–79
Solution selling 145–146
Solution strategies 39–40
Strategic business units (SBUs) 59–61
    strategy 62–75
Strategic marketing stage 52–55
Strategic priorities 209–210
Strategic segmentation 60–61
Subcontracting projects 5
    see also Project typology
Supplier benefits 9–10
Supplier uncertainty 24
Switch account 174

Tender preparation 142, 145
Time, attitudes towards 194–195
Turnkey projects 6–7
    see also Project typology

Uncertainties 23
    customer 24–25
    supplier 24
    see also Risk
Uniqueness *see* Project business
    characteristics

Printed and bound in the UK by
CPI Antony Rowe, Eastbourne